Angelina Osborne —
To Gabriel and Tania, my biggest cheerleaders

Patrick Vernon —
*To Alex, my brother-in-law, and the many others
in the community who sadly died of COVID-19*

Contents

Foreword
by David Olusoga

On 7 June 2020, the statue of slave trader Edward Colston, which had stood in the centre of Bristol for 125 years, was pulled down by protestors and dumped in the city's harbour. Despite repeated requests over many years for Colston's statue to be taken down, it had remained in place, perhaps in part due to too narrow a focus on biography – stripped of context and sanitised, much of his life having been deliberately obscured.

None of the other nearby statues were touched by the Black Lives Matter protesters, nor were any of the shops in the vicinity damaged. The protestors deliberately and purposefully targeted the statue of the slave trader. The protesters, who were overwhelmingly young, were well aware of who Edward Colston was and what he had done. As an investor and later as Deputy Governor of the Royal African Company, Colston had been a key figure in the activities of the company which transported more Africans into slavery than any other in British history.

All of this was known to the protesters because they have been the beneficiaries of fifty years of scholarship. They are the first generation brought up in Britain for whom access to Black British history has been relatively easy. Over the previous half-century and more, a great pantheon of Black historical figures have been painstakingly salvaged, one by one, from the hidden recesses of the archives. That history and those biographies are alive in modern Britain, inspiring and motivating a new generation.

Building on those decades of scholarship, this book by Patrick Vernon and Dr Angelina Osborne brings the biographies of Black Britons together and vividly expands the historical back-drop against which these hundred men and women lived their lives. Despite prejudice and racism, they went on to achieve outstanding success in fields from politics to film-making; publishing to teaching; sport to medicine; law to business; and music to architecture.

We share a national fascination with our colourful past, but one colour has been largely missing: Black. The history of Black people is unique in how comprehensively and consistently it has been not just overlooked but denied.

When I was at school in Britain in the 1970s and 80s, there was certainly no such thing as Black history, nothing even about the history of the British empire that might have explained to my classmates why a child born in Nigeria was sat among them. To date, history as taught in British schools has conspicuously failed to make sense of how young Black British people and their families came to be here and to be British. We urgently need a new curriculum that includes all the dark chapters in our shared past, the unsettling stories as well as those we currently celebrate.

There can be no doubt that initiatives such as Black History Month and the 100 Great Black Britons campaign have helped thousands of children – and adults – to understand their place in Britain's story and have become a counterblast to the relentless waves of negative stereotypes that batter Black children growing up in Britain. But we need to be wary of an overreliance on Black British heroes. Constant reassessment must be made of the individuals we venerate, and new heroes will emerge who mean more to the new generation than they did to the last. This book is by no means the final *100 Great Black Britons* – there are many more volumes to come.

Patrick Vernon's original 100 Great Black Britons campaign made a significant contribution to this, and while we need to be wary of the limitations of biography – particularly heroic biography – as history, life stories have their role to play, as they did at the beginning of this process, in revealing and making sense of the past and guiding us into a better future.

Preface:

The Making of *100 Great Black Britons*
By Patrick Vernon OBE

Where are the Great Black Britons?

It must have been in the summer of 2001 when I became aware of the BBC 100 Greatest Britons campaign; I remember seeing a massive billboard one weekend as I was driving from London to Wolverhampton to visit my parents. The poster hoarding was encouraging people to nominate their Greatest Briton of all time, and I saw similar messages as I clicked on the BBC website in the following weeks. My feeling at the time about the BBC's venture was that it was simply another vanity project to bolster their ratings, as they were facing competition from other terrestrial, satellite and emerging cable channels.

At that point in my life, I was busy in my role as senior director for the NHS, delivering a multi-agency partnership public health programme, called Brent Health Action Zone, to residents in Brent, north London. The programme was one of New Labour's strategies to improve the health of the country by targeting twenty-six areas in which there were health inequalities and poor levels of life expectancy. In addition, I was mentoring at Fryent Primary School in Brent, working with dynamic head and deputy teachers who were recruiting several Black professional males to mentor young boys who were not focusing on their schoolwork and were experiencing behavioural problems. For me, it was giving something back to the community; I have some degree of privilege, and I felt a moral responsibility to use it to help empower young people. This led me to develop my first website based on my mentoring experience and my passions for family history, intergenerational learning and Black British history. *Every Generation* was launched on 1 October 2002, on the first day of Black History Month.

However, it was not until the autumn of 2002 that my attention was drawn again to the BBC campaign. Their official list of 100 Greatest Britons was announced along with a ten-part documentary series, which then culminated in a final voting extravaganza and studio debate. Looking though the list, I noticed that the only person of colour was the late Freddie Mercury, lead singer of Queen, born in Zanzibar of Parsi heritage.

I remember reading various articles and commentaries regarding the lack of representation of women and different parts of Britain on the list. I was a member and committee member of BASA (the Black and Asian studies association), which, along with other organisations, had been lobbying the government and education bodies for several years to ensure that the national curriculum reflected the diversity of history – with some success. BASA's membership of academics, community historians, students, activists and writers all complained and castigated the BBC about its lack of Black and Asian representation in their Greatest Britons poll, which we felt was another instance of institutional racism and reinforced the invisibility of Black and Asian British history. Many believed that the BBC had a golden opportunity, as a public broadcaster, to rectify this invisibility. However, when Winston Churchill was announced the eventual winner of the Greatest Briton poll during Black History Month 2002, numerous people felt this was game over again.

Nevertheless, I became fixated by this overall creative process of engaging the public – how to use online content and films, involving celebrities and people in public life, to create a narrative of British history. I decided an intervention was required. I was going to create my alternative campaign focusing on people of African descent, showing their contribution to the creating and shaping of Britain going back 1,000 years. However, I had no idea how I was going to do this – how I was going to compile a comprehensive list of individuals and develop a public media campaign. I sent a message to the BASA group that we should all do this together and develop our alternative list of Black British achievers. Only one person responded, however, who wished me well in my venture.

Undeterred, I started to plan how I could deliver this project – what resources I would need, as well as the timescale. I came to the conclusion that this campaign had to be ready by the first anniversary of the BBC announcing the results of its 100 Greatest Britons, which was also during Black History Month. I employed Pamela Adjei, who I had previously worked with in the NHS, as a full-time web designer and editor for *Every Generation* and my new website *100 Great Black Britons*. I secured a small office space, and acquired the franchise to design websites for companies and charities in order to generate the income required to pay freelance staff and to support our work on Black history. Through a mutual contact, I then approached another website designer called Denise Little to develop the interactive voting function on the website. A few months later, at a creative arts and media networking event in King's Cross, I met Angelina Osborne, who had recently completed her master's degree in history. We got on well and she was looking for an opportunity to use her research. Several weeks later, I approached Angelina and offered her a six-month job as a researcher for the campaign. In the end, though, we became lifelong friends and she is now co-author of this publication, doing the bulk of the research and writing.

To put together the list of individuals, I then approached friend, entrepreneur, board game publisher and walking encyclopaedia on Black history, Jak Beula Dodd. He provided a working list of names to lay the foundations for the website and further research.

Angelina and I set to work, reaching out to various people for further information and advice. During this time, I also referred considerably to the historical genius and all-time hero of mine, the late J.A. Rogers (1880–1966). Rogers wrote several books covering the Black presence in Europe, and his two-volume opus *World's Great Men of Color* (he did cover women too, though!) was written during the time of the Second World War and was based on his extensive travels in Europe. It was also a rich source of material for the Black Britons project as it was one of the few books covering the Black historical presence in the UK. Other books of great interest and inspiration were *Black Britannia* by Edward Scobie (I was actually tempted to use this name for the campaign) and *Staying Power* by Peter Fryer. In particular, Rogers's book *100 Amazing Facts About the Negro* became the template for how we designed the website and how we ran the campaign, seeking to educate people that Black British history is also part of British history.

Our aim was to highlight Black individuals who had occupied the same space as white British heroes but who had either been ignored or whose identities were never mentioned or discussed. We also sought to bring to the foreground those who were the first Black people to take on a specific role or appointment that broke the mould and paved the way for others. In addition, we wanted to cover multiple time periods over the last 1,000 years. In the end, by the time we finished the campaign in February 2004, the number of biographies on the website was in excess of five hundred names under many subcategories – five times the hundred we set out to achieve.

One of the key aspects of the campaign was to inform and engage young people and schools, so we decided to run a school competition for key stages 1 to 4, with students submitting their celebrations of Black British history. This ranged from paintings to videos of school assemblies to booklets showcasing their favourite Great Black Britons. My good friend and teacher Angie Brooks helped to formulate questions for students on the website, and I then approached the *Times Educational Supplement* who reviewed the site and helped to promote the school competition. For the 2020 campaign, we ran another school competition with the support of the National Education Union.

Millennium blues and retromania

The BBC's 100 Greatest Britons campaign took place at a time when Britain was experiencing a wave of nostalgia and retromania after the anti-climax of reaching the new millennium.

Britpop and Cool Britannia of the 1990s had disappeared as Britain saw the emergence of garage and grime in the early 2000s. British sporting achievements were few, and there was a growing movement towards independence for Scotland and Wales, plus mounting demands from northern cities for more regional autonomy, which were all threatening to fracture the Union and the whole notion of Britishness.

For the Black community, there was not much to celebrate at the start of the millennium apart from the successful campaign by Doreen and Neville Lawrence to bring the Macpherson Report to light, with its damning indictment of institutional racism within the Metropolitan Police, which would eventually result in the Equality Act of 2010. Also, the community lost Bernie Grant MP after he passed away in 2000, one of the most respected and revered individuals in mainstream politics and media; although, in his place, local boy and lawyer David Lammy was selected as the next MP for Tottenham.

However, over the course of the following years, gains were made. In 2002, Paul Boateng was appointed as Chief Secretary to the Treasury and David Lammy as Junior Minster for the Department of Health. In 2003, Baroness Valerie Amos was made Leader of the House of the Lords, and Baroness Patricia Scotland as Attorney General in 2007. It felt as though this was another chapter in the history of Black representation since 1987, when Paul Boateng, Diane Abbott, Keith Vaz and Bernie Grant were elected to the House of Commons as MPs.

The impact of 100 Great Black Britons

100 Great Black Britons has become one of the most successful campaigns to raise the profile, history and achievements of

Britons of African and Caribbean descent over the last 1,000 years. Such was the impact of the campaign that I was invited by *Channel 4 News* to announce the results of the poll live in February 2004. The BBC also did extensive news coverage about Mary Seacole as the winner of the 100 Great Black Britons campaign.

It is difficult to assess comprehensively the impact of 100 Great Black Britons since it began, but we can point to several successes and milestones:

- Mary Seacole and many other Black historical figures were included in the national school curriculum. In 2013, when the then Secretary of Education, Michael Gove, tried to remove Seacole from the syllabus, more than 40,000 people signed a petition to overturn this, and a letter to *The Times* was signed by politicians, celebrities, academics, activists and public- and voluntary-sector leaders.
- Mary Seacole was adopted into the Royal College of Nursing and given the same status as Florence Nightingale.
- The campaign kickstarted the Mary Seacole Memorial Statue Appeal chaired by Lord Soley, raising over £500k for a statue that was unveiled in 2016 in the grounds of St Thomas Hospital (facing the Houses of Parliament).
- More statues, memorials and blue plaques from the 100 Great Black Britons list were erected, including Oliver Lyseight and Walter Tull.
- There was greater public awareness of Black British history in schools and in the media.
- Children and young people were being encouraged to have greater self-pride and confidence about Black history and belonging to Britain.

- More publications and radio and television programmes on Black British history have been commissioned and developed (including David Olusoga's successful book and accompanying television series *Black and British* [2016]).
- More work on Black heritage was undertaken by museums, archivists and public institutions.
- As of 2020, the *100 Great Black Britons* website still has more than one million visits per month. It is used extensively by schools (being recommended in the national curriculum), adults for educational purposes, and the general public.

Sixteen years after 100 Great Black Britons began, in 2019 we relaunched the campaign against the backdrop of Brexit, the rise of right-wing politics, the 2018 *Windrush* Scandal and the continuing inequality facing Black people in the UK. As we were working on the book, COVID-19 was also having a disproportionately devastating impact on the Black community, and I was campaigning for Mary Seacole to be named as the NHS COVID-19 recovery hospital in Birmingham.

The year 2020 also saw the resurgence of the Black Lives Matter movement as a result of George Floyd's murder at the hands of the police in the United States. More white people, it seems, are starting to understand that everyday and structural racism is not a figment of Black people's imagination, with marches, demonstrations and vigils taking place in defiance of the government lockdown due to COVID-19. The debates around white privilege, how to be an ally to Black and Brown people, and mainstream bodies issuing statements of solidarity to the Black Lives Matter cause are all welcomed. For many years race was off the agenda, despite the atrocities of Grenfell Tower and the *Windrush* Scandal, and it remains to be seen whether this discourse on race relations in Britain carries on. However, I believe that the removal of the Edward Colston statue in Bristol in June 2020 was an iconic moment reminiscent of the fall of the Berlin Wall in 1989. It has served to kickstart a nationwide conversation about Britain's colonial past, especially when it comes to the national curriculum, the role of statues and revisiting national heroes like Winston Churchill.

Since the first 100 Great Black Britons campaign in 2004, academics and independent scholars have discovered more Black British historical figures, and new role models and icons have emerged. Like the Black Lives Matter movement, this fresh iteration of the 100 Great Black Britons campaign provides an opportunity for reassessment and reflection. What makes a Great Black Briton? How do we recognise unsung heroes who may not have had the same profile and coverage about their impact and legacy? I believe that this new campaign and publication have the potential to further educate, inform and advance the contributions of Black people in Britain, and inspire the next generation of role models and achievers. I hope that it will be a further marker that Black people belong here, that our historical and current contributions are making a difference, despite us not always having been valued and respected.

Criteria and selection for 100 Great Black Britons 2020

To be a Great Black Briton for this publication, we have laid down the following criteria building on the 2003 campaign:

- To identify as being of African or African Caribbean descent
- To have used their platform, privilege or status to support the advancement of the Black British community while being a British resident and/or citizen
- To have overcome racial, faith, gender or social barriers

We have also endeavoured to have a spread of nominees who reflect the diversity of Black Britons, with individuals who are:

- Female, male and LGBTQ+
- From across the United Kingdom
- From a range of sectors: faith/spirituality, music, politics, academia, science, medicine, public administration, technology, business, charity/philanthropy, social justice/civil rights, arts, media, sports, entertainment

In total we had over a thousand nominations submitted via email, social media, the website and at events. We hope that this book and its final selection will lead you to explore further both the better-known icons in this book and those included who have previously been marginalised. We hope that, once more, *100 Great Black Britons* will provide role models to Black communities and emphasise that the history and achievements of Black Britons are an integral part of our shared heritage in this country.

Introduction

I N 2001 THE BBC commissioned a poll inviting the public to vote for who they thought should bear the title of Greatest Briton Ever.[1] It was a poll that immediately captured the public's imagination. Over 30,000 people responded via telephone or the BBC website; and from those nominations, a list of 100 individuals was drawn up. The list featured men and women identified as the nation's favourite Britons, representing the fields of science and technology, literature, royalty, politics, the arts, sport, exploration and defenders of these shores throughout Britain's history. The achievements of Winston Churchill, Sir Francis Drake, Charles Dickens, Alexander Graham Bell, Charles Darwin and many more became the subject of lively debate in living rooms, pubs and workplaces across the country.

On the basis of that first poll, BBC Two commissioned ten programmes, one for each of the top-ten nominated individuals as they appeared in the poll; each nominee was assigned a champion to argue their case: why that person ought to be declared the greatest. Each champion made an impassioned case for the greatness of an individual, attempting to convince viewers to vote for their nominee.

Each film was framed by a television debate, hosted by Anne Robinson, at the time one of the BBC's highest-profile presenters, who had achieved considerable fame as host of *The Weakest Link*, a quickfire general-knowledge quiz show in which she adopted a forbidding and stern persona with the purpose of intimidating the contestants. Her presenting style was well suited to chairing a debate about who was the greatest Briton, since it was likely to become robust as it spoke to deeply held personal beliefs and preferences over which people have contributed most to Britain's might as a nation.

The ten programmes, broadcast twice a week over five weeks, concluded with a second public poll to vote for the greatest-ever Briton. Within forty-eight hours of the poll opening in October 2002, over 170,000 people had voted; by the time the poll closed, 1.6 million people had cast their vote. As the BBC noted in the book that accompanied the series, a button in the national psyche had been pressed: the poll had provoked passionate conversations and had 'opened a window on all they abhor and all they hold dear'.[2]

The list was not without its detractors; there were complaints that it was too England-centric and too male-dominated. Irish newspaper the *Sunday Tribune*, disappointed with the dearth of Irish nominees (5 out of 100), published a list of 100 notable Irishmen and women. The BBC shrugged off all criticisms, pointing out the list's legitimacy lay in the fact it was devised by the public and they had chosen the nominees.

Widely tipped to win, former Prime Minister Winston Churchill duly topped the poll with 456,000 votes, 35,000 more than engineer Isambard Kingdom Brunel.[3] Churchill's contributions to the nation are ingrained in the national consciousness – the statesman, military officer and writer had long been a well-loved British icon, best known as the man who helped the country hold its nerve throughout the most difficult moments of the Second World War. His success in this forum was confirmation of the regard in which he is still is held.

The BBC had an enormous hit on its hands, an incredibly successful factual series, the success of which lay in its engagement with the public.

This was precisely what Jane Root, then controller of BBC Two, had envisaged would be the outcome. Root was credited with the success of the format of public-vote programming, a format which was eventually sold to other countries. In an interview with the *Guardian* newspaper she spoke enthusiastically about how the series' key selling point was its legitimacy as it was based on public opinion rather than conceptualised solely by the BBC: '[The series] engages with the many different passions of our audiences . . . we have to trust the intelligence of our audience to make the important decisions.'[4]

Root capitalised on the burgeoning popularity of history programming that has existed since the 1990s. Simon Schama's BBC series *History of Britain* had, for example, been extremely popular, leading the viewer through a tour of the history of the British Isles and its links to the wider world. The final series concluded in June 2002, making room for another series that could benefit from its popularity.

The ease of access to historical information via the internet, and the growing numbers of those accessing that information and watching the television programmes, reflected a long-held public interest in history. *Great Britons* was certainly part of this trend; there were, however, other contextual factors that explain why it took hold of the nation's imagination in the way that it did. The poll and the fact that Winston Churchill won can be viewed with hindsight as deeply resonant at a moment when the world became more complex and perilous.

In September 2001 the world was left reeling by the attacks on the United States by the terrorist group al-Qaeda, in which the World Trade Center in New York was destroyed and thousands of people were killed in a single day. Subsequent attacks in the following years around the world created an atmosphere of heightened public fear and anxiety. In the UK, this level of uncertainty was characterised in the terror threat levels that came to dictate British ways of life in a way not seen since the Troubles loomed large in the British consciousness between the 1970s and 1990s; 9/11 changed the world and people's perspectives of it.

In October 2002, at the time when *Great Britons* was being broadcast, a terrorist attack at a nightclub in Bali killed 202 people, injuring hundreds more; many of the victims were British and Australian. At that time, Britain was yet to experience an attack on its own soil of that severity, but the awareness that the safety of its citizens around the world was under greater threat from an enemy that transcended borders, operated without any understandable structure, and had a willingness to kill others and themselves was a terrifying new reality to digest. People became frightened and suspicious of their fellow citizens – British Muslims found themselves under intense scrutiny by the security services and a terrified public, as Islam wrongly became synonymous with extremist ideologies and terrorism.

Nostalgia acts as a coping mechanism in times of great uncertainty and anxiety. When the future or even the present is unclear, a typical response is to attempt to control or predict one's environment and to seek comfort in what is familiar. A national debate on who should be the greatest Briton was arguably a way to reattach to the familiar, to what was known. In celebrating national figures and their virtues, the series was able for several weeks to bring the nation together, to celebrate its shared history and identity. Little wonder that *Great Britons* was a television phenomenon, that it engaged and inspired so many. And little wonder that Churchill topped the poll. It was the perfect salve for a nation struggling to make sense of new ideologies and attitudes that threatened its way of life.

One of the most notable criticisms of the *Great Britons* list was that other than Freddie Mercury, who was born in Zanzibar, a former British protectorate, there were no people of African or Asian descent included. In an interview with the *Radio Times*, Anne Robinson defended the omission: 'We're talking about a world where you could go to parts of America in the fifties and Blacks or Asians weren't allowed in golf clubs. So, you can't say how disgraceful it is that there are so few Black or Asians without reminding everybody that it reflects history.'[5]

Robinson's remarks are reminiscent of those made in 1963 by the historian Hugh Trevor-Roper, who maintained there was 'no African history, only the history of Europeans in Africa . . . the rest is darkness'. There is no Black British history, Robinson appeared to be saying; Black people could not make history because they had not been permitted by white people to do so. They had done nothing; contributed nothing; therefore, they were invisible from history and consequently had no place in the poll. Robinson's reaction was typical in the way that Stuart Hall had often remarked upon – that the idea of Britishness, and by extension British history, carries largely unspoken racial connotations, meaning that it is usually imagined as white. What was also evident from her comments was the belief that it wasn't necessary to reinterpret British history because it was fine as it was.

The BBC publication written to accompany the series acknowledged the lack of non-white faces less stridently, but in a manner that implied a similar ignorance of an African historical presence in Britain: 'It is inevitable that history has most successfully recorded the efforts of those placed to make a mark . . . were this poll to be conducted in a hundred years' time it is unlikely that this would be the case.'[6] The implication here was that Black people had not been in Britain long enough to make their historical mark. When looking at Britain's past, Black people were not only invisible; they did not even exist there.

The arrival of people from the Caribbean to Britain on the *Empire Windrush* in 1948 has been mythologised as the defining moment that changed Britain from an exclusively white population into a racially diverse one; the beginning of a constant Black British presence in this country. The fiftieth anniversary of the ship's arrival, commemorated in 1998, four years before the series was broadcast, may well have informed the assumption that Black people simply haven't been here long enough to make any mark on history. Yet there is substantial evidence of an African presence in Britain since the Roman period, and a constant presence since the sixteenth century, living far more integrated lives in British communities than previously understood. Evidence exists of Black British men and women who have made their mark historically in many ways, comparable to those discussed in the series; however, the public, by and large, had little to no knowledge of who they were.

Using data from parish records and letters, historians have shown that there was a substantial African presence in Tudor Britain that extends into the thousands. Their presence was large enough for Elizabeth I to remark upon it in two letters signed by her in 1596. As Britain's involvement in the trade and trafficking of Africans in the seventeenth and eighteenth centuries expanded, so did the Black population. Based on marriage and baptismal registers, historians estimate there were 10,000 Black people living in Britain in the eighteenth century. Black sailors who served in the British navy established communities in the port cities of Britain. By 1918 there were perhaps as many as 30,000 Black people living in Britain, many of whom had migrated from different parts of the then empire. Certainly, there were enough in the 1930s for the Jamaican-born civil rights campaigner and physician Harold Moody to establish the League of Coloured Peoples in an attempt to overturn the discrimination experienced by Black British people living in Britain at the time.

'The trouble with the English,' ponders the character Whisky Sisodia in Salman Rushdie's novel *The Satanic Verses* (1988), 'is that their history happened overseas, so they don't know what it means.' History, as a key subject in the national curriculum, has been an important way of reaffirming British identity and engendering national pride. It has been difficult to move beyond the intrigue of Tudor politics, for example, and to adopt a more reflective approach, asking more critical and complex questions about Britain's imperial past. Currently, we utilise and engage with a very narrow version of British history, culture and identity, where English narratives are centred and prioritised as the only version of history children are required to know and learn.

In 2010, the Conservative Secretary State for Education Michael Gove both caused controversy and received considerable support when he outlined his vision for the school subject, which would give a more narrative-driven view of history that would focus on kings, queens and wars, downplaying the more so-called unsavoury aspects, 'so that our students have a better understanding of the linear narrative of British history, and Britain's impact on the world and the world's impact on Britain . . . this trashing of our past has got to stop.'[7]

In its report *Making British Histories*, the Runnymede Trust critiqued the policies made by the Conservative/Liberal Democrat coalition government (2010–15) and its predecessor, the New Labour government (1997–2010), on history education as marginalising the experiences of non-white British people, and largely not addressing the issue of Britain's broader ethnic diversity.[8] The consequences of a lack of inclusivity – that is, a more purposeful engagement with Britain's imperial past and centuries of migration – means that a significant part of Britain's story remains untold. The *Great Britons* series, in which the public were invited to name the greatest, did not name anyone of African descent because there was not, in 2002, nor in 2019 for that matter, a national treatment of British history as a global phenomenon.

Therefore, the 100 Great Black Britons initiative was a response to the absences and silences within what appeared to be a nationally sanctioned televised campaign on Britishness. Patrick Vernon, a genealogist and community activist, was determined to prove the BBC wrong about their claims that there were, as far as they could tell, no contributions made to the national story by people of African descent, an assertion that is as false as it is dangerous. As a subject, Black history had been taught, researched and shared within community spaces for many years. Discrimination against African Caribbean children in mainstream education led their parents to set up supplementary schools to enable children to have additional educational support and to learn about their cultural heritage, history and language, encouraging them to have a positive sense of identity and belonging. Many people who attended these schools as children credit them with empowering them with self-knowledge and an alternative to the narratives with which they were being inculcated at school, in which they did not see themselves. The rapper and author Akala, for example, has written in his excellent book *Natives* about the impact that attending a supplementary school had on the development of his Black consciousness and sense of identity, how it shaped his sense of self-worth and esteem and 'imbued me with a community-oriented moral compass'.[9]

David Olusoga has brought Black British history to a mainstream audience with great success. His award-winning television programmes detail the ways in which African and Caribbean peoples' histories are interwoven into the British national story and have made inroads into raising awareness of these histories. He has acknowledged he stands on the shoulders of earlier historians who have used their research to dispute standard representations of history that have tended to exclude African and Caribbean people. Furthermore, these historians were pioneers in their work to establish Black British history as a respectable and valid field of study, rather than a fragmented treatment of the African historical presence, which was often reduced to a passing footnote or ignored altogether. Edward Scobie, a Dominican-born historian and journalist, documented the first full-length account of the Black experience in

Britain in his book *Black Britannia: A History of Blacks in Britain* (1972). Two excellent narrative studies by Folarin Shyllon – *Black Slaves in Britain* (1974) and *Black People in Britain* (1977) – explored the Black experience of enslaved and free people living in Britain from the sixteenth to nineteenth centuries, offering a new chapter in English social history.

Ron Ramdin's *The Making of the Black Working Class in Britain* (1987) is a classic study that traces the roots of Britain's Black working class in the nineteenth and twentieth centuries, and the role of Black radical ideology in working-class struggles. *Staying Power* (1984) by Peter Fryer presents a radical historical interpretation of Black people in Britain and remains to this day a foundational text of that history.[10] Other important accounts by scholars and community historians around the country from the 1970s to the present have helped to advance knowledge of these communities; despite these advances, inclusion of these narratives has been insufficient in national or academic curricula.

The ground-breaking studies of the African and Caribbean presence published in the 1970s and 1980s sit within a wider movement that has spanned at least fifty years. This has been led by scholars, teachers, archivists, educational activists and parents who have been the principal agents behind a series of institutional and community-based initiatives exploring Britain's global 'island story', with its complex patterns of migration and diaspora. This work has been produced, as Hannah Ishmael has noted, 'through the convergence of the politics of race and the politics of heritage'.[11] It has set out to revise and unsettle the Anglo-centred definition of heritage, which featured so dominantly in the *Great Britons* campaign, with its focus on established national figures, historic houses and monuments. These activities of transforming national memory have been described by Stuart Hall as part of a 'deep slow-motion revolution'.

There was a resolve to demonstrate a shared heritage and identity, and to counter the negative effects of excluding African, Caribbean and Asian experiences from Britain's historical narrative, and the way it was being taught in the classroom. This movement has spawned some important initiatives that have become an integral part of Britain's heritage landscape, negotiating spaces in which Black people have been empowered to tell their own stories.

The aftermath of the uprisings in London, Bristol, Liverpool and Leeds in 1980 and 1981, born out of frustration, anger and despair over years of racial and social injustices, was a pivotal moment which saw the emergence of organisations and associated projects concerned with documenting, displaying and disseminating the history of Black people in Britain. These organisations had a shared vision: to develop a strategy to take Black British history from the periphery and integrate it into the narrative; and to use history as a tool to fight against inequality. This strategy of effecting change at a local level has over time begun to have some impact at a national level.

In 1981, Len Garrison, a community activist and historian who had been collecting Black historical materials for several years, used his collection to create the Black Cultural Archives in London. Its mission to catalogue the Black British presence has seen it develop into a national archive and it has been disseminating Black History materials, creating exhibitions and conducting research for nearly forty years.

Black History Month has become an important event in the UK calendar to recognise the economic, cultural and political contributions of people of African heritage. Originally developed in the United States in 1926 to counter the negative historical representations of African Americans, in the UK in the late 1980s a similar phenomenon was taking place where students of African and Caribbean heritage could not find themselves represented in any meaningful or positive way. There was deep concern over the misinformation about African British people, that they had made no contribution to history, which was having negative effects on African British schoolchildren, giving them a lack of racial esteem. At its conception in 1987, the organisers secured the commitment of London boroughs to recognise these contributions in a way that would instil pride in students of their heritage and to create an inheritance for the future.[12]

The Black and Asian Studies Association (BASA), a nationwide network of archivists, teachers, historians and parents, has since 1991 fostered research on people of African and Asian origin; through its newsletters and conferences it has made considerable progress in the dissemination of Black History material. In addition, BASA has persistently lobbied successive governments for a history curriculum that is representative of the histories of African and Asian people, and lobbied museums, libraries and archives to make histories of Black people more accessible.

BASA brought into consciousness the importance of establishing a more accurate and inclusive history of Britain. For nearly thirty years, it has held public bodies to account and championed the work of Black historians. The materials it has produced have inspired innovative ways of presenting more accurate and inclusive historical narratives.

Consequently, Tony Warner of Black History Walks has been leading guided tours and film nights that explore the

African and Caribbean presence for well over a decade. His work fills an important gap that mainstream guided tours leave in their telling of the history of Britain's built environment. Warner has attracted many people to his walking tours who have described the experience as enlightening and inspiring, and has spoken of how the research undertaken by BASA members helped him in developing and designing his walks. Miranda Kaufmann and Michael Ohajuru's work on identifying and promoting new research on Black history through their conferences comes out of the tradition established by BASA.[13] The work of S. I. Martin, Robin Walker, Black History Studies and many others demonstrated that historical research has always taken place outside of formal educational space that challenged established narratives about Britain and its people, as well as exploring African people's place in world history.

The 100 Great Black Britons campaign in 2003 was both critically informed by and built upon these earlier works and interventions. The compiled list of 100-plus people aimed to celebrate and acknowledge the contemporary and historical contributions of people of African heritage to the life, culture and history of Britain. On reflection, there was a lot at stake – the list not only acted as a tool for raising awareness about a more diverse British history; it also sought a re-examination of what it meant to be British. It aimed to disrupt and complicate the constructed national self-image and encourage more attention to understanding that Black British history was as global as empire, shifting attention towards geographical spaces beyond the British Isles.

The writer A. Sivanandan's answer to the question often asked of immigrants, 'Why are you here?', was a succinct 'We are here because you were there.' ' "Here",' as Colin Prescod noted, 'is an uncomfortable place of consequences ... of forgotten, unknown, hidden, covered-up beginnings. "There" turns out to be a time and a history.'[14] A history and a time that birthed a global capitalist system based on enslavement and exploitation that enriched Britain and devastated Africa and its peoples. It is this 'trashing of Britain's past' that Michael Gove was anxious to sidestep, preferring to focus on keeping the 'great' in Great Britain; the same history that during the television campaign in 2002 was uncritical and unquestioning of its exclusions.

It is with this perspective in mind that the original 100 Great Black Britons list did not utilise the same framework or criteria used by the *Great Britons* campaign – that is, what made these Britons 'great' by virtue of established tropes; or whether they were born in Britain – the global nature of British history meant their place of birth could be Britain, the Caribbean or the African continent.

It had a framework of 'greatness' that was characterised by the nominees' resistance and resilience, and the ways many of them challenged and overcame racial barriers to make significant and notable advances in the fields in which they excelled. The individuals featured were not all nationally or internationally recognisable – many occupied the space of community histories and were recognised for the ways they resisted racism as well as building community cohesion in their respective regions.

The 100 Great Black Britons campaign was launched in March 2003, and like the BBC campaign, the public was invited to vote for the greatest Black Briton via the website and to make additional nominations. The purpose behind this was to discover more Black Britons whose contributions had been hitherto unrecognised, thus creating a database that could act as an important resource in the gathering of data on people who had made contributions in their community.

The campaign immediately attracted media attention for the breadth and scope of the list, which included many well-known Black British people and introduced the public to little-known people who nevertheless had made their mark historically. It opened a door to a world of excluded stories taking centre stage and its impact was felt long after the campaign ended. Books, documentaries, exhibitions and conferences have helped make changes in how many people perceive this island's story. The arrival of the *Windrush* as the defining moment of a multicultural Britain was turned on its head as the public was confronted with 'new' information demonstrating that Britain had Black communities long before. And there was more.

Two English queens, Philippa of Hainault, mother of Edward, the 'Black Prince', and Charlotte, wife of George III, made the list because some historians and genealogists maintain that they have Black or Moorish ancestry.

The historian J. A. Rogers was one of the earliest people to make this remarkable claim in his three-volume series *Sex and Race*, first published in 1940. Their inclusion was therefore controversial and questioned the concept of race and racial difference, and highlighted the fact that groups of people had been mixing for so long that the idea of a 'pure race' was false.

African anti-slavery activism challenged the belief that the abolition campaign was led by white men and women and highlighted how African people added their voices to condemn and campaign against British enslavement in the Caribbean. Mary Prince, Olaudah Equiano and Ottobah Cugoano all spent part of their lives as enslaved workers, and their experiences made them authentic and vocal critics of slavery and its devastating effects on Africa and Africans. Their narratives gained new interest and, in the years after the campaign, research was undertaken to learn more about the people that wrote them. Equiano, for example, became the subject of a new biography and an exhibition in Birmingham in 2006 that explored his extraordinary life. The *Equiano* exhibition, produced in partnership with the Equiano Society and Birmingham Museums and Art Gallery, was the first major exhibition on the eighteenth-century African British writer and anti-slavery campaigner.

The campaign brought attention to the work of historians who had been writing about the Black presence in sport. Further myths were shattered as Black men were discovered to have been professional players as far back as the nineteenth century. Walter Tull, of Barbadian and English heritage, was inside forward and half back for Clapton, Tottenham Hotspur and Northampton Town. Tull also served in the British Army during the First World War, rising to the rank of second lieutenant, the first man of mixed heritage to become a commissioned officer. Black soldiers' service began to be recognised, their almost total exclusion from the history books is gradually being reversed, and by the time of the First World War centenary commemorations that took place in 2014 many different projects and publications were addressing this oversight, their service and sacrifice at last receiving recognition.[15]

The campaign was hugely successful because it initiated a discourse on Black achievements and contributions to the country; it compelled people to rethink concepts of identity and Britishness. And it introduced the public to people and stories long forgotten or hidden, shattering the myth that there was no Black British historical past. The campaign enabled a way to refute misconceptions about the Black experience and presence in Britain.

The top-ten Great Black Britons reflected the way that those who voted embraced the campaign and what it stood for. Queen Philippa of Hainault, Mary Prince and Olaudah Equiano's inclusion demonstrated a need for broader explorations in British history beyond a narrow focus and well-trodden themes. The inclusion of Wilfred Wood and Oliver Lyseight reflected the centrality of religion in the lives of many Black British people. Bishop Wood, the first Black bishop in the Church of England, and Dr Lyseight, credited with founding the New Testament Church of God, stand on either side of an important narrative of how Caribbean Anglicans responded to their racist rejection from the Church of England, which led to the creation of more welcome spaces of worship, and how that institution began to make gestures to become more inclusive and welcoming.

Courtney Pine, world-famous jazz musician and composer instrumental to the revival of Britain's jazz scene in the 1980s, earned his inclusion in the top ten, along with newsreader and broadcaster Sir Trevor McDonald and Lord Bill Morris, the first Black General Secretary of the Transport and General Workers' Union. The glamourous Welsh singer Dame Shirley Bassey, known for her powerful voice and as the singer of three James Bond theme songs, was also included. The MP and activist Bernie Grant, who in 1987 became one of the first Black MPs to enter Parliament and had spent his life fighting against social and racial injustice, also made it into the top ten. Cultural theorist Stuart Hall, who through his work shifted debates on the media, race, politics and critical theory, could not be denied a place for his academic contributions.

The person who received the most votes and was named the Greatest Black Briton was the Jamaican nurse and Crimean War heroine Mary Seacole.

Seacole was celebrated in her lifetime for her great courage and skills as a doctress, with her ability to heal ailments using herbal remedies. Travelling alone to the Crimea after her offers of service were rejected by the War Office because of her race, she set up the 'British Hotel', where she took care of sick and injured soldiers. Seacole's advances in the field of what Helen Rappaport called a holistic practice of nursing – influenced by the Caribbean tradition of healing and treating illnesses using herbal remedies – and her service to the soldiers faded from memory after her death. Winning the Great Black Britons poll set into motion a sequence of events that helped restore Seacole to public consciousness. She became the subject of a new biography and, by an extraordinary stroke of fortune, the only known painted portrait of her was discovered and acquired by the National Portrait Gallery on a long-term loan.

In 2004 the Mary Seacole Memorial Statue Trust was established to raise money for a statue, which was installed in the grounds of St Thomas' Hospital in June 2016, the first statue of a named Black woman in the UK.

Unquestionably, Seacole winning the 100 Great Black Britons poll influenced the success of the memorial statue campaign and, more broadly, created a small shift in perceptions about British history and its inclusion of diverse narratives. A conversation had been started – attempts were being made to restore the traces of a Black past that had been removed or forgotten, demonstrating they were part of the British future, in a way that should be fixed in the national memory.

Britain's decision to leave the European Union in June 2016

has plunged the country into one of the most fraught and divisive periods in its history. Anti-immigration sentiment appears to have been a key factor in people's decision to leave, along with belief in a threat to Britain's sovereignty from Brussels who supposedly wield control over British laws and its borders. The language of the leavers was persuasive and pernicious, offering dehumanising narratives of Muslims, asylum seekers and immigrants. With the resurgence of far-right nationalist groups capitalising on the rise of populism, their rhetoric has been co-opted in mainstream political discourses and driven by a hostile media. It is no surprise that hate crimes, race-related and xenophobic, increased by 17 per cent in the twelve months leading to March 2018.[16]

Studies of the people who voted to leave have shown that they have a tendency to support conservative policies and have a traditional view of Britain; they are likely to have a less critical and more rosy view of the country's past, a nostalgia for a time when Britain had a more homogenous population and an empire.[17] Those who voted to leave may have understood that to leave the EU was to 'take back control' over the country's destiny, and who it could permit to enter and exit its borders.

The Conservative Party's resolve to protect the public from illegal immigration saw the then Home Secretary Theresa May introduce a 'hostile environment' policy in 2012 to expedite their removal. Although the impact of the policy wasn't brought to national attention until 2018, almost immediately the policy disproportionately affected African and Caribbean-born citizens and their descendants who were unable to provide documentary proof of their Britishness. The so-called '*Windrush* Scandal' in 2018 resulted in wrongful deportations and the loss of jobs, homes, access to medical treatment and benefits because the burden of proof of Britishness was placed on the people caught up in it. That the *Windrush* Scandal occurred in the seventieth year of the docking of the SS *Empire Windrush* was as depressing as it was shocking. Men and women who had travelled as children with their parents, who had answered the call to come to the 'mother country' to help rebuild it after the war, had their lives destroyed for not being able to 'prove' their Britishness.[18]

As the 'justification of presence' gains traction, and against the backdrop of uncertainty, hostility and turmoil, reviving the 100 Great Black Britons campaign could be one way to remind Britain that it benefits significantly from what Paul Gilroy has termed the 'rich diversity of convivial culture'.

A new campaign that celebrates African British people, past and present, is necessary in bringing people together, to challenge current ideas of Britishness, and assert that it can be expressed within a multitude of ethnicities and cultures. This book, which accompanies a fresh campaign that has taken place between 2018 and 2020, places the nominees in context, offering a comprehensive narrative study of the lives and contributions of Black British people, past and present. A few of the profiles are doubled up due to the fact they belong to the same profession or are contemporaries.

The list features not only the so-called 'great and good'; it also celebrates individuals who are well known within their communities and explores the ways in which they have enriched those communities. For every Stormzy, there is an Eric Irons – there are countless men and women who form part of community narratives of survival, resistance and cultural and political change.

Diane Abbott

(b. 1953) politician

I N April 2019, Diane Abbott was photographed unwinding,
after a long day's work, with a mojito while travelling on
public transport. Abbott apologised after the photos were circulated on social media. Many people, however, stood in solidarity
with Abbott, photographing themselves on trains enjoying the
premixed cocktail; 31,000 people even attended a Facebook
event 'Sipping a cheeky mojito on the underground'.

The incident was another in a long line to embarrass and
shame the embattled MP, who, in the years since the referendum to leave the EU, has suffered more racist and sexist abuse
than at any time since she entered politics over thirty-five years
ago, receiving ten times more abuse than any other MP in the
weeks leading to the 2017 election.[1] This is an astonishing
statistic, giving an indication of her position in relation to her
peers as a high-profile Black woman.

She went public with the vile nature of some of the abuse,
which she described as 'debilitating, corrosive and upsetting',
aware that the roots of the abuse lay in the fact she is a female
and Black politician, a stark example of misogynoir.[2] In 2018
research undertaken by Amnesty International found Black

women in journalism and politics were 84 per cent more likely to face online abuse than white women, a chilling statistic.[3]

The personal, racial and political attacks on Abbott, which she attempts to transcend by 'putting one foot in front of the other', often take focus away from the fact she is a trailblazer who has spent her career bringing gender equality and race to the forefront of British politics, and who votes according to her conscience, sometimes not in line with official policy.

Abbott's life and career have been marked by a series of significant firsts. She was the first of her family to attend university (Cambridge); the first Black woman to enter Parliament in 1987, elected in that year along with Paul Boateng, Keith Vaz and Bernie Grant. She is also the first Black woman to become Shadow Home Secretary and to lead Prime Minister's Questions in Parliament.

Her career has been defined by the desire to affect social and political change. As a student she realised she wanted to change the world for working-class people. The daughter of Jamaican immigrants, and an attendee at one of the country's leading universities, she understood her life experiences differed significantly from her fellow students – an understanding that has influenced her politics ever since.

As for many other prominent women in politics today, feminist politics was the framework in which she began her career. She recalls attending the first Black feminist conferences in the 1980s, sharing platforms with emerging female council leaders, such as Margaret Hodge (leader of Islington Council, Labour MP) and Linda Bellos (leader of Lambeth Council). She also cites Ken Livingstone, who, as leader of the Greater London Council, pursued trailblazing policies including supporting women's and LGBT rights.[4]

Abbott has used her platform to find ways to close the attainment gap among Black pupils. She founded the Black Child Initiative to raise educational achievement among Black pupils in London, hosting an annual conference for educators, children and their parents. She is an eloquent and articulate communicator, winning the Parliamentary Speech of the Year in 2008 for her speech on civil liberties in the counterterrorism debate.

For Abbott, the immigration scandal affecting the so-called *Windrush* generation has been personal as well as political. At the time the 'hostile environment' policy was being debated in Parliament, Abbott expressed her concerns to Theresa May, the then Home Secretary, about the danger of the targeting of people who may on paper present as being here illegally, but in reality were not. How the scandal has played out has laid bare the deep flaws within the system, and its conflation of immigration with race. Of the hostile environment policy, Abbot remarked that 'it's almost impossible to produce a hostile environment for immigrants and not produce a hostile environment for people who look like immigrants'. She argues that the nature of the debate on immigration needs to change from problematising immigrants to overhauling the system.

Despite the barrage of criticism and abuse levied at Diane Abbott, her contributions to the country are notable and significant. The fact she regained her seat in the 2017 general election with 42,000 votes and in 2019 with 39,972 votes sends a clear message to those determined to bring her down, that she is loved and respected by her constituents and a new generation of young Black women who aspire to enter politics.

Victor Adebowale, Baron Adebowale CBE

(b. 1962) health and social care executive

Victor Olufemi Adebowale was the chief executive officer of Turning Point, a social enterprise that offers adult social care services to people with complex needs in three hundred locations across England, in a range of areas including mental health, drug addiction and unemployment. As chief executive from 2001 to 2020, Adebowale oversaw a significant increase in the number of people the charity serves; by the end of his tenure, turnover had increased from £20 million to £130 million, supporting 100,000 people annually and employing around 4000 people, from doctors and social workers to psychiatrists and counsellors. He has said it's the people he works with, especially those who engage with the public and 'who give a damn', who inspire him.

One of the most dynamic figures in health and social care, Adebowale has been one of the principal movers behind health and social care policy, and as a crossbench peer has advised successive governments on learning disabilities, mental health, social care, inclusion and housing.

Hailing from Wakefield in Yorkshire, Adebowale's interest in these social issues was inspired by his mother, an NHS nurse. A friendship with a young woman with a learning disability then helped to inform his sensibilities around the importance of prioritising the health and welfare needs of those with learning disabilities.

Adebowale came from humble beginnings – his first job was working as a street sweeper, which he said gave him a grounding in understanding people.

He went on to work in the housing association movement, rising through the ranks to become regional director of the largest Black-led housing association, Ujima, while still in his twenties. He was chief executive of the homelessness charity Centrepoint for five years before taking the helm at Turning Point. In late December 2019, it was announced that Adebowale would be leaving that charity to take up the role of chair of the NHS Confederation, the non-partisan health charity, in April 2020.

One of Adebowale's concerns is that there is 'a striking absence of diversity' within the leadership of health and social care charities, who serve people of colour disproportionately but with a mostly white leadership making decisions about their needs. Minority groups, he argues, don't have access to the networks that make them visible to head hunters, which means little has changed – although more women are in leadership roles, they are not women of colour.

'I could not imagine,' Adebowale writes, 'a black exec of the National Trust . . . similarly I could not imagine a black exec of Macmillan or the Red Cross, and that is an indicator of how little has changed over the years.'

How talent is defined needs a radical rethink, says Adebowale: where to find it and how to encourage it. It is diversity of thought that matters, and the presence of Black and ethnic minority people in leadership positions would be an excellent indicator of this.

Adedoyin Olayiwola Adepitan MBE

(b. 1973) Paralympic athlete, broadcaster

I N 2013, ADE Adepitan travelled to Nigeria, the country of his birth, to make a documentary to understand why it was one of only three remaining countries in the world where children still contracted polio. Adepitan, who contracted polio aged fifteen months, leaving him unable to use his left leg and having only partial use in his right, learned that religion, a suspicion of outsiders, terrorism and terrible sanitation were the principal reasons. Angered and saddened, Adepitan knew that thousands of children were at risk from contracting a disease that was easily preventable, condemning them to lives of great hardship, lack of opportunities and exclusion.

Ade Adepitan is a television presenter and broadcaster, former wheelchair basketball player and junior powerlifting champion. He was the face of the 2002 BBC ident *Hip Hop*, featuring three wheelchair dancers spinning and doing wheelies. He has presented documentaries and programmes for Channel 4 and the BBC, and has been part of the presenting teams for the Paralympic Games since 2008.

When Adepitan went back to Nigeria to make his documentary, he thought about what his life would have been like had his parents decided to remain there. The decision made by his parents to move to Britain achieved what they hoped – that Adepitan would have greater disability support. Little did they realise that their son would lead such a remarkable life.

Two physiotherapists who had set up a wheelchair basketball team in Newham, London, introduced Adepitan to wheelchair basketball when they saw him being raced about in a shopping trolley by his friends, the fastest way for him to keep up with them. They asked if he wanted to swap the trolley for a wheelchair and be part of a basketball team.

Adepitan was initially reluctant to participate, however, because when he was a teenager his preconceptions of wheelchairs were negative. He has admitted that 'as a young thirteen-year-old kid, when you're told you're going to watch wheelchair athletes, I was like nah! I don't want to have anything to do with this! I almost felt embarrassed . . .'[1]

Adepitan wanted to be like everyone else, and walked with the assistance of callipers. He went to Stoke Mandeville Hospital (renowned for developing wheelchair and amputee sports after the Second World War) in Aylesbury where he saw the British men's wheelchair basketball team in action and was astounded at how good they were. The other thing that amazed him was the physicality of the sport. 'It seems counterintuitive,' he recalled, 'when you think of disability you don't think of physicality, you think of people trying not to hurt themselves . . . these guys were crashing into each other's chairs. Imagine for the first time you see a guy with no legs flying down the court, and he smashes into someone else's chair, he flies out the chair, rolls down the court . . . within five minutes of watching these guys I knew this was the sport for me.'[2]

Adepitan found his wheels empowering. 'I could do more than walking, I moved around faster, I felt so much more able, it helped me believe in who I was.'[3] He described his team-mates on the Newham Rollers as giving him a sense of belonging, and from the moment he joined the team it was his ambition to play for the national team.

After being rejected for the national team seven times, in 2000 Adepitan was selected to compete at the Sydney Paralympic Games. During those times of rejection, he said he had to dig deep within his well of determination and self-belief to keep going. He won a bronze medal in the Athens Paralympic Games in 2004, and scored the winning basket that helped the team win gold at the Paralympic World Cup in 2005.

Adepitan believes that the increased coverage of the Paralympic Games has helped to change perceptions about people with disabilities, with Paralympians becoming household names. Channel 4's *The Last Leg*, which was first broadcast during the 2012 London Paralympics to reflect on each day's events during the competition, is today a popular comedy and late-night television programme that features interviews with Paralympians and celebrities. Adepitan himself played a wheelchair basketball coach in the 2007 CBBC drama *Desperados*, which followed the journey of a young footballer who, following a disabling accident on the pitch, finds meaning and purpose when he joins a wheelchair basketball team.

In 2019, Adepitan hosted a four-part documentary for the BBC, *Africa with Ade Adepitan*, which saw him exploring countries across the continent in ways that reflected his enthusiasm, fearlessness and sense of adventure. Adepitan said that as far as he knew, there had never been a major four-part documentary series hosted by a Black disabled TV presenter, and he was excited at the prospect of putting his stamp on four hours of TV. 'I could finally make the type of documentary that I wanted to make,' he wrote, 'which was both educational, challenging and most importantly, entertaining.'[4]

Dr Maggie Aderin-Pocock MBE

(b. 1968) space scientist, television presenter

THE FILM *HIDDEN Figures* (2016) brought to light a story that had remained secret for decades. An African American mathematician, Katherine Johnson, was responsible for calculating the launch and landing coordinates for Alan Shepard and John Glenn's historic space travels in the 1960s. In the film, Johnson (played by Taraji P. Henson) and her colleagues Dorothy Vaughan (Octavia Spencer) and Mary Jackson (Janelle Monae) are the central characters in this true story of space exploration's early days. Here we see Black women in roles representing science, technology, engineering and mathematics (STEM) on screen. Off screen, visible representations of Black women in STEM are elusive; the latest statistics show that 6.2 per cent of students enrolled on to STEM-related subjects at UK universities are BAME; and although BAME girls are more likely to study STEM at A level, further exploration of those statistics indicates that girls of African Caribbean heritage are least likely to study a STEM subject at A level, and that they are disproportionately encouraged to study vocational subjects.[1]

Black women leading their fields in STEM are, just like the characters in *Hidden Figures*, helping to make the dreams of

Black girls interested in sciences a reality through their visibility and advocacy. By extension, Dr Maggie Aderin-Pocock demonstrates that careers in science and technology for Black women are attainable.

Dr Aderin-Pocock is passionate about science and technology and making them accessible to the general public. She is heavily involved in public engagement activities: through her company Science Innovation Ltd, she delivers many public lectures to children and adults, translating the complexities of science into a language that everyone can understand. Having the skill to explain complex ideas to a lay audience is a gift that not many, even the most brilliant people, possess. Her knowledge and her enthusiasm for her field mean that people perhaps not normally drawn to science find themselves captivated by the excitement and wonders of the universe.

In her career as a scientist, she works both in academia and the space industry, making specialised instruments such as parts for telescopes, handheld landmine detectors and optical subsystems. She is also an award-winning broadcaster – her BBC Two programme *Do We Really Need the Moon?* (2011) won the Talkback Thames new talent award at the Women in TV and Film Awards.

Born in London to Nigerian parents, Aderin-Pocock always wanted to be a scientist, working in space and astronomy. As a child she learned to build her own telescope and would plead with her parents to allow her to stay up late so she could watch *The Sky at Night*. Today, Aderin-Pocock is one of the presenters of this much-loved and long-running astronomy programme, which she says has brought her full circle. She has also spoken about her love for the 1970s children's programme *The Clangers*, which she says inspired her interest in space.

Having struggled with dyslexia and being placed in remedial classes, she says she felt 'written off', unable to fulfil her potential since her teachers assumed she wasn't very intelligent. Because of these negative experiences, she's made it her mission to inspire children, particularly Black children, that science as a career is possible, and that being a Black female astronomer can change stereotypes.

After graduating with a BSc in physics and a doctorate in mechanical engineering, she has been involved in many different projects in the space and defence industries, including designing missile warning systems for the Ministry of Defence, leading a group making observational instruments for the European Space Agency and NASA, and helping to build the 8-metre Gemini telescope for the conservatory in Chile that provides coverage for the northern and southern skies.

Keen to chip away at the assumption that scientists and TV science presenters are white and male, Dr Aderin-Pocock's aim is to demystify science by showing Black children that being a scientist isn't strange or unattainable.

Professor Hakim Adi

(b. 1957) historian, author, activist

H AKIM ADI, PROFESSOR of African History at the University of Chichester, is the first person of African heritage to be promoted to professor of history in a UK institution of higher education. That this only happened in 2014 speaks to the continuing predicament of the under-representation of Black British scholars when it comes to attainment and progression in UK higher education. That there are currently eighty-five Black professors, twenty-five of whom are women and only two of whom are historians, reflects the difficulties that Black academics face when trying to thrive within environments that are white and are not structured to embrace difference; as academic Robbie Shilliam has remarked, 'the doors to higher education have been opened, but the architecture of the building has hardly changed'.[1]

Hakim Adi has been at the vanguard of the study of Black British history, working inside and outside of academia to challenge the Eurocentric teaching and researching of history. The absence of Black historians has been for many years supplemented by Black people producing and disseminating their own histories in the community. Adi has been a member of this grassroots organising, which has a long history. In addition he has, since 1991, through the work of the Black and Asian Studies Association (BASA) which he co-founded with Marika Sherwood, campaigned for the growth of Black British history as a way to understand how people of African descent have helped shape the history of Britain, both locally and globally. Together they established a network of teachers, historians, writers and archivists who were committed to educating and disseminating material about Black and Asian people in Britain and lobbying successive governments for this history to be included in the national curriculum. BASA's campaigning has resulted in changes in the national curriculum, and museums and archives have become more inclusive in their interpretations and engagement with their materials.

Professor Adi is one of the few historians specialising in the history of the African diaspora in Britain. He explores the political history of West Africans in Britain, and the influence of Pan-Africanism and communism on anti-colonial activism. The interest in his research and his activism has led to him speaking around the world, and he works with museums, libraries and archives to help them make marginalised histories more visible and accessible.

In 2015, concerned at the alarmingly low numbers of Black students on history undergraduate courses, Adi once again acted, organising a conference called History Matters. Held at the University of London in partnership with the Royal Historical Society and the Historical Association, the conference invited undergraduates, postgraduates, teachers and academics to hear research and participate in discussions on how history was currently being taught in schools. An outcome of the conference was the establishment of the Young Historians Project, a group of young Black British students who research underexplored and overlooked community histories.

Sir David Adjaye OBE, RA and
Elsie Owusu OBE, RIBA

(b. 1966 / b. 1955) architects

S IR DAVID ADJAYE and Elsie Owusu are two of the leading
Black British architects working in the UK. Both are at the
top of their profession, leading successful practices that have
won major commissions in the UK and internationally to
design public buildings and private residences. Adjaye, arguably the world's most celebrated Black architect, was the creative force behind the Museum of African American History
and Culture in Washington, DC, which was named Beazley
Design of the Year in 2017, with the judges selecting it 'as a
reminder that design enables a diverse conversation and can
challenge the dominant political discourse'. Inspired by
Yoruban art and architecture, the museum explores the history
of America through the African American experience.

Owusu, a specialist conservation architect, has won plaudits
for her work as co-lead architect on two major projects: the
refurbishments and renovation of the UK Supreme Court and
the entrance to Green Park Underground Station.

Adjaye and Owusu are among a handful of Black and Asian
architects who have succeeded against the odds, breaking

through the barriers often imposed by an industry that, according to a survey conducted by the *Architects' Journal* in partnership with the Stephen Lawrence Charitable Trust, struggles with 'unacknowledged racism', and is slow to dismantle the barriers to progression and offer support for Black and Asian architects who believe their skin colour is hindering their career. The survey is a stark indication of the level of the problem; almost a quarter of Black and Asian architects (23.4 per cent) said they thought that racism was widespread in the profession, with almost a quarter saying they had been a victim of racism at work.[1] Another stark message from the survey was that Black and Asian architects still feel they have huge hurdles to overcome to reach the profession's more senior levels, with seven out of ten respondents saying that being Black or Asian created barriers to career progression.[2]

To be an architect requires years of education and training. It involves three stages of study, which includes undergraduate and postgraduate degrees and diplomas, work placements, specialist training and a final qualifying exam. It is expensive, so mentoring and financial support are essential, and mentoring schemes and bursaries are often critical to the success of aspiring Black and Asian architects. The Stephen Lawrence Charitable Trust honours the architectural legacy of Stephen, who had hoped to enter the profession before his tragic death, by providing bursaries and mentoring schemes for many aspiring architects who would not have broken through without its support. Despite this, the number of Black and Asian architects is shrinking – for every ten BAME students that begin training, only one emerges.[3]

In their own ways, Owusu and Adjaye endeavour to change the rules of the game; they have broken through the glass ceiling by establishing their own practices, providing opportunities for aspiring and talented architects of Black and Asian heritage. Adjaye lets the quality of his work speak as a way to challenge the system. Despite early public projects such as the Ideas Store in Tower Hamlets and the Stephen Lawrence Centre in Deptford receiving a lukewarm reception, his design of the Nobel Peace Centre in Oslo (2005), the Museum of Contemporary Art in Denver (2007) and the Skolkovo School of Management in Moscow (2010) are significant commissions that reflect, as his former partner William Russell has remarked, 'his ability to think big, pushing the client beyond their limits'.[4]

Owusu, who is very much in demand as a conservation architect and interior and urban designer, is on a mission to open up the profession. The co-founder of the Society of Black Architects, she campaigns for the profession to modernise and open itself to men and women of all backgrounds and ethnicities. In 2017 she launched, along with the Stephen Lawrence Charitable Trust, the RIBA (Royal Institute of British Architects) 25+ campaign to increase diversity – an initiative that resulted in raising the number of non-white members of RIBA's governing council from one (Owusu) to a historic twelve.[5] She also risked her professional career by bringing the charge of institutional racism and discrimination to the door of RIBA. In 2018 she ran for the institute's presidency, and during her campaign she claimed that it was institutionally racist and sexist.

Sir David Adjaye and Elsie Owusu reflect the best of British architectural talent and innovation. Their work demands they be judged on their skill, and their activism demands that architecture cannot remain an old boys' club.

Akala

(b. 1983) rapper, poet, author

Akala is a polymath; a modern-day Renaissance man who has enjoyed a multifaceted career as an award-winning hip-hop artist, bestselling author, poet, educator and cultural commentator.

His first book, *Natives: Race and Class in the Ruins of Empire* (2018), quickly made the *Sunday Times* bestseller list, raising his profile and revealing a depth of range of a person who is interested in many diverse topics: Shakespeare, political economy, sociology, culture, music, history and much more.

Part memoir, part social and cultural history, and part political commentary, in the book Akala used his life experiences to explore, among many other topics, the impact of structural racism on the life chances for Black people; the intersections of race and class; how empire is still extolled as beneficial to the countries who suffered under it, while its dreadful legacies are largely ignored; identity politics; and the excluding, damaging nature of the education system that many readers who are of African heritage will recognise. Much of what Akala writes about, in terms of his life as a young Black man, resonates, and therefore he gives voice to the experiences of many Black British men and women who have had difficult but predictable inter-actions with whiteness, as it operates in the institutional frame-work of schools, policing and employment. *Natives* is also an impressively researched book, extensively referenced, which unpicks imperial transgressions such as enslavement and its legacies, as well as Britain's inability or unwillingness to confront issues of race and class in a meaningful and constructive way.

Born Kingslee Daley, he performs under the name Akala, a Buddhist word that means 'immovable'. The younger sibling of the Mercury Prize-winning artist Ms Dynamite and of Jamaican and Scottish parentage, Akala grew up in Kentish Town, London, and developed a love for theatre and music while seeing numerous productions at the Hackney Empire, where his stepfather worked as stage manager.

His love of performance is evident in his music, which is influenced by the philosophy of Afrika Bambaataa and KRS-1, early hip-hop pioneers who envisaged the art form to educate as well as entertain. Preferring this more intellectual (and some might say less popular) branch of hip-hop, his music references cultural icons and historical figures such as Malcolm X and Marcus Garvey, encouraging the listener to seek self-knowledge and to question everything, especially how the history of African people has been distorted or hidden. His scepticism about how history is taught and disseminated, and the intention behind it, stems from attending a Pan-African Saturday school as a child, where he learned a different interpretation of history – one that focused on how enslaved people were the agents of their own liberation, and about Pan-African leaders who fought to liberate themselves and their countries from the grip of imperialism.

Akala is also a sought-after political, social and cultural commentator and has lectured at many universities in Britain and around the world. His appearances on *Question Time* and *Good Morning Britain*, as a guest whom Piers Morgan did not shout over, were shared thousands of times over various social media platforms. What is celebrated is his eloquence, articulacy and knowledge on topics under discussion, while challenging many viewers' perceptions and assumptions about the intelligence of young Black men.

Akala created a series of short films for the *Guardian* on race and imperial history, and his YouTube channel discusses the books he is currently reading and encourages his viewers to read widely and think critically, and he speaks about his own creative process and the books that have helped him to write. As a broadcaster, he presented *Akala's Odyssey* for BBC Four, exploring the story of Homer's *Odyssey*, and gave a performance piece for BBC Two entitled *The Ruins of Empire*, using animation to present an abridged version of his poem.

John Akomfrah CBE

(b. 1957) writer, artist, filmmaker

I N THE 2010 film *The Nine Muses*, John Akomfrah uses
archive footage of a 'West Indian Man' newly arrived in
Britain reflecting with an English interviewer on how isolation
was generally impacting upon him and others in their new
home. 'The initial experience,' he says, 'is [not being able] to
call on the hundreds of people around him . . . for the first
time, he is alone.'

Anxious to put a positive spin on this depressing assessment
and thinking, perhaps, of how the film would be received by
the mainly white audience, the interviewer replies, his tone
hopeful and assured, 'Eventually, you get settled.'

'You get settled,' agrees the man, 'and then you too become
part of the strangeness.' The 'strangeness' the man speaks about
can be defined as how Caribbean immigrants had to face and
negotiate the combination of expressions of acceptance and
tolerance and a contrasting environment of hostility and othering, as played out in this filmed exchange.[1]

In this segment, the interviewee may be speaking of the
effect these contradictions are having on him and how he is
attempting to adapt to them, as opposed to the effect his

presence was having on British culture and way of life. In this film, as in Akomfrah's other works, the key themes driving them is the centring of the experience of the African diaspora in Britain and the world. He juxtaposes newsreel and archive material and intersperses them with contemporary film, modern and classical literature to create poetic documentary essays and features that explore race, identity and memory.

Akomfrah, who was born in Accra, Ghana, and moved to London with his parents as a child, is a co-founding member of the Black Audio Film Collective. Formed in 1982 at Portsmouth Polytechnic, the members of the collective – Akomfrah, Reece Auguiste, Edward George, Lina Gopaul, Avril Johnson, David Lawson and Trevor Mathison – created a series of experimental works exploring identity and the popular and political culture that defines the Black and Asian British experience. Using the works of Stuart Hall and other social and post-colonial theorists as an intellectual framework, they offered new interpretations of the Black British experience through documentary, video and film, with a distinctive Black voice.

Akomfrah, through his work with the collective and his solo work, has established himself as a pioneer of British film and one of the most influential figures of Black British culture from the 1980s to the present.

His first film, *Handsworth Songs* (1986), was a counter narrative to the mainstream media's biased depictions and analysis of the 1985 Handsworth uprising, which ignored the root causes of the disturbances, and the death and funeral of Cynthia Jarrett, which sparked the Broadwater Farm uprising in London. Akomfrah's film was a response to descriptions of Black youth involved as a mindless mob clashing with the police, looting stores and attacking members of the Sikh community. Using montage, recurring images, reggae and voiceover poetry, and undercutting newsreel shots of West Indian immigration in the 1950s with shots of the uprising, Akomfrah communicated a sense of what it meant to be Black in Britain in the 1980s.[2] Commissioned by Channel 4, the film made a considerable impact when it was shown a year after the uprisings, and won seven international film awards, including the BFI John Grierson Award for Best Documentary.

His documentary *Riot* (1999) reflects on the events surrounding the uprising in Toxteth, Liverpool, in 1981, which is told from the perspectives of the people involved, including residents, journalists, local activists and police officers. Each of them thinks back on the events that led up to what was one of the most turbulent examples of civil disobedience of the late twentieth century.

Akomfrah's distinctive method of combining archive footage, soundscapes and contemporary shots can be seen throughout in his work, whether this is confronting the impact of climate change on our planet (*Purple*, 2017), exposing the brutality and disorder of the whaling industry (*Vertigo Sea*, 2015) or tracing the life and work of the pioneering academic and intellectual Stuart Hall via video installation (*The Unfinished Conversation*, 2013). His work *Mimesis: African Soldier* debuted at the Imperial War Museum in 2018, exploring the overlooked role of soldiers serving across the African continent during the First World War.

Ira Aldridge

(1807–67) actor

I RA ALDRIDGE WAS the first major Black Shakespearean actor
in Europe, and one of the greatest actors of his day. No
other performer travelled as widely, enacting the plays of
Shakespeare throughout Europe and as far as Moscow, Kiev
and St Petersburg. He interpreted Black and white roles in classical plays to international acclaim, gaining some autonomy
over representing a Black character in mainstream theatre. Yet,
even after he established his reputation in Britain and Europe,
and won many awards and honours for his acting, Aldridge was
seldom invited to perform in London and never performed in
the United States. He succeeded against tremendous odds in a
profession not open to Black people; he was an anomaly in the
era of slavery in the Americas, contradicting the stereotypes
that white people in the nineteenth century preferred to hold
of Black people. His dignity and intelligence came as a great
surprise to audiences who expected someone cruder and clum-
sier, quickly finding the joke was on them.

Born in New York in 1807, Aldridge was drawn to the
theatre as a teenager, becoming involved in a number of
dramatic productions put on by the African Theatre. He

developed a deep passion for the stage and aspired to become a professional actor. As the movement towards the abolition of slavery was more established in Britain and Europe than in the United States, Aldridge saw an opportunity to realise his ambitions, and he left for England on a ship bound for Liverpool, intending to perform on the English and European stages. In the spring of 1825, aged seventeen, he made his debut in *The Revolt of Suriname, or a Slave's Revenge*, at the Royal Coburg Theatre (the site of the Old Vic) in London. Although he had the audience on his side, critics reacted to a Black actor playing a Black role with hostility. It wasn't until eight years later that Aldridge was invited to perform again in a major London theatre; during that period, he honed his craft in the English provinces. Developing a repertoire including roles in *Othello*, abolitionist melodramas, comedies and musical farces, Aldridge could perform as many as sixteen different roles on demand, and back then actors would sometimes play three different roles in one evening. The playwright Lolita Chakrabarti, whose play *Red Velvet* (2012) deals with Aldridge's life and his performance as Othello, has noted that by the end of his career he had a repertoire of forty characters in his head, showing just how talented, hardworking and tenacious he was.[1]

In 1833 Aldridge returned to London to play Othello at the Covent Garden Theatre, performing the role for only two nights; the critics again savaged his performance, complaining about his manner, his voice, his accent and his colour. Once again, although the critics hated him, he won praise from his audiences. He performed for the next nineteen years in the provinces, extending his Shakespearian repertoire with white roles, including Shylock, Richard III and Macbeth. In 1852 he embarked on his first European tour, and after three years abroad returned to England laden with honours and awards, but still unable to find regular engagements in London. Further tours in Europe made him world famous, but success on the London stage continued to evade him. He spent his final years performing in France and Russia where he was acclaimed as one of the greatest tragedians of all time, and died while on tour in Poland in August 1867.

Aldridge's life and career are remarkable in ways that today are still not fully appreciated. Of his own volition, he transcended the roles that, as a Black man, he would have been expected to play. He was the first Black man to play white roles in Shakespeare's plays – roles that are considered the ultimate test for an actor. He performed bilingual productions when he toured Europe and Russia, and must have been aware that his race drew customers to his performances. That said, it was his talent that kept audiences returning.

Aldridge adopted the stage name 'African Roscius', and it remained his trademark throughout his life. 'Roscius' was the middle name of the eminent Roman actor Quintus Roscius Gallus and had become a word used in the nineteenth-century theatre world to describe an actor of great talent and skill. The name suggests classical poise and refinement, and was wholly appropriate for the style of Aldridge's performances. As well as being a clever way for Aldridge to promote himself, the title also helped to challenge expectations and assumptions; Aldridge was an African in a race-conscious society, who was not expected to attain excellence in artistic interpretation, but did.

Valerie Amos, Baroness Amos CH

(b. 1954) politician, diplomat

VALERIE AMOS HAS had a distinguished and impressive career in politics and diplomacy. She was the first Black woman to serve as a minister in the British cabinet, as Secretary for International Development. In the House of Lords, she served as Leader of the House and Lord President of the Council, presiding over meetings of the Privy Council, the formal body that advises the monarch.

She has also served as High Commissioner to Australia and was Undersecretary General for Humanitarian Affairs and Emergency Relief Coordinator at the United Nations. In this role, she called for a UN resolution to allow access for aid to reach Syria; Resolution 2139 was adopted unanimously by the UN Security Council in February 2014.

In 2015, Amos was appointed as director of the School of Oriental and African Studies (SOAS), the first Black woman to head a university. In August 2020, she took up the post of Master of University College, Oxford, becoming the first female master of that college and the first Black head of any Oxford college.

In the ground-breaking research project 'The Colour of Power', undertaken by the *Guardian*, Operation Black Vote and Green Park Recruitment, it was discovered in a study of a thousand top jobs that only 3 per cent were held by Black and minority ethnic individuals and 23 per cent held by women.[1] Given that Black and minority ethnic people make up nearly 14 per cent of the population and women around 50 per cent, it means that top jobs, such as high court judges, senior police officers, advertising executives and university vice-chancellors, continue to be held predominantly by white men. Consequently, Amos, who is at the top of her profession, represents someone who has broken through formidable barriers, holding particularly challenging jobs with composure and competency.

Born in British Guiana (Guyana), Valerie Amos came to Britain as a nine-year-old and was brought up in the suburbs of Kent. She was the first Black pupil at her selective grammar school, with her sister following her three years later. She credits her parents, who were both teachers, with helping to build her confidence to navigate living in a new country. They also encouraged her to have an opinion, teaching their daughters how to become good debaters, to think logically and develop their arguments.

Passionate about equality and social justice, Amos read sociology at Warwick University and studied for a master's degree at the Centre for Contemporary Cultural Studies at the University of Birmingham in the 1980s. There she became involved with a new collaborative cohort of scholars of Black and Asian heritage, including Hazel Carby, Paul Gilroy, Errol Lawrence and Pratibha Parma, who, under the guidance of Stuart Hall, director of the centre, produced publications exploring race, racism and social inequality. These publications became the staple of reading lists on sociology courses on race and ethnicity, and on other social science disciplines. Noting that analyses of race were absent from feminism, Amos co-authored an article with Pratibha Parma called 'Challenging Imperial Feminism' (1984), which was published in the *Feminist Review*. A Black feminist critique of the women's movement of the early 1980s, it argued that many gains made by white women had been at the expense of Black working-class women, and that their biases had prevented Black women from participating in the movement in any meaningful way.[2]

Amos's career trajectory has moved some distance from the radical intellectualism of the 1980s, yet she has retained her interest in how organisations and their cultures work. She once said she wanted to work inside organisations, to enable them to become the best they could be. After working for several London local authorities, she was appointed chief executive of the Equal Opportunities Commission in 1989, tackling sex discrimination. Amos transformed the commission, giving it a more active and aggressive role, regularly challenging the government on judicial review of employment legislation that discriminated against women.[3]

After that breakthrough appointment, Amos co-founded the consultancy Amos Fraser Bernard, and became an advisor to Nelson Mandela's South African government on public service reform, human rights and employment equality. Being good at running things prepared her for later roles in politics and diplomacy.

She says she is still passionate about the same things: issues of equality, social justice and reform, pushing for change on the inside quietly, and walking towards challenges and not away from them.

Kehinde Andrews

(b. 1983) academic, activist, author

KEHINDE ANDREWS HAS emerged as one of the most prolific Black political voices speaking on racism and inequality in Britain today. He is one the developers of the degree in Black Studies at Birmingham City University (BCU), the first course of its kind in Europe, centring the experiences, perspectives and contributions of people from the African diaspora. A course of study that has been a mainstay in American universities since the 1960s, its introduction into a UK university in 2017 is remarkable, revealing two things. Firstly, a lack of Black scholars in UK universities, which has been often remarked upon, but little has been done to instigate change. Secondly, lack of interest and engagement on the part of universities in studies on Black British perspectives, histories and contributions. The fact that BCU had six Black scholars in the same department – an extreme rarity – made the Black Studies course possible.

Andrews can be described as a scholar activist, who uses his position as an academic to bring attention to racial inequalities in Britain. His idol is the human and civil rights activist Malcolm X, whose writings and speeches Andrews frequently references to make points and suggestions of ways in which Black communities can organise and unite for the protection and wellbeing of those communities.

Andrews is in demand as a social, political and cultural commentator, offering sharp critiques on how the legacies of slavery and colonisation manifest themselves in the modern era, from the institutional racism in higher education, to Black people's invisibility in art, to the criminalising and homogenising of young Black men. He is unafraid to attack Britain's role in slavery and colonialism, arguing the West was built on racism, and that modern ideas of science, capitalism and democracy were formed at the expense of Black suffering.

Andrews has been honest about his ambivalent feelings towards universities – although working at one has helped to give him the freedom to write and teach, he is conscious of them being as racist as other institutions in the way that they erase and distort blackness. He argues for everyone, not just students and academics, to be brought into university spaces, which are publicly funded – for people to use these spaces and resources for debate and discussion, and to hold academics to account. He argues that whiteness in the administration, staffing and course content in higher education only reproduces a universal white consciousness, upholding the structures that benefit white people and disadvantage Black and Asian people. As one can imagine, his detractors view him as provocative and divisive; those more supportive of his views see him as speaking truth to power. He has appeared on *Good Morning Britain*, sparking a row when he questioned Winston Churchill's revered status, calling him a racist who believed in white supremacy. Piers Morgan's reaction to Andrews's assertions indicates the degree to which Churchill is ingrained in the national consciousness as above reproach or criticism. In that interview, the contrast of Morgan becoming more and more irritated and Andrews calmly making his point, faintly amused at the vitriol aimed towards him by Morgan and the other guests, was compelling to witness.

Professor Dame Elizabeth Anionwu DBE

(b. 1947) nurse, health activist, campaigner

D AME ELIZABETH ANIONWU gained recognition in the 1980s as one of the pioneering specialist nurses of sickle cell anaemia, leading the first UK nurse-led counselling services for the disorder. As a nurse and later an academic, Dame Elizabeth led the field of sickle cell anaemia and thalassaemia counselling services and education.

Dame Elizabeth's early years sit within a time of sweeping social, cultural and political changes for Britain. Born in 1947, Dame Elizabeth's birth was only one year away from the passing of the 1948 Nationality Act, the arrival of the *Windrush* and the creation of the National Health Service, the institution in which she was to play a significant role. These three events are intricately linked: Caribbean and African immigrants answered the call of the 'mother country' and began to settle in Britain to help rebuild it, including helping to build the newly established NHS, which was suffering from a staffing crisis.

Dame Elizabeth was born to an Irish mother and Nigerian father, who met as students at Cambridge University. Her mother was a promising classics student, the first of her family to attend university; her father was a law student who, like many Nigerian young men of that country's independence generation, would eventually return home to use their education to help their country transition from colony to independent nation. Her father later became a barrister and ambassador to the Vatican.

According to Dame Elizabeth's memoir, the realisation that her mother, from a devout Catholic family, was pregnant out of wedlock was a great shock to her family; to then realise that the child she was carrying was of Nigerian heritage was scandalous. It is estimated that, during the Second World War, around two thousand babies of mixed heritage were born to British women and African American GIs.[1] Although many of the children were kept by their mothers, around a third were placed into care. Consequently, the stigma of Dame Elizabeth's mixed heritage meant that she spent her first nine years at Nazareth House in Birmingham, a home run by Catholic nuns, with her mother visiting regularly. As a child, Dame Elizabeth suffered from severe eczema, and one of the nurses would use humour to distract her from the pain of removing and changing her bandages. The kindness and skill this nurse displayed towards her inspired her to become one herself.

In her memoir, Dame Elizabeth has spoken frankly about her turbulent early years – the rejection and violence meted out by her stepfather, being rescued by her grandparents, her ambivalent feelings towards her mother, and eventually being returned to her mother and stepfather when she was sixteen. A job as a nursing assistant at a residential school provided an escape. She undertook her nursing training at Paddington General Hospital, London, becoming a state-registered nurse in 1968. As a health visitor, working in the community and visiting families in their homes appealed to her, and a friend-ship with a French African nurse and eventually reuniting with her father were crucial to her embracing her African identity and igniting her political awakening. She described herself as a 'radical health visitor', not just interested in health but the overall wellbeing of her patients, including any social and financial problems they might be experiencing. She developed an interest in sickle cell anaemia, a blood disorder that affects people of African, Caribbean and South Asian heritage, as she began to come across it in her work as a health visitor. She was encouraged by her friend, the rights activist and publisher Jessica Huntley, to learn more about the condition, wondering whether it was because it affected marginalised groups that it was a neglected illness. This inspired her to set up a support group, and she became a sickle cell nurse counsellor and infor-mation officer for the Sickle Cell Society, in which role she campaigned for better services for sufferers and their families. Visits to the United States and the Caribbean allowed her to study sickle cell services, as well as general attitudes towards and health beliefs about the illness. She applied her findings to the services she established at Willesden Hospital, London, the first service of its kind in the UK.

Dame Elizabeth's research into sickle cell was ground-breaking. Through her work she successfully positioned herself within the community, the health service and academia, in which she has attained significant respect for her expertise. She was inducted into the *Nursing Times* Nursing Hall of Fame for her work in the development of nurse-led services, and received a Chief Nursing Officers' Award for Lifetime Achievement.

Her campaign for the recognition of the nineteenth-century Jamaican British nurse Mary Seacole raised awareness about her life and the work done by Black and minority ethnic nurses nationally. She established the Mary Seacole Centre for Nursing Practice to establish a multi-ethnic philosophy into the processes of nursing, education and research.

As trustee of the Mary Seacole Memorial Statue Appeal, Dame Elizabeth helped to realise the dream of having a statue of Seacole in front of St Thomas' Hospital in London.

Dr Elaine Arnold

(b. 1927) social worker, academic, researcher

S INCE THE LATE 1940s, Elaine Arnold has been interested in the legacies of broken attachment, separation and loss upon people, and particularly their effects felt upon the reunion of mothers and children of African and Caribbean heritage due to immigration. She has explored these legacies' impact on children and their mothers' emotional health and how that impact typically manifests as behaviours that are often interpreted negatively, and frequently as cultural characteristics. Arnold argues, however, that these reactions to loss are applicable to all children and adults, regardless of their ethnicity or background. Her ground-breaking research has raised awareness of how attachment issues develop within families who have experienced separation and loss.

Her interest in attachment issues and separation was sparked while working as a teacher in a children's home in Trinidad, which housed children for various reasons, including emigration of parents to Britain. She noticed that children cared for by a succession of carers were unable to form deep attachments with adults and would fail to thrive, and when older children were given the opportunity to experience family life with surrogate families, their self-esteem improved. The experience of working at the home and noticing how separation and loss impacted the children's behaviour inspired Arnold to leave teaching and to embark on a career in psychiatric social work.

Her research found that parents who left their children in the Caribbean when they migrated to Britain during the 1950s and 1960s believed their children would be safe and well while raised by family members; that they wouldn't be harmed. What they did not understand, however, was that leaving their children caused them to experience grief and loss, and when the children were reunited with their parents, the grief and loss were compounded when they had to leave their primary caregiver in the Caribbean. Arnold applied John Bowlby's work on children and attachment to demonstrate 'Attachment Theory', showing how Caribbean children were not prepared for these separations and experienced grief as a consequence. They received no help to process their grief, which manifested itself in three stages: protest (crying, often secretly), despair (sadness, lack of interest in school) and detachment (emotional detachment, lack of trust). According to Dr Arnold, these stages are often misinterpreted by the parent as the child being ungrateful for the sacrifices made to bring them over to Britain after having done their best. Unable to understand their children's feelings, they could not help them to process them. A lack of communication led to deeper detachment and insecure relationships between parent and child. Some children found it difficult to develop relationships with their teachers, and the effects of their grief manifested as anger or withdrawal. These behaviours became racialised, regarded as typical behaviour exhibited by African Caribbean pupils.

Arnold has argued that poor attachment can be passed on to the next generation and, to break the cycle, interventions must be made to understand it. She founded the Separation and Reunion Forum in 1999 to raise awareness and to promote a discourse on the importance of secure attachment in children. The forum holds annual conferences for people with personal and professional experiences of issues arising from broken attachments, separation and loss.

Amma Asante MBE

(b. 1969) filmmaker, screenwriter

Amma Asante's directorial debut in 2004, *A Way of Life*, won seventeen international awards, including a BAFTA, and established her as one of Britain's most celebrated directors. One of the few Black British filmmakers working in the industry, her most recent films have explored interracial relationships in different historical periods, and the political, social and personal consequences of love across racial divides.

Born in Streatham, London, to Ghanaian parents, Asante attended stage school at the behest of her father, who believed she needed to overcome her shyness.[1] In the 1980s she became a regular in the school drama *Grange Hill*. She was part of the anti-drug campaign inspired by a harrowing storyline of addiction in the show, and was one of the cast members who took the campaign to the White House.

After appearing in hit television comedies *Desmond's* and *Birds of a Feather*, Asante turned her hand to screenwriting and established her own production company. She wrote and produced the BBC series *Brothers and Sisters*, a drama revolving around the lives of the members of a Baptist congregational choir in Liverpool. The series was notable for featuring some of the best-known Black British actors, including the future Oscar-nominated actor David Oyelowo.

The move into directing occurred when Asante was encouraged by the UK Film Council to direct a film based on a script she had written that challenged the myth of the idyllic rural village, places which in reality are often environments harbouring poverty, inequality, racism and isolation.

Released in 2004, *A Way of Life* is a study on these themes told through the story of a young single mother who goes to increasingly desperate lengths to survive and to keep her daughter from being taken by social services. A confrontational relationship with her Turkish neighbour, whom she believes is trying to get her daughter taken into care, escalates, culminating in him being murdered by her brother and his friends.

The film won Asante the BAFTA's Carl Foreman Award for a debut by a British filmmaker, and the Alfred Dunhill UK Film Talent Award at the London Film Festival. Asante has said that, in her films, she wants to present a point of view with which you may agree or disagree. In *A Way of Life*, she wanted to understand what would motivate the kind of hatred that would lead to murder.[2]

Her second film, *Belle* (2013), tells the story of Dido Elizabeth Belle, daughter of an enslaved African woman, and John Lindsay, a British naval officer. Brought to London as a young child by Lindsay, Belle was brought up by William Murray, 1st Earl of Mansfield and Lord Chief Justice of England, in Kenwood House. Mansfield is known for his legal ruling on two landmark cases involving slavery in Britain: the 1772 Somerset decision and the *Zong* case of 1781. The film considers the possible influence Belle had on her great uncle's rulings, as well as her efforts to find a husband. Asante illustrates how

Britain's involvement in slavery produced so many contradictions and complexities that were played out not only on the plantations, but also in English society.

Asante has since gone on to helm bigger films on the strength of these successes. Her third film, *A United Kingdom* (2016), made her the first Black British director whose film opened the London Film Festival. It is based on the true story of the prince of Bechuanaland (Botswana), played by David Oyelowo, who fell in love with and married a white office clerk (played by Rosamund Pike), which creates tensions between Britain and Bechuanaland, at that time a British colony.

In her work, Asante tells the stories she wants to tell that might not have been made had she not been in the position to do so. 'As a woman of colour who makes movies in a world that is the privilege of the white male,' she once said, 'I represent 0.4 per cent of my industry. It would be great to be remembered as someone who broke boundaries and made way for others who look like me.'[3]

Winifred Atwell

(1914–83) musician, entertainer, broadcaster

IN HIS MEMOIR *Me*, the singer Elton John describes Winifred Atwell as one of his musical heroes, a hugely popular recording star during his childhood. It is said he was playing her songs by ear on the family piano when he was three or four years old – at which point his mother decided he needed lessons.

'My hero had been Winifred Atwell,' he wrote, 'a big, immensely jolly Trinidadian lady who performed on stage with two pianos . . . I loved her sense of glee, the slightly camp way she would announce, "and now, I'm going to my other piano"; the way she would lean back and look at the audience with a huge grin on her face while she was playing like she was having the best time in the world. I'd never experienced anything like it in my life.'

In the 1950s and 1960s, Winifred Atwell was known as 'The Queen of the Ivories', one of Britain's most popular entertainers, with a string of boogie-woogie and ragtime hits. She sold over 20 million records, was the first artist to have three million-selling records, and was the first Black artist to have a number-one hit; she had eleven top-ten hits in the UK singles charts between 1952 and 1960.

At the height of her fame her hands were insured for £40,000, she made numerous television appearances, and she had her own shows on ITV and the BBC. She was one of the first African Caribbeans to become a television star; the media historian Stephen Bourne called her 'a folk hero for the British working classes', as her music was played in many working-class homes.

Born in Tunapuna, near Port of Spain, Atwell was a child prodigy who began playing the piano aged four. As a young woman she worked in her father's chemist shop and was expected to become a chemist herself. She preferred to play piano for her friends, however, and during the war she would perform for the US servicemen based in Trinidad, where she developed her talent for ragtime and honkytonk music.

In the early 1940s she moved to New York to study piano technique with the celebrated concert pianist and teacher Alexander Borovsky. That she was even accepted as one of his students indicates the level of her musical abilities. This is further demonstrated by the fact she gained a place at the Royal Academy of Music, London, where she was the first female pianist to be awarded the highest grade in musicianship. Atwell played ragtime in London clubs to supplement her income while studying, and was spotted by Bernard Delfont, a leading theatrical impresario. Her first booking was for a charity concert at the London Casino, which made her a star overnight. She developed a routine of having two pianos on stage, a beautiful one and an old battered one, which she had discovered in a Battersea junk shop. First, she would play classical works, and halfway through her stage act she would tell the audience, 'Now I'm going to play my other piano,' and would then play boogie-woogie and ragtime, happy tunes that helped to lift the depression of the post-war years.

In 1952, Atwell performed at the first of three Royal Variety shows before Queen Elizabeth II, and was invited to Buckingham Palace to play for the royal family. That same year she recorded 'Black and White Rag' by ragtime composer George Botsford, which was a big hit. Years later, the BBC would use that recording as the theme tune for its snooker series *Pot Black*.

For his book on the Black experience in British film and television, Stephen Bourne interviewed many of Atwell's friends and fellow entertainers from the Caribbean, all of whom described her as warm, funny and down to earth. She was very supportive of the artists who had settled in London, giving advice on how to present themselves at auditions and advising Black female performers how to style their hair.

Although she became famous for playing popular music, classical music was her first love. In 1954 she performed at the Royal Festival Hall with the London Philharmonic Orchestra, playing Greig's *Piano Concerto in A Minor* and George Gershwin's *Rhapsody in Blue* to critical acclaim. The advent of rock and roll contributed to the decline of her popularity in Britain, but she remained extremely popular in Australia and undertook her first tour there in 1958. She eventually made Australia her home, where she died in 1983.

Dame Jocelyn Barrow DBE

(1929–2020) anti-racist campaigner, community activist, educator, politician

D AME JOCELYN BARROW was a fearless champion for racial equality in Britain for over five decades, making a tremendous impact on British political life. She worked both in high-profile appointments and at the community level to make small and large institutions more diverse, initiated innovative developments in education, challenged racial discrimination in housing, employment and education, and paved the way for activists in the broader political and community fronts. Before Sharon White made headlines as the first Black woman appointed to head Ofcom in 2015, Dame Jocelyn founded its forerunner, the Broadcasting Standards Council, in 2003 and served as its chair. Many years before that, she was part of the vanguard of African, Caribbean and Asian activists who established the Campaign Against Racial Discrimination (CARD) in 1964, which lobbied to establish race relations legislation against the colour bar and racism against Black and Asian people.

Born in Port of Spain, Trinidad, Dame Jocelyn became involved in politics as a teenager. Her parents imbued her with great confidence; she once remarked, 'My parents brought me up to feel that nobody could stop me from doing what I wanted to do.'[1]

In the Caribbean during the 1940s, organised movements emerged calling for autonomy against British colonial rule and towards independence. Aged sixteen, Jocelyn was part of this movement as one of the pioneering members of the People's National Movement, one of the two major political parties in Trinidad and Tobago campaigning for independence. She worked closely with its founder Eric Williams, also a distinguished Caribbean historian, who in 1962 became the now independent country's first prime minister.

A qualified teacher, in 1959 Dame Jocelyn travelled to England to begin postgraduate studies at the Institute of Education in London. Teaching exposed her to the level of discrimination within the education system against children of Caribbean and Asian immigrants, which inspired her to set up the organisation Each One Teach One, to help families navigate the system. Education, however, was only one part of the problem. Racial discrimination and racism were dominant in all areas of life and institutions; a de facto colour bar operated, preventing immigrants from finding decent jobs and housing. Black and Asian people were powerless, and it was clear that legislation against discrimination and the promotion of social and racial equality were essential for the situation to improve and change.

In December 1964, on his way to Oslo to receive the Nobel Peace Prize, Martin Luther King met with a group of activists, Dame Jocelyn among them. He advised them on how to hold the government to account on discrimination. 'King was warm and charming,' Dame Jocelyn recalled, 'and wanted to give us an idea of what we should be doing. It helped crystallise our ideas, and we went on to form CARD.'²

CARD lobbied to introduce legislation outlawing discrimination and worked hard to expose discrimination by providing evidence of it. By June 1965, four hundred people had joined and twenty-eight organisations had agreed to support its aims and objectives, and Dame Jocelyn served as its general secretary.³ Its work with the *Observer* newspaper exposed the levels of discrimination in the employment practices of London Transport, which was critical in influencing MPs that the 1968 Race Relations Act should be much more robust than the 1965 Act.

During this time Dame Jocelyn held down her full-time job as a teacher at Furzedown College and the Institute of Education, where she pioneered the introduction of multicultural education.

Being an anti-racist campaigner is both profile-raising and arduous, leaving one open to verbal and sometimes physical abuse, hate mail and rejection. The discrimination and abuse Dame Jocelyn experienced made her 'more determined and feisty'.

In her subsequent appointments, Dame Jocelyn fought hard to make changes from within, to embed into institutional policy opportunities for under-represented groups. Selected as a BBC governor in 1981, she made sure that BBC journalism policy and practice would not allow for racial segregation in television interviews. This was inspired by an occasion when she was invited to talk about the passing of the 1968 Race Relations Act on the BBC with Enoch Powell, who refused to be in the same studio and have a direct conversation with her and another guest, an Asian psychiatrist. The fact that the BBC accommodated Powell's request to be in a separate studio was not forgotten; she also played a role in ensuring Black talent had positions as news reporters and presenters. It was at her behest that Moira Stuart was moved from Radio 2 to become the face of BBC news from the 1980s onwards. She worked hard to get the BBC to reflect in its broadcasting the lives, struggles and cultural creativity of Black and Asian Britons. For her services to broadcasting she was made a DBE, the first Black woman to receive this honour.

Described as having a mixture of bossiness and charm, Dame Jocelyn was a formidable person who knew how to get things done. As chair for the Camden Community Housing Association, she approached the problem of poor housing in that borough by securing funding from the council to buy up eighty-nine houses on the Calthorpe estate.[4] She was invited by the Inns of Court Law School to chair an inquiry into why Black barristers were not being successful in their training. The inquiry led to a change in the centuries-old tradition of train-ing barristers only in London, making it available in six other parts of the country. She was also a mentor to countless indi-viduals who went on to have important careers in politics, the law, broadcasting, the arts, activism and academia.

Dame Jocelyn Barrow led a remarkable life that was dedi-cated to the struggle for racial equality and social justice in Britain. At the notice of her death, Diane Abbott remarked, 'Without the work of her generation of activists, Black and Brown people in this country could never have achieved the advances we see today.'[5]

Lance Sergeant Johnson Beharry VC, COG

(b. 1979) soldier

THE VICTORIA CROSS is the highest military decoration in the British honours system, given for 'valour in the face of the enemy', and can be awarded to any member of the Armed Forces of British, Commonwealth and former British Empire territories. The cross was created in 1856 to recognise the heroism of all soldiers, regardless of their rank, and has been backdated to 1854 to recognise acts of bravery that occurred during the Crimean War. As of 2020, there are nine living recipients of the Victoria Cross: four from Britain, four from Australia and one from New Zealand.

Johnson Beharry received a Victoria Cross in 2005 for his heroism in Iraq in 2004. While serving as a Warrior vehicle driver with the Princess of Wales Regiment, he risked his life twice to save thirty members of his unit.

Beharry was born and raised in Grenada, coming to England when he was nineteen, where for a short time he was involved in drug dealing. Ashamed of his life choices, Beharry resolved to change, and joined the Princess of Wales Regiment aged twenty-one. He trained as a driver of Warrior armoured vehicles and served six months in Kosovo and three months in Northern Ireland before being stationed in Al Amarah in Iraq.

In 2004, while driving the lead Warrior armoured vehicle of a convoy, his platoon was caught in an ambush. He was faced with the stark choice of either driving over a mine and taking his platoon to safety, with the likely loss of just his own life, or doing nothing and losing everyone. Beharry realised he would probably die when the mine went off, because he was sitting next to the engine. He decided to drive the engine over the mine to take most of the blast, hoping that only he would die and that his comrades would live. The mine did go off; the vehicle was ablaze but, amazingly, still functional, and he drove on into what he described as the 'killing zone', in which he saw a rocket-propelled grenade coming towards him that destroyed the hatch he was trying to close. While still under heavy fire, he was able to pull six men out of the burning vehicle and carry them to safety. On that day, he managed to save the men in his armoured vehicle and a company of soldiers who had been in a nearby building – twenty-seven of his comrades in total.

Six weeks later he drove into another ambush, and this time a grenade exploded six inches from his face. He managed to reverse his vehicle out under heavy fire, but sustained critical head and spine injuries, losing 40 per cent of his brain, and was given a 1 per cent chance of survival. Beharry survived his injuries and, for the two individual acts of heroism, he was awarded the Victoria Cross.

Beharry has been candid about the mental health problems he suffered since Iraq, having attempted suicide because of depression and post-traumatic stress disorder. He has often spoken about how the army rescued him, and in 2014 he set up the JBVC Foundation with the aim of keeping young people off the streets after they are released from detention, helping with job placements, CV writing and other forms of support.

Dame Floella Benjamin of Beckenham DBE, DL

(b. 1949) actor, author, broadcaster

MOST PEOPLE OF a certain age will remember Floella Benjamin from the BBC children's programmes *Play School* and *Play Away*. Broadcast between the late 1960s and late 1980s, the programmes featured an ensemble of singers and performers who engaged preschool and older children with great enthusiasm and silliness – qualities adored by children. Seeing a Black woman on television in the 1970s was a big event in many African Caribbean homes – it meant being seen, being recognised as part of the population. Benjamin, with her smile, colourful braids and graceful dancing, was a television pioneer who helped pave the way for future presenters of African heritage. Today, Benjamin is a national treasure, a leading campaigner for television programming and children's rights, a successful businesswoman and a life peer.

Born in Pointe-à-Pierre, Trinidad, Benjamin arrived in England in 1960 aged ten to join her parents and siblings, settling in Beckenham, Kent. She has described her early experiences in England as difficult.

Being subjected to racist abuse, being racialised as 'other', was very difficult to accept after coming from a small and loving community in Trinidad. She first dealt with the abuse by fighting with the people who racially attacked her. She recalls eventually learning to fight with her brain, not with her fists, after an encounter with a racist teenage boy whom she was about to give a good hiding. She learned, she said, 'to smile at adversity'.[1]

Abandoning dreams of becoming the country's first Black woman bank manager after leaving school, Benjamin became an actor, appearing in the musicals *Hair* and *Jesus Christ Superstar*, and acted in one of the early Black British films, the comedy drama *Black Joy* (1977), about a naive young immigrant from rural Guyana who is exposed to the hustling way of life in Brixton, south London. Benjamin played Miriam, a single mother and café owner who is in a relationship with Dave (Norman Beaton), a petty crook.

Benjamin began presenting children's television in 1976 as presenter of *Play School* and *Play Away*, through which she became a household name. She said she saw the role as an opportunity to change the world and raise awareness. While working as a presenter, she suggested changes to the imagery so that it included Black and Asian children, challenging the all-white culture of children's television at the BBC.[2]

Benjamin's celebrity also helped to raise national awareness about illnesses that were affecting the African and Caribbean communities – in 1979 she was appointed as one of the patrons of the Sickle Cell Society.

In 1987, she started her own production company, Floella Benjamin Productions, making programming such as travel and cookery shows, documentaries and preschool programmes. In 1995, she published her memoir *Coming to England* as an illustrated children's book about her and her family's life in Trinidad, the journey to Britain and the difficulties they faced as new arrivals into a hostile environment, seen through the eyes of a young Floella. The book was made into a film, which is used as an educational resource to help children understand the experiences of Caribbeans in 1960s Britain. In 2004, the film won a Royal Television Society Award.

A long-time campaigner for children, Benjamin successfully lobbied the government for a Minister for Children and Families role to be created, and in 2010 became a Liberal Democrat life peer. She served on the *Windrush* Commemoration Committee as chair and created, with Birmingham City Council, the *Windrush* Garden as part of the seventieth anniversary celebrations in 2018, which was displayed that year at the Chelsea Flower Show, winning the Gold Medal. In 2019, Benjamin received the Lifetime Achievement Prize at the Women in Film and Television Awards.

Munroe Bergdorf

(b. 1987) model and activist

IN 2017, L'ORÉAL Paris made headlines when it introduced the brand's first transgender model in its latest beauty campaign in Britain, naming Munroe Bergdorf as one of the five new faces representing its five new shades of foundation. Within days of the appointment, Bergdorf, an LGBTQ+ activist who spoke regularly on matters of inclusion, feminism and transphobia, was dropped after a Facebook post she had written in response to the Charlottesville white nationalist rally was brought to L'Oréal Paris's attention.

In her post about the rally, Bergdorf detailed her thoughts on white privilege, and how it was built on violence against people of colour, for which she asserted all white people were responsible. Her comments were picked up by several newspapers, and she was accused of declaring that all white people were racist. The outrage at her 'racist rant' led to her being dropped from the campaign. Invited on national television to clarify her comments, she developed her argument further, explaining that 'socialisation has placed all white people in a certain privilege, meaning that if you are not dismantling racism, then you are part of the problem, because it makes you complicit . . . and when L'Oréal fires me for speaking about the origins of racism, that goes completely against what diversity is. The reason we need diversity is because we have racism.'[1]

In 2014, Reni Eddo-Lodge's blog post 'Why I'm no longer talking to white people about race' outlined the mental and emotional exhaustion she has experienced as she attempted to engage with white people on the topic of race, 'particularly on the legitimacy of structural racism and its symptoms'.[2]

Eddo-Lodge's book of the same name became an international bestseller. Its popularity demonstrated that in some quarters there exists a desire to speak honestly about race; however, when Black and Asian people do speak out, they are shouted down and vilified, and any attempts to achieve diversity are condemned. Consequently, Bergdorf found herself in the midst of a media storm because of her effort as an activist to bring to wider attention the inequalities that structural racism creates. The attacks against her were racist as well as transphobic in their bid to delegitimise her and her critiques.

As a Black trans woman, Bergdorf has said that her body has always been political. Born gendered male to a Jamaican father and an English mother, she has described herself as being an 'effeminate boy' who was bullied and beaten up at school. She transitioned aged twenty-four and taught herself how to DJ, and over time became deeply involved in activism. She began to call out social injustices via her social media presences, commenting on racism, transphobia, mental health and online trolls. Journalist Charlie Brinkhurst-Cuff remarked, 'She is compelled to write these [posts], as many of my Black and LGBT peers are, because the reality of our lives in the UK means we see and experience these things on a daily basis. They are reflected in our interactions with our white friends, the way we are treated on the streets and in the right-wing press.'[3] In 2019, the number of transgender hate crimes recorded by police forces in England, Scotland and Wales rose by 81 per cent; LGBT charity Stonewall estimates that two in five trans people have experienced a hate crime or incident in the past year.[4] Bergdorf uses her influence in the LGBTQ+ community and her national profile to bring attention to these injustices.

Jak Beula Dodd

(b. 1963) activist, musician

JAK BEULA DODD, the founder of the Nubian Jak Community Trust, seeks to create spaces to acknowledge the African and Caribbean presence in Britain, both past and present. Beula, a former model, musician and songwriter, was a social worker in the 1990s, and was raised by his grandmother, a Pentecostal evangelist.

Working with young people at risk from social exclusion, Beula noticed many of them had a negative self-image, which he attributed to an exclusion of Black British history in the curriculum. He thought it was important to redress that by creating a game that would give them a sense of positivity and highlight the contributions made to Britain by Black people. He created the game *Nubian Jak* which, when it was first released, outsold both *Trivial Pursuit* and *Monopoly*. Over time the concept expanded from a board game into books, an educational academy and a heritage plaque scheme.

In 2006, the Nubian Jak Community Trust unveiled a plaque honouring the reggae icon Bob Marley. The plaque was erected at Ridgmount Gardens, London, between Tottenham Court Road and Gower Street, where Marley and his band the Wailers moved in after finding themselves stranded, with no money, while promoting records for their then label. Thirteen years later, English Heritage erected a plaque to Marley at 42 Oakley Street in Chelsea, where he lived in 1977, arriving from Jamaica after an attempt was made on his life. While living at this address, he and the Wailers recorded the classic album *Exodus*. Both these addresses were significant to Marley's life in London, where he knew he could connect and find support within the Jamaican community in London, particularly Rastafarians.

These two addresses were notable for how they framed his evolution from relatively unknown musician to global superstar, alongside his growing political influence back home in Jamaica that saw him loved and feared in equal measure.

By erecting the plaque in 2006, the Nubian Jak Community Trust, with support from the Mayor of London, was making a statement. It decided it wasn't going to wait for English Heritage, the organisation responsible for awarding blue plaques in London, to validate the historic contributions of such an important cultural figure. It decided instead to create the opportunities to highlight Black British history in the local environment themselves, with the support of the communities in which the plaques are located.

Since 2006, the Nubian Jak Community Trust has erected over fifty plaques and memorials celebrating the contributions of men and women from the African diaspora to British history. It has taken the initiative in identifying not just residences, but community halls, theatres, open spaces and sites where original buildings once stood to bring the history of the African diaspora in Britain to a wider audience.

The trust's activities are in contrast to the English Heritage blue plaque scheme, which tends to focus on well-known individuals from mainstream British history and is arguably less aware of Black historical and contemporary figures and organisations that have been central to the history of Black Britons.

Of the nine hundred plaques erected by English Heritage, only 4 per cent are dedicated to Black and Asian figures from history. This dearth is explained in part by a strict criterion established by English Heritage, which includes the necessity of there being a surviving building associated with the person considered for the plaque, which means that Black and minority ethnic people are often excluded. London's constantly changing landscape, and the racism and institutional barriers Black Britons have faced, means they often were not included in official records that could link them to a specific building. The criterion serves as a baseline that is usually met by white historical figures, on account of the details of their lives and accomplishments being well documented, and those accomplishments are compatible with the general population's identification of what British history should look like. Black British historical figures who are not world-famous remain unknown outside of the community, unable to capture the heights of recognition, nor able to meet the requirements that would earn them an internationally recognised blue plaque.

The lack of integration of Black British history in the mainstream narrative means that these stories stay within the communities or are unknown, or disregarded. Consequently, the history of Black theatre companies in the 1970s and 1980s, for example, remains virtually unknown. By placing a plaque on Longford Hall in Brixton – home of the first publicly funded Black theatre company in the 1970s, the Dark & Light Theatre

Club – the Nubian Jak Community Trust helped the history of Black British theatre to gain wider recognition.[1]

Similarly, African and Caribbean service in the world wars has been overlooked until quite recently, and it has been revealed by historians that there were conscious decisions by the governments at the time to ensure that memorials to the war would not include these contributions of African and Caribbean soldiers. The 2018 centenary of the First World War provided the opportunity to redress this, and Jak Beula Dodd did this by creating a memorial dedicated to African and Caribbean armed forces that has been erected in Windrush Square in Brixton, next to the Black Cultural Archives.

It's Beula's intention to continue highlighting Black British history in the built environment through his heritage scheme.

Karen Blackett OBE

(b. 1971) creative leader, advertising executive

KAREN BLACKETT IS a trailblazing creative leader and the most senior Black woman in UK advertising. Formerly the chairwoman of MediaCom, the UK's largest media company, in 2018 its parent company WPP appointed her as the first UK country manager. This made her the most important agency leader in the British advertising industry, working with 17,000 staff in dozens of agencies, spanning media, creative, design, branding, data and public relations across WPP's £2 billion-a-year UK operation.

Blackett has been described as 'exceptional and inspirational' and has been named by her peers as the industry's most admired leader. She has appeared five times on the Powerlist, the annual ranking of the 100 most influential Black people in the UK, topping that list in 2014, and was named race equality business champion by the former Prime Minister Theresa May.

Blackett's mother and father came to England from Barbados and worked as a nurse and telecoms engineer respectively. She credits them and particularly her father for equipping her with the values she has attributed to her success in the world of advertising. As a child, she was more excited by the adverts than the programmes, coming up with ideas that she thought were more creative while having no idea that it was an industry or how to get into it.

The day Diane Abbott was elected as MP in 1987, her father told her and her sister that there was a Black woman in Parliament, and that with hard work they could be anything they chose to be. One of his favourite sayings was 'you have two ears and one mouth – use the ears more and the mouth less', which she has said is the most important skill of a marketer: to listen. He also told his daughters to embrace difference, to be 'comfortable with being memorable, because he knew we would be one of few in any room we walked in to. He knew we'd be either one of the only women in the room, or one of the only people of colour in the room.'

After graduating with a degree in geography from the University of Portsmouth, Blackett has advanced to more and more senior roles over the course of her career. Since 2017 she has served as Portsmouth University's chancellor. Advertising, she realised, was like many other industries, in which familial connections were often the route in. It didn't make sense to her that an industry that needed people from different socio-economic backgrounds to sell products to others was so white, male and middle class.

As chair of MediaCom, she championed diversity as good business sense; ensuring that advertising staff, from junior to senior levels, are from different backgrounds and ethnicities guarantees diversity of thought and innovation. It 'future-proofs' one's business by covering all the ways customers are represented, tapping into the significant purchasing power of Black and minority ethnic consumers, which increased from £30 billion in 2001 to £300 billion in 2010.

Looking beyond race and gender and considering social background will, according to Blackett, create truly diverse teams, enabling companies to reap the benefits of this purchasing power. It's essential to build empathy, Blackett has argued, to understand what would motivate someone to choose one brand over another. You need to walk in their shoes.

In 2012, Blackett established the first government-backed scheme for eighteen- to twenty-four-year-olds which would lead to a national vocational qualification. Working in collaboration with the Institute for Apprenticeships, MediaCom has found full-time roles for 90 per cent of its apprentices to date.

Blackett's leadership style is to 'bring her whole self to work': to accept that sometimes she doesn't have all the answers, to show vulnerability as well as courage, and to have a great team.

Karen Blackett received the OBE in 2014 for services to the media industry and was appointed as a trustee of the Prince Harry and Meghan Markle's charitable foundation.

Malorie Blackman OBE

(b. 1962) author

MALORIE BLACKMAN IS a multi-award-winning writer of imaginative and convincing stories for young readers, which show that there are many tales to be told about children of colour beyond racism. A prolific writer, she has written seventy books, including novels, short-story collections and television screenplays. Her achievements in literature saw her appointed as the UK's first Black Children's Laureate (2013–15).

Growing up in Clapham, south London, of Barbadian parentage, Blackman was writing stories and poems at the age of eight. A voracious reader, she found it curious that there were no stories written by Black writers or characters who looked like her, and it did not occur to her that she could get her stories published. She recalled that, growing up, 'too many people were ready to set my limits for me'. Black children were often discouraged from pursuing jobs and professions they were deemed not to have the imagination or competency for; pushed into jobs more 'suitable' that would stagnate and eventually kill their dreams. For Blackman, a university reference was refused when the school's career advisor learned of her desire to become a teacher. Blackman had said that discovering and reading Alice Walker's prize-winning *The Color Purple* planted the seed of an idea: that maybe she could 'be part of the rich cultural heritage' of her country.

Eighty-two rejections over two years did not deter her; in fact, it strengthened her resolve. 'I made up my mind I was going to be a writer and I wasn't going to give up,' she recalls in an interview. 'I made a deal I'd carry on writing and sending my work to publishers until I reached my one thousandth rejection letter.'

Blackman has said that editors, booksellers and librarians told her that 'no white child will read a book with a black child on the cover'; or 'white children can't relate to black issues' – whatever this means. More than thirty years since Malorie Blackman published her first book, the UK publishing industry still struggles in diversifying children's and young adults' literature; Blackman herself has had only one Black editor in her whole career. The Centre for Literacy in Primary Education's report 'Reflecting Realities' found that of the 9115 children's books published in the UK in 2017, only 391 featured Black and minority ethnic characters; only 1 per cent of the books published in the UK had a main character who was Black or minority ethnic. In 2018, 11,011 books were published for children, of which 743 had a Black or minority ethnic 'presence', which suggests those characters weren't protagonists or central to the narrative. Given that the percentage of BAME pupils at UK schools currently stands at 33.1, the findings of the report are as depressing as they are unsurprising. Life continues to be viewed through the experiences of white, English and middle-class children, aimed at white audiences, sending a message to BAME children that their lives don't qualify as being important enough to write about.

In her tenure as Children's Laureate, Blackman addressed these disparities and discussed how greater diversity would be beneficial and enriching to all readers, saying that although 'you want to escape into fiction . . . and read about other people, other cultures, other lives, other planets . . . [there] is a very significant message that goes out when you cannot see yourself in the books you are reading. I think it's saying, well you may be here, but do you really belong?'

Sky News, which interviewed Blackman, claimed that Blackman had said that 'children's books had too many white faces', which resulted in Blackman receiving racist abuse on social media. Blackman, who did not use that phrase, complained to Sky, who apologised and changed their head-line.[1] Unbowed, Blackman vowed she would not be silenced by 'hatred, threats and vitriol', writing in an opinion piece that 'when children and young adults see their lives and concerns reflected in the homegrown books they read . . . they feel they and their lives are not invisible.'

Blackman has shown that stories that address racism can engage younger readers. In her breakthrough novel *Noughts and Crosses* (2001), the idea of the book came from wanting to explore the legacies of slavery, and how the past still influences lives and perspectives today. Discouraged from addressing a history that is, for many people, in the past and no longer rele-vant, and drawing on some personal experiences such as not being able to find plasters that represented her flesh tone, she decided to apply an interesting and challenging premise by turning the tables on racialisation in British society. Blackman created an alternate world in which Europe is colonised by Africa, and white people (known as Noughts) are the under-class, and Black people (known as Crosses) make up the dominant ruling class. All Black people hold positions of power and their culture dominates. No Nought has ever been prime minister, and they are under-represented in politics, business, literature and art.

This upside-down literary device addressing race was first employed in film, with Desmond Nakano's 1995 film *White Man's Burden*, starring John Travolta and Harry Belafonte, which also worked well to make people's assumptions and prejudices visible. The world in *Noughts and Crosses*, seen through the eyes of Sephy, a Cross, and Callum, a Nought, shows how perspectives influence thinking about race. The books are prescient in the way they explore how inequality and oppression impact people and the decisions they ultimately make, addressing issues such as radicalisation, knife crime, terrorism and anti-immigration tensions.

The *Noughts and Crosses* series extends to four books and was adapted for television in a flagship BBC drama, broadcast in 2020.

John Blanke

(16th century) trumpeter

Archival records of John Blanke, containing details of his likeness and his position in society, have made him the most widely recognised African in Tudor England. The circumstances of his presence at the courts of Henry VII and Henry VIII are not completely known; it's been suggested he arrived in England from Spain with Catherine of Aragon when she came to marry Arthur, Henry VII's eldest son and the Prince of Wales, in 1501.[1] While Blanke's presence aligns with the trend for European royalty to employ Africans as musicians, entertainers and servants, Africans were not only living in Tudor England as immigrants. Many were born here, occupying positions varying from household servants to dignitaries for overseas territories.[2] They lived and were baptised, married and buried here. Evidence found in early modern parish records and other primary documents is changing perceptions that the early African presence in Britain is linked solely to the transatlantic slave trade. Research undertaken by Dr Onyeka Nubia, a historian specialising in Africans in Tudor and Stuart England, shows in his study of parish records that Africans were locals, part of their communities, buried alongside white residents with their information duly recorded by officials in the same way.

The historian Sydney Anglo first brought John Blanke to academic attention in the 1950s, recognising the connection between his likeness depicted in the 1511 Westminster Tournament Roll paintings and references to him in the accounts of John Heron, the treasurer to Henry VII and Henry VIII.

Audrey Dewjee brought his image into the public domain when she and Ziggy Alexander included him in an exhibition they developed for Brent Council, entitled *Roots in Britain: Black and Asian Citizens from Elizabeth I to Elizabeth II*, having seen the image of him in an exhibition on heraldry.[3] Peter Fryer included him in his important book on Black people in Britain, *Staying Power*, after seeing the touring version of the exhibition. Blanke's image of himself riding on a grey horse wearing yellow and grey livery, his head covered by a turban while his companions are bareheaded, has become an iconic image registering an African presence in a period previously assumed to have none.

Yet John Blanke remains a mystery. His presence is now quite well known; his life less so. His last name is an ironic joke, his first name an English one; did he have an African name? The documents tell us he was one of eight royal trumpeters who played at the funeral of Henry VII in May 1509 and at the coronation of Henry VIII in June that same year.[4] In 1511 he played at the special tournament in Westminster to celebrate the birth of Henry's first short-lived son.

The documents also suggest Blanke had agency – he petitioned the king to permit him to take the position of a deceased trumpeter and to double his wages from 8 to 16*d* per day. He complained his current wage was 'not sufficient to mayntaigne to doo your grace lyke service as other your trompeters doo', and asked that his 'true and faithfull service' be considered.[5] Blanke had confidence in his skill as a trumpeter – was the dead trumpeter, referred to as Domynyk Justinian, a musician of higher rank whose position Blanke believed he could assume with ease? The success of the petition means Blanke was the first African recorded to have his wages doubled; and when he married in 1512, Henry presented him with gifts: a gown of violet cloth, a bonnet and a hat. What is known about John Blanke from these entries in the royal records indicates that he held a prominent position in the royal household. The glimpses into Blanke's life are part of the fascinating stories of people of African descent; that he was one of many who made a life and a place for himself in sixteenth-century England.

Dennis Bovell

(b. 1953) reggae artist, producer

As LONG As there has been reggae, there has been reggae in Britain. It's as prominent as the rock music that was inspired by R & B in the 1950s; it formed the basis of bass and rave culture, a significant reference in the making of pop music in this country. From the moment of Jamaican migration to Britain, ska music began to top the charts. In the 1970s reggae exploded, finding a fanbase among punk rockers, who took the music into the mainstream.

Of the many reggae pioneers who injected reggae music into popular culture, Dennis Bovell is certainly one of the most important and influential figures in British music. He revolutionised the sound of reggae and dub music in Britain and was a key figure in the early days of the sub-genre of lovers' rock. He is also renowned as an accomplished multi-instrumentalist (playing guitar, bass and keyboards), a composer, bandleader and sound system leader. He has played a huge part in getting Britain to fall in love with reggae music and influencing other musical genres.

Growing up in Barbados, Bovell was introduced to Jamaican music via his uncles. When he was twelve, he reluctantly joined his parents in London – reluctantly, because his uncle, who was in a soca band in Barbados, had just started teaching him how to play the guitar. His parents' friendships with many Jamaicans, however, meant he became more immersed in Jamaican music and culture. While at school he joined his first bands, influenced by the music of Otis Redding and Jimi Hendrix, who Bovell thinks was responsible for the first dub record – 'Third Stone from the Sun' on the album *Are You Experienced?* features the values and techniques common to dub, such as echoes and delays.

It was the Desmond Dekker hit '007' that inspired him to form his band Matumbi – the name coming from the Yoruba word for 'reborn', reflecting his growing Black consciousness in the period when racism was being legitimised by the National Front and speeches by Enoch Powell. A reggae cover version of the 1973 Hot Chocolate song 'Brother Louie', about an interracial couple, got Matumbi signed to Trojan Records, and the band became Britain's leading reggae act, just as reggae was starting to gain international recognition. Their songs 'After Tonight' and 'The Man in Me' are considered British reggae classics and are still very well received on the revival circuit.

Matumbi's dubplates – the dub versions of their songs – got the band invited to be part of the sound system Sufferah's Hifi. Other sound systems of that time were Trojan, King Tubby and Mombasa. Brought to the UK from Jamaica, sound system culture defined the music scene for Black Britons. Created by sound men and their crews, they specialised in playing the latest music out of Jamaica. For Black British people they were the place to hear reggae music, which was seldom played on the radio. A fracas at a gig in 1974 put Bovell's career on hold when he was falsely accused of affray. After two trials he was found guilty and spent six months in prison before his conviction was overturned on appeal.

He began to build his reputation as a musician, producer and sound engineer, collaborating with great reggae artists such as I-Roy, Steel Pulse, Errol Dunkley and Johnny Clarke. At a time when the children of the *Windrush* generation began to seek a sound that wasn't purely Jamaican, reflected Black British culture, and was more romantic and softer than dub, Bovell was behind the creation of lovers' rock, writing and producing Janet Kay's 1979 song 'Silly Games', which got to number two in the charts. He began a long collaboration with the poet Linton Kwesi Johnson, producing classic albums including *Forces of Victory* (1979), *Bass Culture* (1980) and *Tings and Times* (1991), and has toured internationally with Johnson and the Dub Band.

Bovell's reputation as a soundman and a reggae pioneer has attracted some of the most influential bands and artists, seeking to inflect their sound with dub. The Thompson Twins, Bananarama, Fela Kuti, the Slits, Orange Juice, Madness, the Boomtown Rats, Dexys Midnight Runners and more have sought to develop their sound using his expertise. With Bovell producing the Slits' 1979 album *Cut*, band member Viv Albertine spoke about reggae's influence on their music, remarking that 'reggae taught us about space, leaving gaps . . . a relief after the strictness and minimalist of punk'.[1]

Bovell was musical director and acted in the 1980 classic film *Babylon*, about a man who worked as a mechanic during the day and was part of a sound system by night. He has also worked in television, writing the theme music for the ground-breaking Channel 4 current affairs series *The Bandung File* (1985–91), presented by Darcus Howe. In 2011 he was featured in the BBC Four documentary *Reggae Britannia*, and helped coordinate the accompanying concert held at the Barbican, which finally recognised reggae as the music that changed Britain.

Sonia Boyce OBE, RA

(b. 1962) artist, curator, academic

I N HER SELF-PORTRAIT *She Ain't Holding Them Up – She's Holding On (Some English Rose)* (1986), the artist Sonia Boyce places her image front and centre in a meditation on being caught between the past and the present, between the Caribbean and England, and her identity as both Black and British. Like the mythical god Atlas, condemned to bear the weight of the heavens, Boyce is using muscular arms to hold up her family, dressed smartly either for church or for a family photograph, suggesting she is holding up the image of her family as a representation of unity or is bearing the emotional weight of her responsibility as daughter. Children who grew up in second-generation Caribbean families can relate to the responsibilities placed on older children, who often bore the responsibility of looking after younger siblings while parents worked, and were burdened with the role of family representative when encountered by family friends and acquaintances outside of the home. In the portrait, Boyce stands between these two worlds wanting to assert her Black British identity; her dreadlocked hair and her dress, adorned with black roses and the words 'some English rose' written on the hem, interrogate the definition of the

'English rose': the assumption that beauty and Englishness are exclusive to white skin. As an artist who had no Black models for life drawings, she used self-portraiture to, as she once explained, 'open up the possibility of constructing the sort of images I wanted'. Self-portraiture, as academic Celeste-Marie Bernier has asserted, 'catalysed an investigation of hidden social, political, historical and cultural realities of Black lives'.[1]

Sonia Boyce literally drew herself into the British artistic canon, from which Black artists had historically been excluded. A critically acclaimed artist, and the first Black female artist to be elected as a Royal Academician and to have a painting exhibited at the Tate Gallery, she was part of the vanguard of Black British artists in the 1980s that began putting their work into the spotlight, examining the reasons behind the absence of art representing the Black experience in galleries, and the impact of colonial legacies on art, identity and race through sculpture, paintings and exhibitions. This movement, initiated by the radical BLK Art Group and comprising several artists studying at Wolverhampton Polytechnic, challenged the art world to acknowledge the complexities of the human experience, and rejected institutionalised representations of Black people. Attending the group's National Black Art Convention in 1982 was a turning point for Boyce, who as a third-year degree student felt isolated, unable to locate any information on works of contemporary Black art in Britain, or to meet other Black artists. Feeling 'a sense of relief and exhilaration' at seeing so many Black artists at the convention, the following year she exhibited her work at the *Five Black Women* exhibition at the Africa Centre in London.

Since the 1990s, Boyce has moved on from exploring the past and present, history and lived experiences through portraiture, focusing instead on collaborative projects that mix sound, video, text, performance and other media. Her collective work *The Audition* (1997) features scores of photographs of people wearing afro wigs. Seeing a connection between afro hair, minstrelsy and parody, the work explores the unconscious response to what Boyce has called 'a deep historical joke', and the afro, as a signifier of the African body, 'occupies both desire and parody'.

In 2018, Boyce caused unintended controversy during a retrospective of her work at Manchester Art Gallery, when the performative act of the week-long removal of John Waterhouse's painting *Hylas and the Nymphs* (1896) was interpreted as censorship. Invited by the gallery to reflect on its eighteenth- and nineteenth-century collections, Boyce organised the removal of the painting as part of a wider discussion on the supposed political neutrality of gallery spaces and curatorial decisions: how verdicts are reached on which paintings are displayed, and which aren't. A discussion with the gallery staff revealed there was discomfort with Waterhouse's painting, which depicts Hylas being lured to his death by seven semi-naked nymphs. Boyce explained the reasoning behind the act in an opinion piece around the controversy, arguing it was important to reflect on how paintings of this period that represent the female form, sometimes in problematic ways, are understood in the twenty-first century. 'Some museums,' Boyce wrote, 'consider the museum as a place to explore new meanings and forge new relationships between people and art . . . the removal of *Hylas and the Nymphs* can be seen in this context.'[2]

Boyce combines being an artist and curator with a distinguished academic career; she is currently professor of Black art and design at the University of the Arts. She is working on producing artwork for the 1.8 km wall for Crossrail in the Royal Docks, and in 2020 was selected to be the first Black female artist to represent the UK at the Venice Biennale in 2021.

Dr Aggrey Burke

*(b. 1943) psychiatrist, academic,
specialist in mental illness*

AGGREY BURKE'S CAREER has been dedicated to understanding the cultural contexts of mental illness in African and Caribbean communities, and he is a pioneer in this field. He was one of the first Black consultant psychiatrists in Britain, and his research has exposed the links between deprivation and mental illness within Black communities, and has uncovered the barriers that affect Black mental healthcare.

There are numerous reports that outline the ways in which the mental health system is failing Black and minority ethnic people. The findings are especially critical of how Black Britons fare within this system, demonstrating how factors including institutional racism and a lack of cultural competency have a devastating impact on the care and treatments they receive.

These reports find that Black people are four times more likely to be detained under the Mental Health Act than white people and are ten times more likely to be subjected to community treatment orders. They are seven times more likely than white patients to be sent to medium-secure units and are more likely to receive higher dosages of anti-psychotic medication, rather than undergoing talking therapies.

Aggrey Burke's research has exposed the prejudices that affect the mental healthcare of economically deprived Black communities. His experiences undertaking his medical training during a period of profound political and social change in the Caribbean and Britain influenced his research and thinking, leading him to apply historical, social and cultural contexts to Black mental health.

Aggrey Burke was born in Clarendon, Jamaica, to politically active parents. His parents named him Aggrey after the Ghanaian missionary and teacher James Emman Kwegyir Aggrey, known as the 'father of African education'. His father, the Revd Eddie Burke, was involved in social reform of the then colony in the 1940s; as one of the leaders of the Jamaica Welfare Association, he worked to improve the education of rural Jamaicans, and also assisted in the development of welfare in Barbados, Tobago, St Kitts and Nevis. In 1958, as tensions between white Britons and Caribbean immigrants erupted in London and other cities, Revd Burke was dispatched to Britain by Jamaican statesman Norman Manley to improve Black and white relations; his family joined him a year later.

Aggrey Burke's experiences of growing up Jamaican in England made him conscious of the constant judgements made about African Caribbean people and the practical disadvantages they suffered, which contributed to many forms of discomfort of *being*.

Burke undertook his medical training in Britain, Ethiopia and the Caribbean, exposing him to the political upheavals taking place in those regions. He then became involved in the political movements precipitated by the banning of Guyanese university lecturer Walter Rodney from returning to his teaching post at the University of the West Indies. Returning to England to complete his psychiatry training, Burke came to understand the struggles of the Black British communities as the threat of death or extinction. Overt and covert racism, discrimination in health, housing employment and education – he recognised these negative stimuli as hazardous to mental health.

In 1981, Burke helped set up the support group for the families who had suffered bereavement and injury from the New Cross Massacre in London, providing them with counselling and support. The group was the first of its kind in Britain. It was in this period that he also noticed how few Black and Asian students were studying medicine at St George's Hospital, where he worked, and other medical schools in London. He and Joe Collier, a pharmacologist, began studying enrolment details at other medical schools and saw that the low numbers were too consistent to be explained as accidental. Their paper, 'Racial and sexual discrimination in the selection of students for London medical schools' (1986), exposed St George's practice of keeping out Black and Asian students. Revealing this practice came at a price; Burke was never promoted to professor, despite his reputation. However, his and Collier's research led to St George's Medical School being found guilty by the Commission for Racial Equality (CRE) of practising racial and sexual discrimination in its admissions policy, finding that as many as sixty applicants each year among two thousand may have been refused an interview based on their gender or race. The CRE made recommendations on how other schools could avoid these discriminatory practices. St George's cooperated with the inquiry and took steps to ensure this practice wouldn't happen again. Previously unsuccessful applicants were offered places and attempts were made to contact people who had suffered.

Burke has been critical of the huge disparities in standards of treatment between what Black Britons receive and what can be expected by white people, and the way psychiatrists pigeonhole Black people as difficult or dangerous, in need of restraint and not healing. As a therapist, Burke has done seminal work on the impact of deprivation, exclusion and rejection in the work, housing, schooling and everyday lives of Black and minority ethnic people. He has highlighted the difficulties facing both people living here and those who have repatriated, as well as the issues of access to treatment and care.

Vanley Burke

(b. 1951) photographer

Hailed as the 'Godfather of Black British photography', Vanley Burke has created a critical visual documentary of the lives of Black Britons in Birmingham over the past fifty years. His photographs chronicle the everyday activities of the Black community, capturing how those lives were and are lived, presenting an authenticity of experience through weddings, funerals, church festivals, playing in the street, sound systems, playing dominoes and just sitting in the park, giving each of these activities meaning.

Born in Jamaica, Burke was given a Brownie box camera by his mother when he was ten. Arriving in Handsworth, Birmingham, as a teenager to join his parents, he used the camera gifted to him by his mother to study his new home and surroundings; his first subjects were his younger siblings, family friends and people who would come into his parents' shop.[1]

Burke has spoken about the 'magic of photography' that first attracted him and encouraged him to explore its possibilities, while looking at people and how they lived. In 1967, he made the decision to document the Black community in England; to capture the lives of the people around him, and at the same time create and preserve a social historical commentary on migration and settlement in Birmingham.

A job as a technician in the photography department of Birmingham Polytechnic (now Birmingham City University) gave him the opportunity to further develop his craft. A Kodak bursary in 1979 made him realise photography could be a professional pursuit.[2]

His photographs of 1970s Black Britain have become iconic. *The Boy with the Flag*, his depiction of a young Black British boy, half smiling into Burke's lens as he stands alongside his bike from which a Union Jack flies, has become memorable for what it represented and what it challenged. Winford Fagan, the young man in the photo, has said that he was asked at the time why he didn't have a Jamaican flag on his bike. 'I didn't know about Jamaica. I was born here,' was his answer.[3] The image has become a meditation on Britishness, identity and belonging.

Burke has captured some of the most significant historical events in Black British history in his most acclaimed images. He was at Handsworth Park at the African Liberation Day celebrations in 1977, where he photographed crowds of young people, many of them wearing the colours and hats associated with Rastas, listening to a speech. The 1970s were the time of political awakening for many of the first-generation young Black British people, who were questioning their parents' beliefs around identity and Britishness. Many had adopted Rastafarianism and liberation politics in the face of harassment and discrimination. Despite the large number of people at the African Liberation Day celebration, it received no press coverage at the time, making Burke's work even more valuable and important for how it captures the social, cultural and religious ways of life of the Black community for future generations to see, enabling them to understand and write their own histories. That he has made this his life's work demonstrates his love for his community. 'I have been absolutely penniless,' he has written, 'but I have never felt poor. I don't know how it is possible to make lots of money from documentary photography. It is a real pauper's life and I liken myself to a jester in a court of kings.'[4]

Margaret Busby OBE, FRSL

(b. 1944) publisher, editor, writer, broadcaster

M ARGARET BUSBY IS a revered editor, publisher and literary critic, who has been hailed as the 'doyenne of Black
British publishing'. She was the youngest and first female Black
publisher when she co-founded Allison and Busby Ltd, and is
known in Britain and internationally as a major cultural figure
who has played a significant role championing the work of
authors throughout the African diaspora.

Margaret Busby was born in Accra, Ghana, to George and
Sarah Busby, a doctor and nurse who had lived and worked in
England before moving to the Gold Coast. Her familial connec-
tions speak to a legacy of political activism and significant liter-
ary accomplishments – her father, who was a general practi-
tioner in Walthamstow in the 1920s, attended school with the
Trinidadian intellectual C. L. R. James and was a friend of the
Pan-Africanist and journalist George Padmore. Her maternal
grandfather, George James Christian, was a delegate at the first
Pan-African Conference (forerunner to the Pan-African
Congresses) held in London in 1900.[1]

Busby's career as a publisher started after meeting Clive
Allison at a party in Bayswater while they were both still

undergraduates. They discovered they both wrote poetry –
Busby edited her college literary magazine, and Allison was the
president of the Oxford Poetry Society. They decided after they
graduated to start a publishing company that sold affordable
poetry paperback editions.[2]

Allison and Busby Ltd (A & B) launched in 1967 with three
poetry titles, and in 1969 the first novel they published was *The
Spook Who Sat by the Door*, a thriller by African American writer
Sam Greenlee, about a Black man who uses his CIA training to
lead an underground guerrilla movement, which had been
rejected by many publishers. Its success with A & B led to the
subsequent publication of many writers from the African diaspora whose work received critical acclaim, among them Buchi
Emecheta, C. L. R. James, George Lamming, Andrew Salkey
and Ishmael Reed.

After A & B was taken over by WH Allen in 1987, Busby
became editorial director at Earthscan Publications, publishing
the works of Frantz Fanon, Carolina Maria de Jesus and
Nuruddin Farah, before becoming a freelance editor and writer,
and continuing to promote the work of African and Caribbean
writing through her work with literary organisations in Britain
and Africa.

In 1992, Busby edited *Daughters of Africa: An International
Anthology of Words and Writings by Women of African Descent*.
The collection was a literary first, featuring works from over
two hundred women writers from the African diaspora, spanning fiction, poetry, essays, memoir and children's writing.
Busby described the compiling of the collection as 'trying to
catch a flowing river in a calabash'. *Daughters of Africa* was a
pioneering work, as it highlighted the voices of Black women
who are often silenced, ignored or underrated. Twenty-five

years later, Busby reworked the anthology for a new generation, bringing together two hundred writers from fifty countries, exploring race, gender politics, romance and intersectional feminism.

Busby continues to campaign for diversity in the publishing industry and is patron of Independent Black Publishers; in 2020, she was appointed as the chair of judges for the Booker Prize.

Dawn Butler

(b. 1969) politician

D AWN BUTLER, THE third Black woman to become an MP after Diane Abbott and Oona King, is a senior Labour MP who served as Shadow Women and Equalities Minister in 2017–19 and was the first Black woman to speak at the dispatch box in 2009.

Formerly the race and equality officer at the GMB (General, Municipal, Boilermakers) Union, and an advisor to the Mayor of London, Butler was elected MP for Brent South in 2005 and served as the Minister of State for Youth Affairs in Gordon Brown's government.

As Butler's colleague Diane Abbott can well attest, being a Black female MP can be difficult and challenging; their jobs are performed in the face of significant abuse levelled by the public, the media and sometimes fellow MPs. As in most workspaces, Black women are both hyper-visible and invisible, and constantly have to navigate a workspace that can be hostile to both identities of being Black and female.

In a white-male-dominated House of Commons, with 430 male MPs sitting in 2020, justifying your presence in a trad-itionally 'white' space can be a constant and exhausting battle.

In facing these challenges, Butler has been uncompromising in her demand to be seen and respected for the job she does and the people she represents. She has used her platform to call out her experiences of discrimination in politics, highlighting how Black people in traditionally white spaces are often called upon to justify their presence. As a newly elected MP, she was told not to use the MPs' lift as cleaners were not allowed in there. Accused of lying about the incident by a Liberal Democrat staffer, Butler demanded an apology, asserting that the denial of Black and minority ethnic people's lived experiences of racism legitimises and promotes it.[1] 'It's exhausting to constantly fight that battle,' she remarked in an interview with the *Guardian* newspaper, 'or constantly have to justify your presence in a space. When it happens to me, sometimes I can ignore it . . . but I have a responsibility to all of the other African Caribbean women coming in behind me. So, I take that responsibility seriously and that is why I was so willing to call it out.'[2] An apology was eventually issued; however, Butler insisted on an inquiry into the incident. To date, no such inquiry has been conducted.

She has also spoken about being mistaken for other Black colleagues after the BBC confused her with fellow MP Marsha de Cordova in February 2020 and was forced to issue an apology, which brought the issue of a lack of diversity in newsrooms to the forefront once again.[3]

In 2017, Butler became the first MP to sign a question using British Sign Language in order to highlight the need to give the language legal recognition, and founded the Parliamentary Black Caucus, a cross-party group concerned with ethnic minority issues.

She is a supporter of transgender rights, maintaining that minority groups should stand together to fight for each other's rights.[4]

During the 2019 general election campaign, Butler, along with Jeremy Corbyn, launched the Race and Faith Manifesto, an ambitious and unprecedented pledge for more inclusivity and fairness.

Although Butler was unsuccessful in her bid to become deputy leader of the Labour Party, there is no doubt she will continue to make her voice heard in the ongoing battles for social and political change.

Earl Cameron CBE

(1917–2020) actor

THROUGHOUT THE 1950s and 1960s, Earl Cameron appeared in British films that were notable for their examination of the racism that defined African Caribbean relations with wider British society. Often cast as the decent, dignified Black man, the sensitive outsider, Cameron added a touch of class to these productions. He was held in high regard by his fellow Black actors and gave each role he played grace and moral authority.

Earl Cameron said that becoming an actor was a 'virtual accident, a means to an end – a way out of washing dishes, kitchen portering, things like that.'[1] Born in Bermuda, Earlston Cameron joined the British Merchant Navy in the 1930s and arrived in England in October 1939. The outbreak of war meant he could not return home so he needed to find work, but he quickly realised a colour bar existed in London and 'it was impossible for a Black person to get a job'. Eventually he found work as a hotel dishwasher. Becoming an actor never crossed his mind, but he seized the opportunity when a walk-on part in a production of *Chu Chin Chow,* a musical comedy based on the story of 'Ali Baba and the Forty Thieves', became available. 'And that night,' he remembered, 'I went on stage for the first time, my knees buckling like mad, sweat pouring down, but I was determined to get through it ... all I was thinking about was that lousy job that I had escaped from!'[2]

In 1947 Cameron was introduced to Amanda Aldridge, the daughter of the famous Black nineteenth-century Shakespearian actor Ira Aldridge, and took lessons in elocution and voice projection from her for about two years. He then worked on developing his craft in repertory theatre and he got his big break when he landed a major role in *Pool of London* (1951). In this noir crime thriller about a merchant seaman who gets involved in a diamond-smuggling racket, Cameron's character Johnny is a more sensitive foil to the brash Dan MacDonald (played by Bonar Colleano). The film was notable for the inter-racial romance between Johnny and Pat (played by Susan Shaw), and Cameron was praised for his performance that presented his character as the film's moral centre.

Reflecting on this 'delightful part, the best part I had in film', Cameron did not land another major film role until 1955, appearing in the drama *Simba* (1955), a somewhat heavy-handed portrayal of the conflict between the Kenya Land and Freedom Army (Mau Mau) and the British settler population and authorities. Filmed at the height of the conflict, when British forces were clearing the Mau Mau cadres in the infamous Operation Anvil that would result in the imprisonment of 27,000 Africans, *Simba* boasted a distinguished British cast, including Dirk Bogarde, Donald Sinden and Virginia McKenna. Cameron and Orlando Martins, who played the leader of the local Mau Mau gang, were the leading Black characters and the only ones who had substantial speaking roles.

In an interview with the film historian Stephen Bourne, Cameron said *Simba* wasn't a happy film to work on. He didn't get along with the director, Brian Desmond Hurst, who he says racially abused him on set. The film itself reflected contemporary British stereotypical attitudes towards Africans in general and the Mau Mau specifically. Similarly, Cameron and Martins's characters represented alternative images of Africa; Martins as the backward-looking, evil Mau Mau leader Simba, and Cameron as the Western-educated doctor Peter Karanja, who represented progress and cultural transformation.

A few years later, two of Cameron's pictures, *Sapphire* (1959) and *Flame in the Streets* (1961), became landmark films that examined race in Britain, particularly in the wake of the Notting Hill and Nottingham race riots, and the daily tensions that existed between white and Black Britons in the era of Commonwealth immigration. *Sapphire* is a bold police procedural; an investigation into what turns out to be the racist murder of a young woman who is discovered to have been mixed race after her brother, played by Cameron, comes to identify her body. It transpires that Sapphire had been leading a double life, passing for white in the last months of her life. The film portrays the commonplace racial hostility towards Caribbean immigrants; Cameron reprises his role as the decent and dignified Black man.

Flame in the Streets focuses on the relationship between Kathie (Sylvia Sims), a teacher and the daughter of a trade union activist Jacko (John Mills), and Peter (Johnny Sekka), a Black teacher who works at the same school. Cameron plays Peter's friend, Gabriel Gomez, who works at the same factory as Jacko, who has been campaigning for Gomez to be promoted to the level of foreman, to which many white workers are opposed. Jacko successfully fights the colour bar on the factory floor, convincing his colleagues to promote Gomez, but struggles with his own prejudice when Kathie tells him she wants to marry Peter.

Cameron convinced the director Roy Baker to dispense with stereotypical representations of Black working-class people, telling Baker that assumptions of Black people being dirty or living in overcrowded rooms were false. He told him to go and visit Black people and see how they lived, to add reality to the story.[3]

Cameron, an ambitious and talented actor, should have been more successful; unfortunately, though, Black British actors in this period were usually typecast, finding work only in 'race specific' films. He refused to take roles that perpetuated derogatory racial stereotypes. 'One has a choice,' he said. 'I was quite prepared to sacrifice my whole career rather than do something so degrading.'[4]

Betty Campbell MBE

(1934–2017) community activist, headteacher

B ETTY CAMPBELL WAS a Welsh community activist and race
education champion who put Black history in the Cardiff
curriculum. She was committed to the history and heritage of
Butetown, where she was born, and the celebration of Welsh
cultural diversity. She was described by Carwyn Jones, First
Minister of Wales, as 'a pioneer and an inspiration'.

Butetown, commonly known as Tiger Bay, was one of the
UK's first multicultural communities. By the outbreak of the
First World War, people from over fifty countries had settled in
the area, which was built up around the docks to the south of
Cardiff, where many of them found work. Her mother was
Welsh Barbadian; her father, who came to the UK from Jamaica
as a teenager, was killed in the Second World War when his
ship, the *Ocean Vanguard*, was torpedoed by a German U-boat
off the coast of Trinidad in 1942.

Campbell, a fan of Enid Blyton's Malory Towers books,
dreamed about being a student at the fictional boarding school.
Winning a scholarship to Lady Margaret High School for Girls
in Cardiff made that dream come true. Campbell had an ambition to become a teacher, and confided to her headmistress that

this was the career path she wished to follow. She was immediately discouraged from doing so. Her headmistress told her 'the problems would be insurmountable'. That her headmistress believed her ambition of being a Black teacher was impossible devastated Campbell but also strengthened her resolve. Becoming a mother and wife deferred but did not end her dreams. In 1960 she enrolled at Cardiff Teacher Training College – one of six female trainees – and juggled raising her four children with her studies.

Campbell's first teaching post was in Llanrumney, and when a teaching post became available at Mount Stuart Primary in Butetown, she jumped at it. But parents, unused to a Black teacher and assuming her ethnicity meant she could not be competent, were hostile towards her. She proved her detractors wrong, however, becoming a headteacher in the 1970s, the first Black woman in Wales to hold this position. In 1971, Bernard Coard's polemical book *How the West Indian Child is Made Educationally Sub-normal in the British School System* was published. Caribbean students were being mistreated and placed in educationally subnormal environments based on culturally biased IQ tests. Coard recommended that schools employed more Black teachers, that Black Studies should be taught in school to make the curriculum more inclusive, and that the ill treatment of Black pupils needed to be addressed by the local education authorities. Whether Campbell had read this report is not known; however, her remarks on the subject suggest she understood only too well the importance of Black self-actualisation, and the effects of racial discrimination on Black pupils' learning. 'As a child there were always people coming in from outside to manage things in our lives,' she once remarked, 'and I thought there must come a time when we can

Margaret Busby in her office at Allison & Busby, Soho, London, in October 1977.
(© Mayotte Magnus/National Portrait Gallery, London)

Victor Adebowale, 2004.
(© Sal Idriss/National Portrait Gallery, London)

Ade Adepitan concentrates for a penalty shot i
the preliminary group basketball match betwe
Canada and Great Britain on 24 September
2004 for the Athens 2004 Paralympic Games.
(© George S de Blonsky/Alamy Stock Photo)

Maggie Aderin-Pocock speaks on stage during a discussion about *The Sky at Night, 60th Annivers*
Edition, at the BFI & Radio Times TV Festival at BFI Southbank in London on 9 April 2017.
(© Tabatha Fireman/Getty Images)

n Akomfrah, Birmingham, UK, 1985. Photographer Pogus Caesar remembers: 'We were in the
centre and some young boys were riding bikes. John asked if he could have a go, they agreed.
s was during the 1985 Handsworth riots. Capturing that moment of joy after so much tension
unfolded was very important to document.'

Ira Aldridge by Miklós Barabás, 1853.
(© National Portrait Gallery, London)

Valerie Ann Amos, 2004.
(© Horace Ové/National Portrait Gallery, London)

Winifred Atwell, 1960. Taken by David Wedgbury, official photograph for Decca Records artists.
(© National Portrait Gallery, London)

hnson Gideon Beharry by Giles Price,
May 2007. (© *National Portrait Gallery, London*)

Sonia Boyce, 24 April 1997. (© *Donald MacLellan*)

ty Campbell, 1981. (© *Media Wales*)

Naomi Campbell at the Dior Ready-to-Wear
Spring/Summer 92 show in France on 21
October 1991.
(© *Pool ARNAL/GARCIA/Gamme-Rapho via Getty Images*)

Sir Coxsone, 1980. *(© David Corio/Redferns/Getty Images)*

William Cuffay by William Paul Dowling, Chartist, portrait painter and photographer, 1848. *(© National Portrait Gallery, London)*

William Davidson by Robert Cooper, publish on 2 May 1820. *(© National Portrait Gallery, London,*

nda Dobbs at the High Court of
stice, Strand, London, 2008.
John Ferguson/Alamy Stock Photo)

s Elba, 2010.
Julian Broad/National Portrait Gallery, London)

Olaudah Equiano by Daniel Orme, published
by Olaudah Equiano on 1 March 1789.
(© National Portrait Gallery, London)

Bernie Grant at the Royal Agricultural Hall,
Islington, London, in May 1987. *(© Geoff Wilson)*

Lenny Henry, 1984.
(© Trevor Leighton/National Portrait Gallery, London)

Lubaina Himid by Sam MacLaren, 1995.
(© National Portrait Gallery, London)

Kelly Holmes, 2005. *(© Harry Borden)*

manage for ourselves. I always felt that Black people were not getting their fair share from society.'[1]

To that end, Campbell made it her mission to develop a curriculum that included the histories of Black people, reflecting the diverse histories of the students of Mount Stuart. Inspired by the history of civil rights activism during a trip to the United States, particularly by the extraordinary life of the nineteenth-century abolitionist Harriet Tubman, she was determined to 'enhance the black spirit and black culture as much as I could'.[2] She introduced the history of the Caribbean, enslavement and its legacies to her pupils, and taught about the ways Black people contributed to British society. She ensured that subjects such as apartheid in South Africa were included in the curriculum. When it was suggested to her that it might be a difficult topic for children, she responded with 'Go ask the black kids in South Africa if it's too difficult.'

Her school became a template for multicultural education, and as an expert on race in education Campbell was invited to be a member of the Home Office's race advisory committee and the Commission of Racial Equality. Campbell also served as councillor for Butetown and advocated fiercely for its residents. She became known outside of her community as a leading academic and education specialist, and taught workshops on the history of Butetown's diverse communities. Campbell's commitment to care for her students through education inspired many of them to rise to achieve great things, proving many people wrong, as she had.

Naomi Campbell

(b. 1970) fashion model, campaigner

NAOMI CAMPBELL IS one of the most recognisable faces in the fashion industry. In the late 1980s and 1990s she, along with five other models, achieved such a level of success and visibility that they became known as 'supermodels', with Campbell the only one of African heritage. Since being 'discovered' at fifteen, Campbell has been considered one of the world's most beautiful women, and the muse, darling and sometimes villain of the fashion industry, with a career spanning three decades. She has attained a level of fame synonymous with the designers whose clothes she has modelled; like her predecessors Beverly Johnson, Iman and Bethann Hardison, she has challenged traditional cultural perceptions of beauty and femininity.

Naomi Campbell was born in Streatham, London; her mother, Valerie, was a dancer, who left Campbell with her mother while she toured Europe and the Middle East with dance troupes, sending money home to pay for her daughter's education. Enrolled in the Barbara Speake Stage School aged five and later attending Italia Conti Academy of Theatre Arts, Campbell was soon being featured in music videos.

While window shopping in Covent Garden she was spotted by a model scout, and within a year she was a modelling sensation.

Campbell's accomplishments are well documented, boasting an impressive list of firsts, including the first Black model to appear on the cover of French *Vogue* and the first to appear on American *Vogue*'s coveted September issue, widely regarded as the most significant fashion publication of the year. She has consistently broken down barriers in the fashion industry, marking the path for the next generation of Black models, many of whom she supports and mentors in order to make their paths a little easier than the one she has had to forge for herself.

Although Campbell is one of the most famous Black models of her time, it has come at great personal cost and struggle. Many of her accomplishments come with a story of racial discrimination behind them. Campbell's beauty has often not been regarded as the right or acceptable kind of beauty by those who control the industry. A widely held sentiment within the industry is that Black women are not their demographic; they do not buy their beauty products or their clothes. Black models, from the industry's perspective, must look like 'white models dipped in chocolate', have skinny noses and thinner lips to sell the product – they must be, from the industry's viewpoint, flawless.

Campbell being featured on the cover of French *Vogue* happened after her friend and mentor, the designer Yves Saint Laurent, threatened to withdraw advertising from the magazine unless it used Black models on its cover. Two of her fellow supermodels, Christy Turlington and Linda Evangelista, risked their own careers by insisting that if designers did not use Campbell, they would not get them either. Campbell maintains she has not earned the same volume of advertising assignments and has had to work harder to be treated equally.

Campbell has been outspoken about racial bias in the fashion industry. In 2013, incensed by the lack of representation, she, along with Iman and Bethann Hardison, created the Diversity Coalition to increase inclusion in runway shows. Sending written complaints to the governing bodies of international fashion, their open letter to the industry stated:

> Eyes are on an industry that season after season watches fashion design houses consistently use one or no models of colour. No matter the intention, the result is racism. Not accepting another based on the colour of their skin is clearly beyond 'aesthetic' when it is consistent with the designer's brand. Whether it's the decision of the designer, stylist or casting director, that decision to use basically all white models reveals a trait that is unbecoming to modern society.

Such interventions forced London fashion houses to acknowledge diversity, with Topshop, Burberry and Tom Ford using higher numbers on their runways. The modelling industry, however, remains at around 82 per cent white, with Black and Asian models at 6.8 and 8.9 per cent respectively.

Campbell also teamed up with the fashion photographer Nick Knight to question why Black models feature far less than their white counterparts and to openly critique the industry over its racism. Knight has stated that he is never permitted to photograph Black models for certain magazines, fashion houses, cosmetic brands, perfumes companies or advertising companies.

While racism in fashion still appears to be tacitly accepted, Campbell continues to champion Black models, making sure they get the same opportunities and fees in advertising, and believing that tapping into Africa's wealth of design and modelling talent, making them part of a bigger network, will redress the balance.

Queen Charlotte

(1744–1818) wife and consort of George III

JAMAICAN AMERICAN HISTORIAN J. A. Rogers (1880–1966)
dedicated his life to challenging racist European and
American scholarship that denied people of African descent
had a history worth writing about. A self-trained historian and
journalist, he popularised African diasporic history in the twentieth century. His research and writings were regarded as
controversial; most of it was rejected by white scholars, as it was
inconsistent with the majority of what they were writing about
Africans in that period. Consequently, most of his information
was disseminated in Black newspapers and self-published books
that became fixtures in Black homes in the United States and
the Caribbean. Rogers spent decades combing through archives
around the world documenting what he referred to as 'Negro
ancestry in the white race' through interracial relationships and
marriage.[1]

His three-volume set *Sex and Race* (1941–44) and *Nature
Knows No Color-Line* (1952) made the assertion that Charlotte
Sophia Mecklenburg-Strelitz, queen consort of George III, had
African ancestry. Rogers said this could be explained by the
significant numbers of Black people in German nobility, 'some

of them with crowns and others as cardinals and bishops', and as indicated in their coats of arms and family names such as Mohr and Moringer, derivatives of the word Moor.[2] A portrait of Queen Charlotte appeared on the front cover of the book, showing her broad nose and full lips, features that many consider to be classically Black.

Over the years, the subject of Queen Charlotte's ancestry has been debated in news articles and researched by genealogists. In 2017 it made the news again after the announcement of the engagement of Prince Harry to Meghan Markle, who defines herself as biracial, having an African American mother and white father. The debate over whether she was the first mixed-raced member of the royal family brought Charlotte back centre stage.

Born in Mecklenburg-Strelitz, a northern German duchy in the Holy Roman Empire, Charlotte married George III aged seventeen and bore him fifteen children, thirteen of whom survived. The city of Charlotte in North Carolina is named after her, she is credited with founding Kew Gardens, and she won public affection for her loyalty and devotion to the king as he struggled with mental illness. The topic of her ancestry makes her interesting and is significant because of the possibility that she passed her African heritage into the royal bloodline.

Historian and genealogist Mario de Valdes y Cocom studies people of the African diaspora and their connections to Europe and the Americas. His fascination with official portraits of Charlotte, whose features he believes are visibly African, led him to undertake a 'systematic genealogical search'. He thinks it's probable that Charlotte had Black ancestors, given her connections to the Portuguese royal family. She was directly descended from Margarita de Castro y Sousa, a fifteenth-century noblewoman nine generations removed, who traced her ancestry from the thir-teenth-century King Alfonso III and his mistress Madragana, reported to be a Moor, a term used to describe people of African descent.[3] Earlier research into fifteenth-century Flemish paintings gives rise to the suggestion that the Black Magi in those portraits may have been based on real people, who were probably members of the Portuguese de Sousa family. According to Valdes, six differ-ent lines can be traced from Charlotte back to Margarita de Castro y Sousa, thus explaining the Queen's unmistakable African appearance.[4]

In her lifetime Charlotte was described as unattractive. Her physician, Christian Friedrich, Baron Stockmar, described her as 'small and crooked, with a true mulatto face'; Sir Walter Scott wrote that she was 'ill-coloured' and called her family 'a bunch of ill-coloured orangutans'. It is possible that those who found Charlotte ugly were simply using racial stereotypes to insult her; in the eighteenth century, racial difference was linked to unattractiveness. Valdes, however, maintains that she had features consistent with someone of African heritage.[5]

Some historians have dismissed this evidence as weak; however, in 1999, the *Sunday Times* published an investigative article with the headline, 'Revealed: The Queen's Black ances-tors, the connection had been rumoured but never proved'. It made the interesting claim that members of the royal family had the credentials to be appropriate leaders of Britain's multi-cultural society, as they had hitherto publicly unacknowledged mixed-race royal ancestors.[6] At the time, the article caused quite a stir; when the American newspaper *Boston Globe* contacted Buckingham Palace, the article was very much down-played. 'This has been rumoured for years and years,' Palace spokesman David Buck told the paper. 'It's a matter of history, and frankly, we've got more important things to talk about.'[7] It was unclear whether Buck was saying the rumours were a matter of history, or whether he was referring to Charlotte's African ancestry.

Valdes, from whom much of the research on Charlotte is derived, started his research after moving from Belize to Boston. He has remarked that his fascination with Queen Charlotte started from a young age; as a child, he heard the stories about her from his Jamaican nanny, Etheralda 'TeeTee' Cole. It's possible that Etheralda had learned about Charlotte from the work of J. A. Rogers, having read *Sex and Race* or *Nature Knows No Color-Line*, and was encouraged by the possibility of Blackness in European royalty.

Edric Connor

(1913–68) singer, actor

EDRIC CONNOR WAS a pioneering singer and actor who was
a major celebrity on radio and television in post-war
Britain, and who personified cultural change in Britain in the
years before Caribbean independence. Throughout his life he
maintained a deep connection with the music of Trinidad and
the Caribbean; like the Jamaican poet and folklorist Louise
Bennett-Coverley, who in 1954 recorded his song 'Day Dah
Light', he had a deep pride and appreciation for Caribbean
language and dialects.

Born in the village of Mayaro, Trinidad, Connor arrived in
Britain in 1944, before *Windrush*, and within a couple of years
was a household name as a broadcaster and singer. He worked
in movies directed by the leading British and American directors of the day, and acted alongside Sidney Poitier, Rita
Hayworth, Robert Mitchum, Gregory Peck and Tony Curtis.
He set up his own film and theatre companies and nurtured
the careers of a generation of Caribbean talent in the UK. He
was the first Black man to be cast in a Royal Shakespeare
Company production. His home was an important centre for
Caribbean and African students, politicians and artists. To

have accomplished all this in the 1940s and 1950s in the midst of a colour bar in Britain, when Black actors suffered from typecasting and other constraints, is remarkable.

Connor's talents as a singer and storyteller were shaped by his family and the community in which he grew up. Aged sixteen he won a scholarship from the Trinidad railway to study engineering, and to ease his homesickness he would sing to himself. 'I suppose,' he wrote, 'my voice really developed against the noise of the machines and the engines of the Trinidad government railway workshop . . . when the machine shop foreman gave me hell, and I was sick at heart, I would sing to soothe the pain, full throated, drowning the noise.'[1]

Working as the *Trinidad Guardian*'s 'industrial reporter', he was noticed and encouraged by a couple of visiting filmmakers. He began to explore the island, collecting folk songs as he went, and became popular as a singer. In 1943, he gave two public lectures on West Indian folk music long before it was a celebrated indigenous tradition. In 1944, he went to England to take an engineering course, and two weeks after his arrival he made his debut on BBC radio in *West Indies Calling*, a programme developed for Caribbean listeners. For the next two years he appeared in various radio productions, including the popular music series *Serenade in Sepia* with Evelyn Dove, a contralto of West African and English parentage.[2] His popularity on that series was so great that it was transferred to television in July 1946, and was one of post-war Britain's most successful programmes.

Connor's wife, Pearl Connor, recalled that in the last years of the war and immediately after, it was relatively easy for Black actors and performers to find work in broadcasting; with people still appreciative of the West Indian contribution to the war, 'doors were open [to Edric], he didn't have to kick too hard . . . there weren't many Black people appearing on radio and television, so it was relatively easy for Edric to attract attention.'[3]

Connor made his acting debut in *Cry the Beloved Country* (1952), a drama about life under apartheid in South Africa. Connor was cast as John, the selfish brother of a minister, Revd Stephen Kamalo, played by Canada Lee. For the next decade Connor acted in small but memorable roles in a number of British and American films: John Huston's *Moby Dick* (1956), in which he played the harpooner Daggoo, *Fire Down Below* (1957) with Rita Hayworth, Jack Lemmon and Robert Mitchum, *The Vikings* (1958) with Tony Curtis, and the biblical epic *King of Kings* (1961) in which he was Balthazar. In 1958 the Royal Shakespeare Company cast him in a production of *Pericles*. Connor played Gower, the chorus/narrator of the play; it was one of the high points of his career in the theatre, and he subsequently campaigned to promote integrated casting.

Throughout his career, Connor sought ways to support Caribbean music in Britain. By late 1945 he had made two recordings of Trinidadian music and in 1946 performed a selection of his folk songs on television. In 1951 he organised many of the concerts for the Trinidad All Steel Percussion Orchestra at the Festival of Britain. The steel band's repertoire of calypso, sambo, waltzes and marches made it a sensation among British audiences. It also appeared on television with Connor in the BBC show *Caribbean Cabaret* (1951), which featured the calypsonian Lord Kitchener, who had famously given a rendition of 'London is the Place for Me' as he stood on Tilbury Docks just after disembarking from SS *Empire Windrush*.

In some of the plays and films he acted and performed in, Connor introduced his viewers to Caribbean calypsos and folk songs. The film historian Stephen Bourne notes that he made an important cultural contribution through his role as Daggoo in *Moby Dick*. Required to sing a sea shanty to inspire the men during the whale hunt, Connor chose 'Hill and Gully Rider', a 150-year-old Jamaican folk song, to describe the undulating ocean upon which they were looking for the whale.[4]

Connor wanted to be influential from behind as well as in front of the camera, as a producer and director. He wished to lead programming about Caribbean people and their culture from a Caribbean perspective. Although he was trained by the BBC, had directed a series of short films about the Caribbean with help from the British Film Institute, and was commissioned by the Nigerian government to direct a film, *Bound for Lagos* (1961), making him Britain's first Black director, he faced opposition from the film industry, which could only appreciate him for his talents as a singer and actor.

In 1956 Connor and his wife Pearl founded the Edric Connor Agency, representing performers from the Caribbean, Africa, Malaysia and India. Pearl Connor recalled that their home was a central meeting place for actors, where they would offer support and a place to sleep; they fought with Equity, the actors' union, to give Black actors work.[5]

The couple was also instrumental in forming the Negro Theatre Workshop, a company of thirty Black actors. The company is best known for its production of *The Road* by Wole Soyinka, which was performed at the Theatre Royal Stratford as part of the 1965 Commonwealth Arts Festival, and a BBC production of the *Dark Disciples*, a version of the Passion of St Luke, which was broadcast in 1966.

Edric Connor died of a stroke in 1968. He was an innovator in film and television, a Caribbean cultural nationalist and an ethnomusicologist who did enormous good for the African Caribbeans in Britain and in the Caribbean.

Lloyd Coxsone

(b. 1945) sound system pioneer, reggae producer

T HE SOUND SYSTEM played a key social and cultural role on the British and Jamaican scenes from the 1950s onwards. It evolved from a source of communal entertainment among working-class Jamaicans in the 1950s to become a major creative force influencing music production, and was the driving force behind the evolution of ska, rocksteady, reggae and other genres, such as roots, dancehall and steppers. It served as a testing ground for new music and had the power to make or break an artist, with audiences having considerable influence over the music's success or failure.

The emergence of sound systems in Britain in the 1950s took on a particular importance as, faced with the harsh realities of racism and exclusion from social spaces such as pubs, working men's clubs and dance halls, Caribbean migrants had to create their own entertainment, which became a refuge from the hostility of white society. To a community restricted in all aspects of life by discrimination, hostility and suspicion, the sound system presented a sacred space; it became a site where blackness could be explored and expressed without compromise.

By the late 1960s, sound systems were established in the major UK cities; in London, nightclubs such as the Roaring Twenties in Carnaby Street, the Marquee and the Flamingo were playing Jamaican sounds and featuring artists from both sides of the Atlantic. In the 1970s, the emergence of roots reggae reflected the growing political consciousness occurring within Britain's Black communities. Sound systems were crucial in the dissemination of the music, providing spaces of spiritual sustenance as well as entertainment, and they produced up-and-coming soundmen who introduced new records and artists for their audiences. These people became known for introducing exclusive bass-heavy dubplates and diversifying into production and discovering new artists and genres. Of all the soundmen who emerged in the 1960s and 1970s, Lloyd Coxsone is regarded as one of the innovators of era-defining music and the leader of arguably one of the UK's most influential sound systems.

Born in Cottage Pen, in the parish of St Thomas, Jamaica, Lloyd Blackwood (as he was then known) grew up listening to the sound systems of Morant Bay, including Commander Springfield, Atomic and Merritone. Joining his father and brother in Balham, south London, as a teenager, he began playing with the Queen of the West, the resident sound system of the West Indian social club that was next door to his home, and later with Barry Skyrocket, developing his skills as a selector (DJ). In 1965, he and his childhood friend Festus set up their own sound, Lloyd the Matador, taking the name of the sonic pioneer of Kingston, Jamaica, who had created the powerful Matador amplifiers. Unfortunately, a fight at a dance destroyed the sound system, and Blackwood, finding himself without a sound, worked for Duke Reid the Trojan as selector. With

Blackwood at the controls, Reid's sound ruled south London. Blackwood fell out with Reid, who refused to give evidence on his behalf when he was arrested for being in possession of a knife, which Blackwood claimed was planted on him by a policeman. After serving six months in prison, Blackwood vowed never to work for Reid again. He built a new sound, calling it Sir Coxsone after the great Jamaican soundman, Clement 'Sir Coxsone' Dodd. The rivalry that followed between his own sound system and Duke Reid the Trojan's recreated in England the legendary rivalry of the Jamaican sound systems, and it was a rivalry that shaped much of the ska, rocksteady and reggae that was recorded.

Extended residencies at the Flamingo, Alphabet and Roaring Twenties in central London, the Georgian in Croydon and the Four Aces in Dalston made Sir Coxsone one of the most successful sound systems. Coxsone was also the first to play dub, pioneering the use of the echo, reverb and equaliser. His sound system's success also lay with playing dubplates – the exclusive music coming out of Jamaica, not yet on general release. The multicultural makeup of the audiences meant that he became adept at playing music that appealed to all tastes.

Sensitive to the shifts in Black British culture, Lloyd Coxsone played a key role in jumpstarting the lovers' rock subgenre, which developed out of the sound system culture as an audience-led movement. The sound originated from the talent contests held during his 'Sir Coxsone Outernational' residency at the Four Aces, where he played a mix of soul and reggae, which attracted a female following. The talent show gave aspiring female singers a platform to perform reggae versions of popular soul hits, recorded by the producer Dennis Bovell. Sensing a new music trend, Coxsone produced a cover of the

US soul classic 'Caught You in a Lie', featuring the vocal talents of a fourteen-year-old schoolgirl called Louisa Mark, which became one of lovers' rock's earliest hits in 1975.

That same year he released one of the best-known dub albums, *King of the Dub Rock*, featuring dub versions of his own productions.

In the mid-1980s, Coxsone went into semi-retirement, giving more control of his sound to the younger members, like Blacker Dread, who released his own productions by artists such as Sugar Minott, Frankie Paul, Michael Palmer and Jah Screechy, cutting some of the best digital dancehall of the late 1980s.

Today, Coxsone's sound remains in demand, a great respect engendered from a remarkable back catalogue and innovation that paved the way for many artists and soundmen. Coxsone has come up against many a good sound and defended the Sir Coxsone sound against the best. He has said that the sound system is like a library; instead of books, people come to hear good music.

William Cuffay

(1788–1870) leader of the London Chartist movement

Accorling to the historian Ron Ramdin, between 1800 and 1850 Black working-class leaders became a central part of the vanguard of the radical working-class movement.[1] Their struggles against poverty, discrimination and disenfranchisement merged into the larger working-class movements of the period where they channelled their grievances and arguments into emerging radical political programmes; among them, political reform and workers' rights. William Cuffay, a tailor whose father was born enslaved in St Kitts, was among the most militant and prominent leaders of the Chartist movement. He was a working-class rebel who received harsh punishment for waging war on the ruling class.

The Reform Act of 1832 had little impact on the lives of the working class. Although it had increased the electorate from 366,000 to 650,000 (18 per cent of the total male population in England and Wales), the majority of the working class was still excluded from voting, and the Act failed to introduce a secret ballot. The Act did, however, pave the way for the

Chartist movement around which working-class campaigns of the late 1830s and 1840s coalesced.[2]

The movement's aim was to gain political rights and influence for the working class. It produced a People's Charter, which called for universal male suffrage, a secret ballot, an end to property ownership as a qualification to be an MP, equal electoral districts and annual elections. Signed by over 1.2 million working people, the first Chartist petition was presented to Parliament in July 1839; its rejection was followed by calls for a general strike and national insurrection. In November 1839 the Newport Uprising was an attempt at armed rebellion, where soldiers shot down around twenty-two Chartists.[3]

It was in this tumultuous period that William Cuffay emerged as one of the leading Chartists based in London. Cuffay's father was formerly enslaved in St Kitts and worked as a cook on board a warship. Cuffay was raised by his mother in Chatham in Kent and learned the trade of a tailor. Although he was born with deformities to his spine and legs, 'he took great delight', according to historian T. M. Wheeler, 'in all manly exercises'.[4]

In the 1830s Cuffay worked as a tailor, most likely in the East End or central London. It's unclear what radicalised him, but the tailors' strike of 1834 was likely a principal factor.[5] Being involved in that strike cost him his job at the shop where he had worked for many years. He joined the Chartist movement in 1839, becoming prominent in its London leadership.[6] He helped organise the Metropolitan Tailors Chartist Association, and early evidence of his militancy is found in his motion on the Newport uprising, offering 'sympathy with their brethren, and condemning the injustice and cruelty of the government'.[7]

As the economic depression worsened in London during the 1840s, Cuffay's reputation rose among the London Chartists, and he was elected as delegate for Westminster to the Metropolitan Delegate Council in 1841. Proud of his working-class roots and his trade, he had an intense dislike of the middle class, aristocracy and industrialists. He advocated the interruption of the middle-class Complete Suffrage Union meetings and Anti-Corn Law League demonstrations. At his trial in 1848 he objected to a middle-class jury, explaining they were not his equals.

In 1842 he chaired a 'Great Public Meeting of Tailors', at which the second iteration of the Chartist petition was formulated. That same year, after the arrest of the movement's national leaders, the Metropolitan Delegate Council appointed Cuffay president of a five-man interim executive.[8]

Predictably, the press frequently attacked Cuffay for his militancy, often working his race into their comments. He was lampooned in *Punch* and the *Illustrated London News*; *The Times* referred to the London Chartists as 'the black man and his party', the bad press leading his wife to lose her job as a charwoman.

Cuffay nevertheless rose to becoming one of the most dynamic representatives of the English working class. Appointed to the Master and Servants Bill Demonstration Committee, he vigorously opposed the power given to magistrates to imprison neglectful workers for two months on their employer's word.[9] He was a supporter of the Chartist Land Plan, which proposed to take the unemployed out of the slums and to allocate families two acres of land. He cared deeply about the plight of the working class, and was committed to improving their lives and the conditions in which they lived.

The year 1848 was the time of revolutions in Europe, and the pivotal year in Cuffay's life. One of three London delegates to the Chartists' national convention, he was criticised for his comments suggesting that if the charter was again rejected by Parliament, England should 'begin to think about a republic'.

He also protested strongly against the banning of the procession after a mass meeting on Kennington Common in April to accompany the petition to the House of Commons.

Parliament's third rejection of the People's Charter was a severe blow to Cuffay and the Chartists. He was a late member of the 'Ulterior Committee', however, that was formed to stage an uprising as the movement's next step. The uprising was planned for 16 August 1848; Cuffay joined the committee only three days earlier. To the ruling classes, however, Cuffay was a dangerous man, and police spies kept a close watch on his activities and infiltrated the committee. On 16 August, Cuffay was arrested and charged with plotting to overthrow the government.

Convicted on the unreliable evidence of police informants, Cuffay and most of the leaders of the London Chartists were imprisoned or transported to Australia. Condemned to transportation, William Cuffay was sixty-one when he arrived in Hobart, Tasmania, in November 1849. Although he was pardoned in 1856, he chose to remain in Tasmania, where he continued his political activities, the only one of the Chartist exiles to do so.[10]

Cuffay was an important figure in London Chartism. His goal was to secure people their rights, which would have been achieved if the charter had become law. His ethnicity, however, made him an easy target for the press. He was a larger-than-life character, and in many ways a true outsider: Black, physically deformed and diminutive. He was scapegoated, identified as the chief conspirator of the plot.

In spite of his conviction, he remained defiant. In a speech before the court he asked for no pity: 'No, I pity the government, and I pity the attorney general for convicting me by means of such base characters. The attorney general should be called the spy general . . . I am quite innocent . . . I am not anxious for martyrdom, but after what I have endured this week, I feel I could bear any punishment proudly.'

Quobna Ottobah Cugoano

(aka John Stuart, c.1757–91?)
African abolitionist, writer

QUOBNA OTTOBAH CUGOANO was one of the most radical campaigners for the abolition of the British slave trade and slavery, who dared to offer a radical solution to the problem of enslavement. A contemporary and associate of Olaudah Equiano, his *Thoughts and Sentiments on the Evil and Wicked Traffic of the Slavery and Commerce of the Human Species* (1787) was a searing criticism of the British trade and trafficking of Africans, making him the first published African critic of the slave trade and the first to publicly demand total and immediate abolition.

Cugoano was born in present-day Ghana in the city of Agimaque (Ajumako), 'on the coast of Fantyn', and was kidnapped around the age of thirteen by African raiders. Transported to the island of Grenada, according to his narrative, he spent 'nine or ten months in the slave gang at Grenada, and about one year at different places in the West Indies, with Alexander Campbell Esq.'[1] Campbell (who was executed in Grenada during an uprising against British rule in 1795) brought Cugoano to England in 1772, where he was baptised

John Stuart under the advice of 'some good people . . . that I might not be carried away and sold again'.

Cugoano arrived in England months after the historic Mansfield decision on the Somerset case, which was met with great jubilation by the African British community. Lord Mansfield, Lord Chief Justice, had ruled that James Somerset, who had been brought to England from Massachusetts by his master, Charles Stewart, could not be legally forced back to the colonies.[2] The ruling was widely but erroneously interpreted as abolishing slavery in England; what it did mean was that masters did not have the power to remove enslaved people back to the colonies: they could no longer enforce their claims of possession because enslaved people in England could legally emancipate themselves by running away.[3]

The circumstances of Cugoano's own liberation are not yet known; it is clear he had received advice from individuals sympathetic to his situation on how to protect himself from being re-enslaved and sent back to the Caribbean, and that he perhaps liberated himself from Campbell, aware that slavery in England had been undermined by the Somerset ruling. By the mid-1780s he was employed as a servant by the artists Richard and Maria Cosway, appearing in several of their paintings and etchings. Through the Cosways, who had the patronage of the Prince of Wales, Cugoano met many of the leading artists and celebrities of the day, including Sir Joshua Reynolds, William Blake and Joseph Nollekens.[4]

Like his contemporary and associate Equiano, Cugoano was part of London's Black community and was actively involved in helping the Black poor and on the larger issue of abolition, working alongside the abolitionist group the Sons of Africa. Both Equiano and Cugoano were co-signatories of letters to leading abolitionists, politicians and others connected with the campaign to abolish the slave trade; they were the leaders of opinion among the free African British community in London, contributing in whatever ways they could. In 1786 Cugoano was able to prevent the transportation of Harry Demane to the Caribbean by getting the abolitionist Granville Sharp to take legal action to rescue him.[5]

In 1787, Cugoano's *Thoughts and Sentiments* was published. Some writers claim that Cugoano couldn't have written it without assistance – that Equiano may have collaborated with him on the book.[6] It ran to three editions in 1787 and a French translation was published the following year. In the book, Cugoano presented the most forceful condemnation of slavery ever made by an African, demanding its immediate end and the liberation of all enslaved Africans. Few abolitionists went as far as Cugoano when he made this demand. It is by this stance that Cugoano's contribution to the campaign against slavery can be judged.

Dame Linda Dobbs DBE

(b. 1951) high court judge

S INCE THE LATE 1980s, there have been several 'firsts' by Black Britons in the legal profession. John Anthony Roberts became the first person of African descent to be made a Queen's Counsel in 1988, and was a Recorder in the Crown Court of England and Wales, and in 1992 was appointed by the British government to be a high court judge of the supreme courts of the British Virgin Islands and Anguilla. In 1991, Patricia Scotland, Baroness Scotland of Asthal, became the first Black woman QC, and in 2007 became the Attorney General, the chief legal advisor to the government, the first woman to be appointed to this position. Grace Ononiwu was appointed Northamptonshire's chief prosecutor in 2005, the first Black woman to hold such a post in the history of the Crown Prosecution Service. And in 2004, Linda Dobbs became the first Black woman appointed to the high court when she joined the Queen's Bench.

As is the case with many professions in the UK, Black British representation at the highest levels in the legal profession is low, especially in the judiciary. As of January 2020, 92.6 per cent of court judges are white (2564), and 1.1 per cent identify as

Black (30).[1] Preliminary research undertaken by the Black Firsts in British Law Project, part of the University of Sheffield Law School, found that barriers along racial lines persist. From their interviews with Black senior lawyers and judges, the key challenges identified were a feeling of not belonging, which affected their confidence, and a lack of formal mentoring. The legal profession still mostly attracts Black and mixed race students from middle-class backgrounds, excluding Black students who are statistically more likely to come from a lower socio-economic background. That said, those interviewed expressed optimism that being the 'first' meant they had created spaces for others to follow.[2]

Dame Linda Dobbs's career was affected by some of these challenges, which she overcame. She was a high court judge – one the most senior judges in the country – from 2004 to 2013, and the first Black woman to be appointed to this role. At the time of her appointment she insisted she wasn't a standard bearer; rather, she was 'a practitioner following a career path'.[3]

Dame Linda was born in Sierra Leone, where her father was a high court judge; however, she was determined not to follow in his footsteps, opting, against her parents' wishes, to study music at Edinburgh University. She quickly realised that she did not have the talent to be a serious musician and chose to read Russian with law at the University of Surrey. She only came around to the idea of the bar after completing a doctorate in law. Called to the bar in 1981, being a Black woman working in chambers could be a challenge. Confused as to why she wasn't receiving briefs, she found that her clerk was removing her name from the diary with Tippex and giving the briefs to the male barristers.

Clients who preferred male (and white) barristers made it clear they did not want to be represented by her – Dame Linda recalled that these incidents 'were never good for my self-esteem . . . I could stamp my feet or make a fuss, or put my head down, work hard and prove my worth.'[4]

She specialised in fraud and regulatory work – banking, utilities investment and communications, among other areas – becoming a Queen's Counsel in 1998. As chair of the Criminal Bar Association, she set up its first equality and diversity sub-committee in 2003.

Dobbs didn't envision herself in the senior judiciary despite being recommended to apply, as most who were appointed to it were men working in commercial law. When the Lord Chancellor told her he wanted her to be one of Her Majesty's judges, she balked at first; however, she believed she had a duty to accept, in the hope that her appointment would create the space for other Black and Asian judges to follow.

She has acknowledged that there is still a long way to go. It took seven years after Dobbs's appointment for Sir Rabinder Singh to be appointed to the high court in 2011, and in 2015, Dame Bobbie Cheema-Grubb became the first Asian woman to take on the role. Although there are many capable senior Black and Asian barristers out there that could be considered, Dame Linda says not many are attracted to the senior bench 'for varied and complicated reasons', which include giving up a successful career for public service, issues with recruitment and being in a culture in which you are often the only person of colour, which may present challenges that some lawyers may not be willing to face.[5]

Since stepping down from the senior bench, Dobbs has pursued her various interests, which include supporting several charities in South Africa, and training lawyers and judges in Africa and the Caribbean.

John Edmonstone

(1793?–1833?) taxidermist

IN 1825, CHARLES Darwin happened to mention in a letter to his sister that he was taking lessons in taxidermy from 'a negro [who] lived in Edinburgh'. Darwin, known for his contributions to the science of evolution, which changed scientific thought forever, was taught taxidermy by John Edmonstone, a former slave from Demerara (Guyana), while Darwin was a student at Edinburgh University.

Like all great scientists, Darwin relied on sources of inspiration from people often overlooked and uncredited for their contribution. Edmonstone is one such individual, almost lost to history, who was hugely influential on Darwin's thinking regarding the fixity of species.

Edmonstone's presence in Scotland speaks to its connections with slavery; how a formerly enslaved man from Demerara ended up in Edinburgh making a living as a 'bird stuffer'. For many years, Scotland celebrated a heroic anti-slavery past and downplayed how enslavement enriched its inhabitants and cities. Recently, it has begun to be reconciled to its slaving past: in 2019, the University of Glasgow, on discovering it had benefitted financially from transatlantic enslavement in the eighteenth and nineteenth centuries, announced it would pay £20 million in reparations to atone for its historical links to the trade and trafficking in Africans, signing an agreement with the University of the West Indies to fund a joint centre for development research.

And what of John Edmonstone? Most of what we know about him comes from Darwin's memoir. He appears and disappears in official records, offering glimpses into where he lived and where he worked. An incomplete historical record means one cannot really know him; until more thorough research is undertaken, he remains a footnote in history, whose association with Darwin is one of the few indications of his existence. We are given only small clues as to how he taught one of the greatest figures in the history of science a skill that played no small part in his thinking about how life developed over time.

John Edmonstone was 'owned' by the Scottish slave owner and wood merchant Charles Edmonstone, who had a timber-cutting estate at Mbiri Creek, on the west side of the Demerara River. He lived in the depths of the rainforest with his wife, who was half Scottish and half Arawak, their children, his brother, nephew and enslaved workers.

Charles Edmonstone was friends and eventual father-in-law to the naturalist and early champion of conservation, Charles Waterton, whose family had a plantation in Demerara. Waterton made several expeditions into the rainforests, and taught several of Edmonstone's enslaved workers taxidermy, including John. He took them on bird-collecting trips, teaching them how to catch, stuff and preserve the birds quickly to avoid them spoiling in the heat. In his memoirs of his travels, Waterton provided a negative overview of John's abilities as a taxidermist:

It was upon this hill in former days that I first tried to teach John, the black slave of my friend Mr Edmonstone, the proper way to do birds. But John had poor abilities and it required much time and patience to drive anything into him. Some years after this his master took him to Scotland, where, becoming free John left him and got employed in Glasgow and then the Edinburgh Museum.[1]

If John was as terrible as Waterton suggested, it's doubtful he would have been able to set himself up as a taxidermist or found work at one of Scotland's most important institutions for natural history.

In 1817, John accompanied Charles and his family back to Scotland, where he resided with the family at their estate Cardross Park for five or six years, and where some accounts say he received his freedom. By 1823, he was living in Edinburgh, where records indicate he lived until at least 1833.

The Edinburgh Post Office directory for 1824–5 records John Edmonstone as living at 37 Lothian Street, where he earned his living stuffing birds at the National Museum and teaching taxidermy to the university students. Charles Darwin, who was living with his brother Erasmus at 11 Lothian Street, came to Edinburgh to study medicine, which he hated, in 1825. More interested in the natural world, he hired John to give him lessons on bird taxidermy, paying him one guinea per lesson. Darwin wrote to his sister of the meeting, that he had found 'a negro lived in Edinburgh, who had travelled with Waterton, and gained his livelihood by stuffing birds, which he did excellently'.

Darwin had hours of conversations with John about Guyana and its tropical rainforests, plants and animals, firing his imagination and his growing interest in tropical regions. His letters to his sister Elizabeth showed he was impressed with John (whom he did not name), with his association with Waterton and with his skill as a taxidermist. 'I used often to sit with him, for he was a very pleasant and intelligent man.'[2]

In 1831, Darwin secured a position as a naturalist on the HMS *Beagle* on its voyage to chart the South American coastline. Tasked with investigating the geology of the region and making natural history collections, he undoubtedly utilised the techniques he learned from John Edmonstone when he preserved the Galápagos finches.

Edmonstone's mentorship and teaching had a profound impact on Darwin; in 2009, a small plaque was mounted on Lothian Street to commemorate John Edmonstone's contribution.

Idris Elba OBE

(b. 1972) actor, producer, director, writer, DJ

I DRIS ELBA FIRST gained international recognition as Stringer
Bell in the acclaimed television series *The Wire* (2002–8).
His portrayal of the charismatic and perceptive drug dealer
who yearned to cross over from the illegal drug trade and create
a legitimate business empire showed that Elba had serious
acting chops and range. Since then his career, spanning over
twenty years, has seen him play a diverse set of characters in
television and in small- and big-budget films.

Born Idrissa Akuna Elba in east London, of Sierra Leonean
and Ghanaian parentage, Elba began his acting career in
Crimewatch murder reconstructions, at the same time managing
his own DJing business. After a series of supporting roles and a
stint in the Channel 5 soap *Family Affairs*, Elba did what many
Black British actors have done to find a way to transcend the
limited roles offered to Black actors in Britain; he moved to New
York in 2001, where he eventually landed the role of Stringer Bell.
Since then, Elba has become a leading Hollywood actor, appearing in blockbuster films such as *Prometheus* and *Pacific Rim*, and
is part of the Marvel Cinematic Universe, playing Heimdall, the
all-seeing, all-knowing protector of the Bifrost Bridge that reached

between Asgard and Earth in the *Thor* movies. Elba also shines in smaller-budget films, such as the BAFTA-nominated film *Second Coming* (2014), a drama about a woman who appears to become inexplicably pregnant following a series of miscarriages and not having been intimate with her husband, played by Elba.

Elba's portrayal of Nelson Mandela in the biopic *Long Walk to Freedom* (2013) was well received; and on television, he has received considerable acclaim for his role in *Luther*, a psychological crime drama, which began in 2010, in which he plays the eponymous brilliant, deeply tortured detective, whose success in capturing some of the most evil criminals suggests a terrible knowledge of how their minds work because his own mind works in a similar way.

Elba's international profile, good looks and acting range meant he was tipped to play the coveted role of James Bond after Daniel Craig's tenure was due to end, which was greeted with disbelief and fury in some quarters. Anthony Horowitz, author of the latest James Bond novel, claimed that Elba was 'too street' to play the eponymous secret agent.[1] Widely interpreted as a comment on Elba's apparent unsuitability to play the role because of his race, Horowitz backtracked on his comments and apologised.

Elba is a visible campaigner and speaker on the issue of the lack of diversity in film and television. In 2016, he spoke to MPs, warning them that, compared to the USA, Black actors were struggling to make progress in the UK, citing his own example of having to move to the USA, which increased his opportunities of securing acting that did not restrict him to best friend or sidekick roles.[2] Elba said that British broadcasting needs a 'Magna Carta' when it comes to casting opportunities for Black and minority ethnic actors.

Elba combines his acting with his music career performing under the moniker DJ Big Driis, appearing in videos with British and American artists including Skepta and Taylor Swift, and featuring on tracks by Macklemore and Sean Paul. In 2018, he performed DJ duties at the wedding of Prince Harry and Meghan Markle. Elba also made his directing debut with *Yardie*, a crime drama based on the 1992 novel by Victor Headley set in Hackney, London, where he grew up, and Jamaica in the 1970s and 1980s.

Edward Enninful OBE

(b. 1972) magazine editor

IN 2017, NAOMI Campbell shared a photograph on her Instagram feed of the British *Vogue* editorial team under its then editor, Alexandra Shulman; the team appeared to be all white, and Campbell criticised the magazine for its lack of representation in front of and behind the camera. The responses to the post were mixed, with many of her followers agreeing with her and others pointing out that race wasn't the issue, commending the team for being overwhelmingly female. While there has been an increase in the number of people of colour being featured on the cover of American glossy magazines since 2017, according to research undertaken by the *Guardian*, of the 214 UK covers published by the bestselling glossy magazines, only 20 featured a person of colour.[1] There was no investigation into the ethnic makeup of the editorial staff of these magazines, but it begs the question as to whether the women of colour who do work on fashion or lifestyle publications are the decision makers, heading up departments, responsible for buying, styling and merchandising.

All of this points to why Edward Enninful's appointment as editor-in-chief of British *Vogue* in 2017 is evidence of some progress. It is also evidence of a natural decision to select an artistic director who had, in the space of five years in his youth, gone from being a thirteen-year-old newly arrived in England from Ghana, to an eighteen-year-old fashion editor of *i-D*, a leading fashion, music and youth culture magazine. Since his appointment, Enninful has added several leading Black names to his list of contributing editors, including Campbell, Steve McQueen and Adwoa Aboah, whom he placed on the cover to celebrate his first issue as editor.

When he was sixteen, Enninful was scouted as a model, and began modelling for *i-D*, where he quickly became a stylist and eventually fashion editor, a significant achievement for a teenager. Becoming an editor of such an influential magazine is an indication of Enninful's prodigious talent; that he possesses an extraordinary understanding of trends and what is popular from a style perspective. As a boy, he would design clothes with his mother, a seamstress and fashion designer, which developed his skill in learning to build character through clothes.[2] It was these early experiences working with his mother that influenced his ideas and developed his instinct and love of style.

As fashion editor, he was inspired by the 1980s club scene, and was one of few editors to feature dark-skinned models – as contributing editor for Italian *Vogue* in 2008, his 'All Black Issue' featuring Black models became one of his most influential works. The original run sold out in the UK and USA within seventy-two hours, with Italian *Vogue* having to reprint 30,000 extra copies for the USA, another 10,000 copies for the UK and 20,000 more in Italy.[3] The success of the issue highlighted the lack of diversity in fashion magazines, and the need for a dialogue in how this could be facilitated.

His directorship at *W Magazine*, a high-end Condé Nast title, helped revive its fortunes by featuring famous people in fantastical imaginings.

When he was appointed editor-in-chief of British *Vogue*, he set out to make it more inclusive and diverse. Knowing that the magazine spoke to a specific demographic – white, upper-middle-class women – Enninful sought to reach out to a wider demographic by featuring more non-white cover subjects, such as Oprah Winfrey and Rhianna, having a diverse staff and advocating for LGBTQI issues.

Meghan, Duchess of Sussex, guest-edited the September 2019 issue, calling it 'Forces for Change', highlighting female trailblazers including climate-change campaigners, artists, politicians and activists around the globe who are breaking barriers and setting agendas.

Enninful's vision for *Vogue* is clear: 'People were ready to embrace something that reflected them. And for me, it was all about bringing *Vogue* back to what it was like in the '70s and '80s when it was about people, and you could see yourself. That's all I ever wanted to do.'[4]

Olaudah Equiano

(1745–97) abolitionist, writer

WHEN EQUIANO WROTE his *Interesting Narrative of the Life of Olaudah Equiano, or Gustavus Vassa, the African* (1789), he presented the story of the life of a truly remarkable man. Published during the emergence of a national campaign to abolish the British slave trade, it provided British readers with an insight into slavery in the Americas, revealing the horrors of what was taking place on the plantations and on slave ships. The book helped shift public opinion on slavery and made Equiano the most famous and wealthiest Black man in Britain. Its subscribers included the Prince of Wales, the Duke of York and the Duke of Cumberland, and in Equiano's lifetime the book went through nine editions, reaching readers as far as Germany, Russia, Holland and New York. When he died in 1797, his wealth enabled him to leave £950, a substantial amount of money, to his daughter Joanna, making her an eligible heiress.

The *Narrative* recounts the life of a man who was not meant to thrive or even survive at a time in history during which millions of Africans became victims of the largest-ever forced migration, made to toil on Caribbean plantations in order to help develop a culture of consumption in Europe with products such as sugar, rum, molasses, indigo and pimento. These commodities meant that by the mid-eighteenth century, slavery was an accepted part of the social and economic structures that sustained Britain and other European nations – the source of their wealth and power. British social life was unimaginable without the produce of slave labour; consequently, from the moment a campaign was established to end it in 1787, West India merchants and plantation owners led the counter campaign and fought, using significant resources at their disposal, to ensure that the institution would never end.

Biographer Vincent Carretta has observed that Equiano's enslavement was unrepresentative of the experiences of the vast majority of enslaved Africans; that he was saved from slavery's worst horrors. Equiano was both literate and had mobility in the jobs he undertook.[1] That said, he was nonetheless an enslaved person, whose life and body were not his own. Even after purchasing his freedom, he maintained a precarious existence and could be re-enslaved at the whim of any white man he encountered. That Equiano always carried his manumission papers on his person indicates how tenuous was his existence.

He was, however, in a unique position to witness how slavery functioned on different islands. He could give an opinion on the impact of slavery on the enslaved and enslaver alike, and his ability to articulate and critique it, to bear witness on behalf of the enslaved in his book, is an indication of his passion for justice and opposition to slavery, while at the same time debunking contemporary assumptions of the lack of intellectual prowess of Africans.

Born in the Igbo Kingdom of Benin (present-day Nigeria) in 1745, Equiano provided a detailed account of his Igbo culture, explaining distinctions between domestic African slavery and chattel slavery. Igbo slaves became part of the family, while chattel slavery rendered a person property for life.

In the early chapters of his narrative, his capture, enslavement and transportation to the Americas are vividly described. The reader learns of his strength of character as he refuses to accept the name given to him by his first master, the naval captain Michael Pascal, who renames him Gustavus Vassa, in the patronising tradition of renaming enslaved Africans after European heroes.[2] Although powerless to control his own fate, as he was sold from person to person, he courageously challenged his status:

> When I came there, Captain Doran asked if I knew him; I answered that I did not. 'Then', said he, 'you are now my slave'. I told him my master could not sell me to him, or anyone else. 'Why', said he, 'did not your master buy you?' I confessed that he did 'But I have served him . . . besides this I have been baptised, and by the laws of the land no man has a right to sell me.[3]

Equiano spent most of his life at sea, acquiring an education in England from two sisters in Falmouth and on board the ships he served while he was enslaved. As a free man he sailed on many voyages: to the Arctic on the Phipps expedition in 1773 as a surgeon's mate; as valet to a gentleman on a tour of the Mediterranean, spending time in Smyrna; and in the Caribbean, assistant to Dr Charles Irving, who was celebrated for turning seawater into fresh water, and living among Miskito Indians in Nicaragua.

The historian Folarin Shyllon maintains that Equiano had become a committed abolitionist from the time of his manumission in 1766, anxious to return to England to begin his campaign against slavery and the slave trade.[4] He became acquainted with the campaigner Granville Sharp, who in 1772 had brought the case of James Somerset, a Black man whose former owner was attempting to return with Somerset from England to the West Indies. The case was heard before Lord Mansfield, the Chief Justice, who made a landmark ruling that English law did not permit slavery on its soil. In 1783, Equiano brought to Sharp's attention the case of the slave ship *Zong*, from which 132 enslaved Africans were thrown overboard on the pretext of a shortage of water, but in truth it was in order to claim the insurance. The case was brought to court, and although no one was held accountable for the horrific crime, the efforts of Equiano and Sharp brought the matter to public awareness. That same year, the Quakers established a committee for abolition and presented a petition to Parliament for the abolition of the slave trade.[5] The historian James Walvin notes that the Quakers in Philadelphia were the first to orchestrate an organised attack on slavery, through tracts written by early abolitionists such as Anthony Benezet, which were printed in London in 1784–5.[6] Equiano had become part of a growing Black community in London which, according to Walvin, 'formed one branch in the Atlantic network for information, gossip and news from Africa, the slave ships and slave colonies'.[7]

Keeping themselves informed of discourse in support of and against slavery was a key aspect of their activities. They drafted a petition of thanks to the Quakers, which Walvin maintains was written by Equiano himself.

As to the debates considering whether the British trade and trafficking in Africans should cease, they were closely followed by Equiano, who led several Black delegations to Parliament to listen to the debates and the examination of witnesses. He drew on his experience and knowledge of enslavement to refute claims made by its defenders, which were widely published. He put forward a case for a trade in commodities instead of humans in a letter to the president for the Privy Council for Trade, which was included in the Privy Council report relating to Trade and Foreign Plantations.[8]

Equiano was a man who understood the politics of his time and who was an excellent and confident lobbyist, comfortable with approaching the most influential people in order to present his case to them.

When Equiano wrote his *Narrative*, he chose to use his Igbo name, reclaiming his African self and presenting it to the public.[9] Through the book he established himself as an African who spoke with authority on the subject of enslavement, as well as a Briton, and showed that the two identities could exist within the same person. In the telling of his life, readers, from the eighteenth century to the present, are introduced to a remarkable person who made a major contribution to the abolitionist cause.

Bernardine Evaristo MBE, FRSL

(b. 1959) author, playwright, poet, academic

IN 2019, BERNARDINE Evaristo made history when she became the first Black woman to win the Booker Prize for her eighth novel, *Girl, Woman, Other*. It is written in a prose-poetry style that Evaristo has termed 'fusion fiction', allowing her to get inside the heads of her characters and flit between past and present.[1] In this way, she presents interconnected narratives that explore the lives and experiences of twelve predominantly Black British female and non-binary characters, whose ages range between nineteen and ninety-three. Set in various locations across Britain and taking place over several decades, the novel covers topics of cultural background, class and sexuality as it tells the stories of these characters' families, lovers and occupations. It is a love song to modern Britain and Black womanhood, while also challenging the stereotypes and invisibility her characters endure.

The Booker Prize gave global recognition to an innovative writer who has long advocated the necessity for more diverse voices in the British literary canon, and whose writings explore the often-hidden narratives of African diasporic lives. Evaristo writes experimentally – her novels are often written in verse – with a devotion to linguistic play and historical detail that draws her readers into worlds that place Black characters at their centre. Evaristo also connects Britain's past with its present by showing that its people were both culturally and racially diverse. She is a mainstream writer whose subject matter is not mainstream; whose work gives attention to the inner and outer lives of Black Britons. She has said that she 'likes to disrupt possible reader expectations through creating characters who defy reductive notions of who we are in this society, in the world'.[2]

Born of English and Nigerian parents in south-east London and raised in Woolwich, Evaristo began her writing career within an alternative arts movement in which Black British artists sought to address the inequalities in mainstream theatre by creating their own spaces to tell their stories and showcase their talent. Co-founding the Theatre of Black Women with fellow drama-school graduates Patricia Hilaire and Paulette Randall, their work sought to provide an opportunity to hear Black female voices in theatre, in order to promote positive and encouraging images of Black women as individuals. The plays written by the collective discussed what it meant to be Black, British and female in the 1980s, the historical exclusion of Black women, and Black self-image, identity and belonging. These themes continue to feature in Evaristo's literary work. She has also spoken about how she was influenced by research undertaken by the Jamaican historian J. A. Rogers, which discusses the scope of historical interracial mixing in Europe.

In her novel *Lara* (1997), Evaristo draws on her own life as the daughter of British and Nigerian parents, and the protagonist's father shares little about her Nigerian heritage. Writing in verse, Evaristo follows Lara's life from childhood to adulthood, as she seeks to understand her ancestry by tracing the roots of her English-Nigerian-Brazilian-Irish family over a hundred and fifty years and three continents, learning about the interconnectedness of her heritage over time and place.

The Emperor's Babe (2001), another verse novel, was inspired by a writing residency at the Museum of London, where she was told there was no evidence of African people living in London in the Roman era. She later discovered that there were Africans living in England in that period. This motivated her to write a novel set two thousand years ago in a multicultural London, seen through the eyes of a young Nubian girl, Zuleika, the daughter of an immigrant who arranges her marriage to an older Roman. Although Zuleika attains status through her marriage, she feels isolated and yearns for a fuller sense of self and accomplishes this in part by hitting London's social scene with her friends during her husband's long absences. The novel plays with the concepts of difference, class, race and gender with vibrancy and verve, winning Evaristo an Arts Council Writers Award.

Soul Tourists (2005) is the tale of a couple who embark on a journey through Europe and encounter Black European historical figures, including Jamaican nurse and war heroine Mary Seacole, Shakespeare's 'Dark Lady', French composer and conductor Joseph Boulogne, Chevalier de Saint-Georges and Alessandro de' Medici. Evaristo's innovative way of weaving in and out of history, drawing attention to these underexposed historical figures, serves to disrupt the myth of a 'white' Western history.

Blonde Roots (2009) is a satire on transatlantic enslavement, which presents its horrors in an alternate universe in which Africans are the enslavers of Europeans. The story of Doris Scagglethorpe, who is enslaved and attempts to escape to return home to her family, upends the racial and colonial prejudices that the transatlantic slave trade produced. By defying established and often unchallenged timelines and hierarchies of key historical moments, Evaristo, like Malorie Blackman with her novel *Noughts and Crosses*, compels the reader to consider how easily things could have been reversed.

In *Mr Loverman* (2013), Evaristo explores the idea of secrets within families. Her protagonist Barrington is a Black British gay man in his seventies who leads a double life – married with children and grandchildren, he has also maintained a decades-long affair with his childhood friend. By centring on older Black characters, Evaristo reimagines the narrative of the older Caribbean male; by making him gay, that narrative is ground-breaking.

Evaristo is a literary advocate of long standing who has raised concerns about the marginalisation of Black British writers and tokenism within major publishing houses. She was the initiator of the Arts Council's 2005 report, *Free Verse*, which found that work by Black British poets represented under 1 per cent of published work. To redress this imbalance, she founded the Complete Works poet mentoring scheme which, over ten years (2007–17), saw thirty poets mentored by some of Britain's leading poets. At Brunel University, London, where she is Professor of Creative Writing, Evaristo founded the annual Brunel International African Poetry Prize, with all the shortlisted and winning poets' work published in the *New-Generation African Poets* series of box sets.

Bernardine Evaristo is one of Britain's most accomplished writers, who shows us that the history of Britain cannot be told without Black people. Britain's landscape and history play central roles in her books to represent the space of movement and of migration.

Sir Mohamed Muktar Jama Farah CBE

(b. 1983) athlete

MOHAMED 'MO' FARAH is Britain's greatest-ever distance runner, and the most successful track athlete in modern Olympic Games history. He is a double-double Olympic champion, having won golds in the 5,000 metres and 10,000 metres in both the 2012 and 2016 Games. He is the second athlete in history to have won long-distance doubles at successive Olympics and World Championships, and the first in history to defend both distance titles in major global competitions – known as the 'quadruple double'. Farah has ten global titles and is the most decorated athlete in British athletics history.

Born in Mogadishu, Somalia, Farah is the fourth of eight children; his father Muktar, who was born and raised in London, was a businessman who, as Somalia descended into civil war, brought his family from Mogadishu to Somaliland, where they were from originally. For a while they lived in a refugee camp, and then moved to Djibouti. Farah's father returned to London and Mo followed aged nine to join his extended family, speaking very little English. He hoped his twin brother Hassan would join them; however, he was quite ill and, unable to travel, had to remain. After war broke out the brothers lost contact – the family with which Hassan was staying moved – and it was twelve years before the brothers were reunited. Farah spoke of the time he was separated from his twin brother as very hard for him.

In Hounslow, where his family had settled, Farah focused on learning English and began competing in cross-country races aged thirteen. Like numerous athletes, Farah's success was many years in the making. Between 1996 and 2008, he was competing and winning junior athletics titles; he won Silver in the European Championship in 2006 and was running fast times. He learned discipline and commitment by training and living with Kenyan distance runners, including Micah Kogo, who was at that time the world number one at 10,000 metres. Not qualifying for the 5,000 metres final in Beijing in 2008 influenced his determination to succeed – in the 2010 European Athletics Championship, he became the sixth man in the history of that tournament to win both the 5,000 and 10,000 metres titles.

In the 2011 World Championship in South Korea, Farah won the gold in the 5000 metres and silver in the 10,000 metres. Having learned to mastermind his races in every way possible – by building up his strength and power, conserving his energy, being much more prepared, varying his tactics and, most importantly, being able to run the last 400 metres in fifty seconds – he achieved ten global wins, a streak that did not end until 2017.

Mo Farah embraces both his British and his Somali heritage. He visits his Somali family annually and launched the Mo Farah Foundation to help support children living in orphanages. He shares his successes with his family to show his appreciation for the sacrifices they make to allow him to compete.

Not only is Mo Farah the most successful British athlete, he is also very popular. In 2017, he won the BBC Sports Personality of the Year, beating the favourite, boxing champion Anthony Joshua. The British public has very much taken Farah to its heart.

Lenford Kwesi Garrison

(1943–2003) educationist, historian, activist

L EN GARRISON WAS an educationist and historian whose
life's work was to develop resources that instilled knowledge of the Black historical presence and contribution to
British and world history. Today he is remembered for the
establishment of the Black Cultural Archives, a lasting legacy to
Garrison's passion and commitment to the importance of the
production of knowledge as a tool for community empowerment. Garrison was one of the many Black education activists
throughout the country committed to the embedding of positive representations of Black British history and culture.

Garrison's work in education was both cultural and political.
In the 1970s and 1980s, he used his political shrewdness to
promote and advocate for a culture-based curriculum in
London and Nottingham as a way to improve opportunities
for young Black people.

Len Garrison was born in St Thomas Parish, Jamaica, where
the 1865 Morant Bay Rebellion had broken out. It was also
one of Jamaica's poorest parishes – a high proportion of post-
war migrants to Britain came from there.[1] Joining his parents
in west London in 1954, Garrison developed an interest in

photography, studying the subject at King's College London, and also trained as a specialist medical photographer working at Guy's Hospital and freelancing for the *West India Gazette*, founded by Claudia Jones.

Black educational activism in London took shape in the late 1960s and early 1970s when parents, community leaders and educators organised themselves into a Black political network, connected by community-based initiatives and radical Black publishing. Garrison was connected to this network, which actively campaigned against the over-representation of Black pupils in educationally subnormal schools. It was within this context of political struggle that, in 1971, Garrison completed a diploma in development studies at Ruskin College, Oxford, writing a dissertation on Rastafarianism, which was eventually published as a book entitled *Black Youth, Rastafarianism, and the Identity Crisis in Britain.* In this work, Garrison noted that, faced with discrimination and racist hostility, Rastafarianism gained currency among many of the first generation of young Black Britons, who rejected the Christianity of their parents that stressed patience and forbearance in the face of such hostility. They turned to Rastafarianism 'in an attempt at self-discovery that constituted an important step in the rise of historical consciousness', which helped them to overcome their personal and cultural insecurities, instilling a sense of direction, self-confidence and spiritual renewal.[2] At around the time Garrison completed his book, Bernard Coard's blistering critique *How the West Indian Child Is Made Educationally Subnormal in the British School System* was published; both studies emphasised the need to nurture a positive sense of self via an appreciation of Black British history and to nurture cultural consciousness.

In 1977, Garrison launched the African and Caribbean

Educational Resource Centre (ACER). Its Black history education packs, which were piloted at Dick Sheppard School in Tulse Hill, just outside Brixton, played an influential role in the development of multicultural education resources. When the Labour Party and Ken Livingstone won control of the Greater London Council (GLC) in 1981, Garrison was able to negotiate with the Inner London Education Authority (ILEA) for funding and resources for this scheme. Until 1988, Garrison worked with teachers and librarians to produce curriculum guides and provided professional development to scores of London teachers about African Caribbean culture and history.

One of ACER's most popular innovations was the creation of the Black Youth Annual Writing Awards, which gave students a platform to write about their experiences as young Black people growing up in Britain. With prizes awarded for entries in poetry and essay writing, winning entries were published in an annual volume that was disseminated in schools.

The Thatcher government, however, dismantled the Greater London Council in 1986, and in 1988 imposed the Education Reform Act, which increased central government's control and reduced local authorities' influence over education policies. With ACER's funding greatly diminished, Garrison moved to Nottingham, where he established East Midlands and African Caribbean Arts. At this centre, he promoted the reclamation of 'hidden histories' and untold stories via community and local history projects, playing a large part in the production of *The Black Presence in Nottingham*, a major exhibition held in the city's museum.

The origins of the Black Cultural Archives grew from the community response to the events of 1981, specifically the response to the New Cross Massacre and the disturbances in

London and other cities. The following year, the African American activist Queen Mother Moore (1898–1997) visited Britain on a speaking tour. An anti-racist activist since the 1920s, involved in the Marcus Garvey and Black Power movements as well as spearheading the reparations movement, Moore urged 'our brothers and sisters here to join in the development and the building of a great monument in memory of our lost ancestors and freedom fighters'. She described the monument as 'a comprehensive international depository of African life and culture, and a meeting place where we could develop the strategies and resources needed to continue the struggle for liberation'.[3]

Like Moore, Garrison believed that collecting and structuring the fragmented evidence of the Black past in Britain as well as in the Caribbean and Africa 'is a major agenda item in the last decade of the 20th century to create a better basis for achieving a fully multicultural British society'.[4] Garrison and his co-founders took up Moore's call for a monument, forming the African People's Historical Monument Foundation, which then began work on the Black Cultural Archives project. Garrison served as chair and steered the project until his death, collecting historical materials sourced from antique dealers and second-hand shops in markets. These materials formed the backbone of the collection, much of which highlighted the contributions of Black communities prior to the *Windrush* narrative. The team collected items for over forty years, with exhibitions in various formats housed in different locations in Brixton and Kennington, south London. Eventually, the Black Cultural Archives centre opened in Windrush Square, Brixton, becoming the first dedicated Black heritage centre in the UK.

The education scholar Lauri Johnson has argued that Len

Garrison was a critical multiculturalist who understood the importance of culture in students' lives.[5] Knowing how institutional racism impacted schools and the curriculum, he never lost sight of his conviction that Black students needed materials that would support their identity development, ground them in African and Caribbean history, and help them to understand their environment and the challenges of growing up Black in Britain. When Black communities around the country erupted in violent protest in 1981, Garrison and other community leaders argued that what young Black people needed was a space with positive representations of their history and culture:

> We need our own archives where important acts of achievement of the past which are now scattered or pushed in the margins of European history can be assembled, where facts presented as negative can be represented from our point of view as positive factors in our liberation.[6]

George the Poet

(b. 1991) spoken-word artist, social commentator

I N THE FINAL episode of the second series of his podcast, *Have You Heard George's Podcast?*, George the Poet reveals he turned down an MBE. Entitled 'Concurrent Affairs', George engages in intimate conversations with personified versions of Uganda and Britain, about the effects of colonialism on both countries. Born to Ugandan parents, George gives his reasons for refusing, explaining that 'the colonial trauma inflicted on the children of Africa, entrenched across our geopolitical and macroeconomic realities, prevents me from accepting the title "MBE" . . . it remains unacceptable to me until Britain takes institutional measures to redress the intergenerational disruptions brought to millions as a result of her colonial exploits.'[1] George thus has joined the tradition of several cultural figures, among them Benjamin Zephaniah, who were unwilling and unable to accept the honour because of the way it supports the legacies of colonialism and empire.

George the Poet (born George Mpanga) is a spoken-word artist who uses his art to make a commentary on social and political issues. His podcasts are remarkable in the way that they defy common and expected formats. They are experimental audio stories, akin to concept albums, which combine soundscapes, rap music, news clips, vox pops and acted-out scenes that are driven by real events such as Grenfell, African slavery in Libya, the 2011 uprisings in London, gun and knife violence, and his own experience of being racialised and searched by the police after a gig. The podcasts also explore the nature of George's creativity and creative process; how ideas that reside within his mind vie for attention to be actualised, and how he overcomes the fears and insecurities which sometimes hinder his process.

Social commentary attracts young people to the news, and the podcasts express this commentary in the way in which young people speak to each other. George has said the series is an artistic exploration of his community and he was going for a 'living-room experience' where people can have difficult conversations in a way that is not combative or defensive. He believes there are different ways to package Black British narratives that do not pander to market forces that seek to commercialise the 'Black experience', such as with artists who are celebrated for their gangster lifestyles.

The episodes are performed live, and George invites the audience to wear eye masks so that they can focus their listening on his beautifully constructed streams of consciousness. The listener is compelled to enter the characters' inner worlds and to consider their individual responses to these worlds – they are immersed in the story, not knowing where it leads, and it never goes where one expects. The series was nominated for a Peabody Award, and won five gold awards, including Podcast of the Year, at the British Podcast Awards in 2019. In May 2019, George opened the BBC's coverage of Prince Harry and Meghan Markle's wedding with a specially commissioned poem, 'The Beauty of Union', which introduced George's poetry to a global audience.

George Mpanga, who grew up on St Raphael's Estate in north-west London, said he 'wanted to be both street and book smart'.[2] Since the age of eleven he has existed between a predominantly Black working-class world and the white middle-class establishment, studying at Queen Elizabeth's School, a selective grammar school in Barnet, and Cambridge University. Spoken-word poetry entered George's life at Cambridge – despite being a talented grime rapper as a teenager, he did not want to present himself as a gimmick, choosing to relay his work more conversationally, without music. His degree in politics, sociology and psychology allowed him to 'become scientific about our condition . . . finding out what seemed like little secrets, little clues as to who I was and why we were in the situation we were in.' This helped with his development as a lyricist and writer.

Although political, George abandoned his ambition to be an MP, becoming disillusioned with the idea when he realised it would restrict him from having candid and unconditional conversations about the situation Black British youth find themselves in. Similarly, he felt unable to pursue a career as a recording artist, walking away from a recording contract because he didn't feel that his social agenda could be prioritised through music. Wanting to be more explorative and elaborative, he saw podcasting as the only medium to give him the space to accomplish this.

Conscious that the narrative about Black British youth is being controlled and shaped by mainstream media, George is adamant that 'telling your own story is the secret to survival'. He believes the option and opportunity exists to be creative about our stories, and that we should reclaim them.

Paul Gilroy

(b. 1956) historian, social and cultural theorist, philosopher

Paul Gilroy has been described as one the most intellectually formidable cultural and social theorists of our time, who has reshaped debates on racism, nationalism and multiculturalism.[1] His scholarship is interdisciplinary, incorporating history, philosophy, cultural studies, anthropology, post-colonial studies, sociology, music and photography, and was highly influential on the cultural and political movements of Black Britons during the 1990s. His seminal work *The Black Atlantic: Modernity and Double Consciousness* (1993) transformed the study of the African diaspora, arguing that the Black Atlantic was a distinctive cultural political space that is not specifically African, American, British or Caribbean, but a hybrid of all of them. He has held professorships at Yale University, the London School of Economics and King's College London, and is the founding director and current Professor of Humanities at University College London's Centre for the Study of Race and Racism. In 2018, Gilroy was elected as a member of the American Academy of Arts and Sciences, and in 2019 was the winner of Norway's Holberg Prize, which is awarded annually to a person who has made an outstanding contribution to research in the arts, humanities, social sciences, law and theology.

Gilroy has remarked that the question often put to him – Where are you from? – and the evolving responses to that question have formed the narrative that explains his work. He has described himself as a creature of a certain moment in the post-colonial life of Britain; his mother, the author, teacher and pioneering psychotherapist Beryl Gilroy, came to London from Guyana in 1951 to study for a diploma in child development, where she met and married his father Patrick, a scientist who was descended from German migrants. As a child of Guyanese and German–British heritage, he has said that the roots of his critical interest lay in attempting to understand the racism directed towards himself and his parents.

As a student he was intellectually restless; he wanted to find a bolder way to engage with problems that interested him, which he found in studying history, sociology and other subjects. Seeing the Centre of Contemporary Cultural Studies at the University of Birmingham as operating outside disciplinary structures, he studied for his doctorate there, under the supervision of Stuart Hall. As a young scholar coming out of the tradition of the new left, Gilroy was a member of a cohort of young scholars, including Hazel Carby, Angela McRobbie and Bill Schwarz, who went on to have successful careers in academia. Gilroy, working within several disciplines, wrote about the way racism was changing the functioning of British political institutions and the operation of British society. His first book, the co-authored *The Empire Strikes Back: Race and Racism in '70s Britain* (1982), was a landmark text in the formation of ethnic and racial studies in Britain and in its focus on the links between state institutions and popular racism. The book remains as powerful and relevant today as when it was first published.

There Ain't No Black in the Union Jack: The Cultural Politics of Race and Nation (1987) made Gilroy's name as a post-colonial intellectual, and still serves as an inspiration to scholars interested in reinserting Black people and their histories into British history. Published at the height of Margaret Thatcher's Conservative government, it is a study of race and racism in Britain that is bound up with a national culture imagined to be only white and Christian in its nature. In his review of the book thirty-two years after its publication, sociologist Les Back wrote that what was distinctive about this work was Gilroy's capacity to anticipate and interpret the damage the British Empire and colonialism did, not only to the colonised, but also to the colonisers. Back highlights Gilroy's observation that, while British imperialism fostered a feeling in the Caribbean colonies of Britain as the 'mother country', it also had a simultaneous desire to keep the Caribbean at a distance and to 'keep Britain white'. Gilroy was, in a way, anticipating the tensions and circumstances that led to the *Windrush* Scandal in 2018.[2]

As the child of migrants, Gilroy found the attachment of culture to nationhood problematic, and his primary interest became how to think about culture differently. *The Black Atlantic: Modernity and Double Consciousness* (1993) explored and critiqued the histories that believed culture belonged in one place. Gilroy considered the process of being forcibly removed from one's home during transatlantic enslavement and mixing with other ethnic groups; it was his position that there were cultural exchanges taking place not just below deck, but above it, that needed to be known and understood. What were the forms of labour and language being developed; what nationalities were being transported, both European and African; and what commodities, such as salted cod, rum or even livestock, had these ships carried? A richer account of cultural interaction and contact between different groups could be understood, argued Gilroy, if the ship is taken as a kind of motif for connecting and reconstructing this history.

Throughout his career, Paul Gilroy has been exploring how to think about race, culture and history in new ways; how migration and movement make cultures anew, and how traditions are not static. On race he remarked, 'for me, a critique of racism and race-thinking provides a route into a clearer, deeper understanding of humankind and its contested nature'.[3]

Bernie Grant

*(1944–2000) anti-racist and social justice
activist, trade unionist, politician*

W HEN BERNIE GRANT wore traditional West African
ceremonial dress at the state opening of Parliament in
1987, he was celebrating his blackness in the midst of what had
been, up until then, the prevailing whiteness of government
and of the establishment, and he was signalling the changes he
intended to make within that space. The gesture was typical of
Grant, who spent much of his parliamentary career demanding
acknowledgement of and seeking ways to repair the historical
wrongs of slavery and colonialism. Before his death, one of his
last interventions in the Commons on this matter in 1999 was
to seek an apology from the then prime minister Tony Blair for
the role the British state played in slavery. He was unwavering
in his belief that, to heal the wounds of the present, you need
to recognise the injustices of the past.

Bernie Grant spent his life campaigning for racial and social
justice – first as a student, then as a trade unionist, and afterwards
as a politician. He was the first Black local council leader and was
one of the first four Black MPs elected to Parliament in 1987. He
was known as a firebrand, an outspoken maverick who

passionately challenged race–class inequalities in Thatcherite Britain. He advocated for his constituents, union members and Black communities throughout Britain, campaigning against discriminatory policing methods and unfair immigration control, about deaths in custody, about institutionalised racism in health, housing and education, for refugees' rights, and for greater resources for inner-city areas. Grant was also an anti-apartheid campaigner, and a supporter of feminist causes, Black studies and a multiracial school curriculum. He was one of the most charismatic Black political leaders of modern times, who was at the forefront of the discourse about race in British society.

Born in Georgetown, (British) Guyana, the son of two schoolteachers, Bernard Alexander Montgomery Grant was educated at St Stanislaus College, a Jesuit-run boys' secondary school. He travelled to London in 1963, aged nineteen, to join his mother, and attended Tottenham Technical College before doing a degree course in mining engineering at Heriot-Watt University in Edinburgh. There he became involved in student politics, leaving the university in protest against the discrimination experienced by Black students.

Grant found employment as a telephonist at the International Telephone Exchange in King's Cross, London, where he quickly become a leading activist in the Union of Post Office Workers, fighting for the rights of fellow workers. He was one of the organisers of the first national Post Office strike in 1971, and stayed on at the Exchange as a representative for the telephonists. Subsequently, he was elected branch chair, campaigning to eradicate racist practices in the workplace. He became a full-time employee of the National Union of Public Employees, representing local authority and health workers. Finding endemic racism within the trade union movement itself, Grant then founded the Black Trade Unionists Solidarity Movement, and worked for it full time between 1981 and 1984.

Having joined the Tottenham Labour Party in 1973, Grant was elected a councillor for the borough of Haringey in 1978. During the 1970s the National Front made alarming political gains in London, particularly in local council elections, and maintained a menacing presence via provocative marches through immigrant neighbourhoods, vandalising Black- and Asian-owned businesses, and violent assaults. As councillor, Grant attracted support in the community for his campaigns against racism in education, policing and within the council's own services and employment practices. His impact was immediate, and within a year he was deputy leader. As a Labour Party member, he was active at grassroots level, particularly with the Black Sections membership, which included Diane Abbott and Sharon Atkin.

His election to Haringey Council occurred in the midst of a conflict between central government, led by the Conservatives and Margaret Thatcher, and local government, which in London was mostly Labour-led. Thatcher was determined to remove powers from these administrations. Grant's policies of allowing greater access for the disabled, and combating racial, gender and sexual orientation discrimination, were seen as highly controversial, and he was personally vilified and was the subject of racially tainted criticisms by the mainstream media. He had overwhelming local support, however, which saw him elected as leader of Haringey Council in 1985. The uprisings on Broadwater Farm, Tottenham, in 1985 brought Grant to national prominence, as he articulated the anger of the youth who faced police harassment daily. His refusal to condemn the youths' actions and his criticism of oppressive policing again earned him a slew of negative reporting and hate mail.

In 1987, Bernie Grant won the Tottenham parliamentary seat, ousting the twenty-year incumbent Norman Atkinson. In his maiden speech, made in a debate on the Local Government Bill in July 1987, he raised racism, privatisation and housing as the most urgent issues. He accused the government of having no interest in improving the lives of people in his constituency, in which up to 80 per cent of young Black men were unemployed.[1] In an interview following his speech, Grant said Thatcherism was hugely divisive, threatening relations 'not only between regions but also between cities, boroughs and even families, separating employed from unemployed, dividing trade unionists, even men from women, Black from White and sick from heathy.'[2]

Grant's vision was for greater Black representation in all sectors, a constant theme throughout his political career. He set up the first Parliamentary Black Caucus with his fellow Black MPs and the peer Lord David Pitt, with the goal for it to become a focus for the political, social and economic advancement of Black people in Britain and to act as a point of contact between African diasporic communities globally. A year later, he convened forty Black British, African Caribbean and Asian academics, local activists and politicians in a series of meetings in London and Warwick, with the aim of creating a policy institute to initiate research on a report on the state of Black Britain. Although these initiatives were short-lived, they demonstrate Grant's regenerative and progressive vision.

Bernie Grant's legacy is the demands he made for equality and social justice. He took the concerns of his community to the highest level of government and was an authentic voice for Britain's ethnic minorities. When asked shortly before he died how he wanted to be remembered, he replied, 'an African rebel'.

Stuart Hall

(1932–2014) sociologist, cultural theorist, political activist

S TUART HALL WAS a seminal thinker around race and the construction of the Black British identity. One of the great public intellectuals of his time, he was an activist for social justice and, through his work and leadership of the Centre for Contemporary Cultural Studies, was a founding figure in the discipline of cultural studies. It's almost impossible to overestimate the significance of Stuart Hall in shaping the field of racial and ethnic discourse. His work has influenced scholars in Britain, the Caribbean and United States in their thinking about race, culture, identity and politics. He was also a significant intellectual force among the visual artists and filmmakers of what became known as the Black Arts Movement of the 1980s and early 1990s, with many participants of that movement citing Hall's influence on their own work, which tended to engage with dialogic questions of identity and race, and the politics of representation.

Hall was one of the first Black scholarly voices who documentary makers used in their work to articulate and give meaning to the struggles of Black people in Britain in the 1970s and

1980s. His own writings developed through the years of crisis in post-war and post-colonial Britain, when the country was going through a period of intense political and social shifts, and when dominant ideologies were being contested by alternative cultures.[1]

The fractures of race and class were evident within Hall's family and upbringing, what he called the 'conflict between the local and imperial in the colonised context'.[2] Born into a middle-class family in Jamaica, his parents, of mixed African and European ancestry, embraced the island's racial and colonial hierarchies. As the darkest member of his family – Hall often shared the anecdote that his sister joked he was a 'coolie', a derogatory term used for poor East Indians – he subsequently developed the identity of an outsider, not quite fitting in, feeling separate from his family and his class, but not having an authentic connection to working-class Jamaica either. Hall found Jamaican racial and colonial restrictions intolerable, and found it difficult to articulate the reasons for his discomfort. 'I could not,' he later wrote, 'find a language in which to unravel the contradictions or to confront my family with what I really thought of their values, behaviours and aspirations.'[3]

Affected by the mental breakdown of his sister as a consequence of his mother's refusal that she marry a young man considered to be too dark, he determined to leave Jamaica lest he be destroyed by the 'colour class colonial dependency'.[4] Escape presented itself in a Rhodes scholarship to study at Oxford in 1951, and Hall became part of the post-war Caribbean migration to Britain that began with the arrival of the *Windrush* three years earlier. He connected with other Caribbeans in England in a way that colour-related social distinctions in Jamaica had not permitted him to do. 'This altered the possibilities,' he wrote, 'for understanding who I was and who I could become.'[5]

Hall was interested intellectually in the question of how culture and politics reinforce ideas. He looked at the power of the media in representing race, gender, class and religion, exposed its ideology and critiqued it. In the classic work *Policing the Crisis* (1977), Hall and his colleagues were troubled by the negative representations of Black youth offered by the state as explanations for Britain's problems, and how this ideology was being reinforced through the media as moral panic and a justification for authoritarianism. These ideas, transmitted through the popular press and television, contributed to the social tensions that emerged in the 1970s and 1980s between the state and the Black British population. Black Britons were facing disproportionately high unemployment, discrimination in education and police harassment, with virtually no way to challenge racist representation through the media. Instead, the media gave preference to nationalist expression articulated by the Conservative government that encouraged British identity as white and supported anti-immigrant rhetoric.[6] Hall coined the term 'Thatcherism', which he described as a historical shift from the social democratic welfare-state moment to the new paradigm of authoritarianism and liberalism, exemplified in the policies of Margaret Thatcher's government.[7]

A campaigner for racial justice, Hall served on the Runnymede Trust's Commission on the Future of Multi-Ethnic Britain in 1998, which analysed the then state of multi-ethnic Britain and proposed ways of countering racial discrimination and disadvantage. The report by the commission, however, was met by a torrent of negative media coverage at its observation that 'Britishness, as much as Englishness, has systematic, largely unspoken, racial connotations.' Hall was said to have been shocked by the media's reaction to the observation that Britain was far from racially innocent.[8]

Hall's involvement in Black British art was considerable. He was chair of Autograph (the Association of Black Photographers) and the International Institute of Visual Arts (Iniva). He helped to secure funding for Rivington Place in London, which houses Autograph's photographic collections and is dedicated to public education of culturally diverse arts.

John Akomfrah's installation *The Unfinished Conversation* (2012), which explores Hall's life and work through images, archive footage and his beloved jazz, brought Hall to the attention of a new generation. Akomfrah's piece takes its title from Hall's discourse on identity, which Hall maintained is not an essence or being, but instead a becoming, which is part of an 'ever unfinished conversation'.

Lewis Hamilton MBE

(b. 1985) racing driver

LEWIS HAMILTON IS regarded as one of the greatest drivers in the history of Formula One racing. A six-time world champion, he has brought some diversity to a sport which is woefully under-represented by drivers of colour and has overcome incredible odds to rise to the top of one of the most brutal mainstream sporting genres. In 2019, he won his sixth title in the Mexican Grand Prix, making him the second most successful F1 driver of all time, one championship behind Michael Schumacher. He is the first Black driver to have raced in F1.

Hamilton's presence in this sport, which is known for its exclusivity, wealth and glamour, means he possesses a level of skill and tenacity that is extraordinary and exceptional, more so because he does not come from a driving background.

Hamilton was born in Stevenage to Carmen, who is white British, and Anthony, who is Grenada-born and was his manager until 2010. Hamilton received his first radio-operated car when he was six, finishing second in the British Radio Car Association championship in 1992. He began karting a year later, progressing through the ranks to Formula Super A, considered to be the karting world's championship class, becoming European Champion in 2000. In 1998 he became the youngest ever driver to secure a Formula One deal when he was signed to McLaren's development programme.

Hamilton won his first championship in 2008 in Brazil when he was twenty-three, making him the then youngest F1 champion in history, and the first British driver to win a championship since 1996.

During his career, Hamilton has been critical of the racial politics and lack of diversity in F1 racing, in which he remains the only Black driver competing at this level. A difficult sport to enter because of the huge expenses incurred, it seems that the only people who can afford to take up the sport are young, wealthy, white men, excluding promising drivers of a more modest background. Hamilton recalled that his father, who took redundancy to support and manage his son's career, spent £20,000 in the first year of his driving career; to finance a professional season of go-karting today costs between £200,000 and £300,000.

As one of the few Black drivers in his entire career, racism has been an ever-present reality; the Mercedes team principal Toto Wolff claimed that Hamilton was racially abused as a youngster and carries permanent scars, which remain a key element in his psychological makeup.[1] The *Guardian* journalist Joseph Harker has noted the exceptionalism of Hamilton in terms of his background and talent, which has seen him secure six world championships, but that he has not yet been embraced by the British public, despite his talent and skills.

Hamilton has said he wants to be a force for progress, to 'shift the diversity a little bit in grand prix racing', saying that many people of different ethnicities tell him his presence in this sport has inspired their children to aspire to be a racing-car driver. Hamilton takes pride in knocking down barriers in sport, just as Tiger Woods and Venus and Serena Williams have done, opening their sports for others to come through.

Lewis Hamilton has proven himself to be an exceptional Formula One talent who has broken into a white sport by virtue of his skill and tenacity, and whose success goes far beyond sport.

Sir Lenny Henry CBE

(b. 1958) comedian, actor, writer, activist

SIR LENWORTH 'LENNY' Henry is one of Britain's most
successful comedians, and has enjoyed a long and
phenomenal career in television, film and theatre. One
cannot underestimate his significance as a Black comedian
and actor, who for many years was one of the few Black
performers regularly seen on television. He is a trailblazer
who has never been content to stay in his lane, moving well
out of his comfort zone on numerous occasions by taking on
theatrical and classical acting roles.

A career spanning forty-five years means that there are a
couple of generations of people who grew up with Henry in
their living room. People of a certain age will remember him
from the zany children's television show *Tiswas*; others will
remember him as the hapless but well-meaning pirate DJ
Delbert Wilkins in his self-titled show in the 1980s. Still more
remember his turn as the arrogant and tyrannical chef Gareth
Blackstock in *Chef!*, and contemporary audiences have howled
at his impressions of Stormzy and Childish Gambino. A
co-founder of Comic Relief, he has participated in its television
appeals for over thirty years.

What is notable about Henry is that many of his characters, such as Delbert or Deakus, were instantly recognisable to Black viewers; he injected into these characters his Jamaican heritage, and there are many who can still remember phrases and jokes that had that flavour of blackness with great warmth and affection. Henry is a national treasure, who uses his profile to take the television and film industry to task over its lack of diversity, both in front of and behind the camera.

Lenny Henry was born in Dudley in the West Midlands, growing up against a backdrop of popular racism, which was being whipped up by right-wing politicians and the press, against Caribbean immigrants. Not far from Dudley was Smethwick, where in 1964 the Tories won the local election with the slogan 'If you want a n****r for a neighbour vote Labour'. Four years later, Enoch Powell gained notoriety by giving racism his blessing with his 'Rivers of Blood' speech in Birmingham in 1968.

As a child, Henry was able to avoid getting beaten up by using humour to charm his would-be bullies, but he had never seen a Black person being funny on television until he saw Charlie Williams, one of the first Black comedians with a national profile. Despite the toxic times in which he grew up, Henry then realised that comedy could be a career for a Black man.

In 1975, aged sixteen, Henry won *New Faces*, a talent competition akin to *Britain's Got Talent*, dazzling the audience with his impressions of Muhammad Ali, Stevie Wonder and Frank Spencer. Henry has said that he once believed that satirising his blackness, as he had seen other Black comedians do, would help him to achieve mainstream success. That he appeared on *The Black and White Minstrel Show*, an extremely popular and racist BBC entertainment programme that featured white performers in blackface, showed that Henry used that form of satire to mitigate his blackness and get work.

More progressive was his appearance in *The Fosters*, the first British sitcom with an all-Black cast. Adapted from the American sitcom *Good Times*, Henry played Sonny Foster, acting alongside Norman Beaton and Carmen Munroe, who were among the most prominent Black actors of the 1970s. The show followed the exploits of a Black family living in south London who were trying to get by despite the odds. Not overtly political, it did offer some commentary on the experience of Black British families in the 1970s.

The lack of Black professionals in the television industry has put Henry on a mission. He has addressed this, and the systemic racism he has witnessed in the industry, by using his platform to effect change. In 2008, his speech at the Royal Television Society castigated the industry for its appalling record on diversity. Although the UK Black and ethnic minority people represented 14.5 per cent of the population, only 5.4 per cent of the creative industries workforce was non-white. Henry warned that if the mainstream channels didn't make their programming more representative, they were in danger of losing a generation of viewers. That Henry is still making similar pleas and critiques ten years later to BAFTA and to the government shows the immensity of the task he has undertaken, and how slowly change is coming.

In 2019, Henry produced and starred in the BBC miniseries *Soon Gone: A Windrush Chronicle*. Consisting of eight short monologues that traced the hopes, aspirations and shattered dreams of one Caribbean family over seventy years, it was both a commemoration of post-war migration and a rebuke to how the past seventy years have embedded hostility and inequality. In this way, Sir Lenny Henry is using his capital to ensure that change stays on the agenda.

Lubaina Himid CBE, RA

(b. 1954) artist

L UBAINA HIMID'S INSTALLATION *Naming the Money* (2004) is made up of a hundred life-size cut-out wooden figures depicting enslaved Africans brought to Europe from the Caribbean in the 1700s to work as servants in the metropole. Each cut-out has a real name, each one is able to say who they are, but each one lives with a new name and a new unpaid occupation. The figures try to tell the audience about themselves, their original names and memories alongside the new names and professions given to them by their European owners. Himid, in centring the lives of these hundred figurative men and women, interrogates the way in which Black servants have traditionally appeared in eighteenth-century British art, as status symbols for the Europeans who 'possessed' them – there to enhance their appearance, and often seen in the margins of the painting. In this installation their voices are restored, their narratives vocalised. Black servants were an unremarkable presence in eighteenth-century Britain – they were both visible and invisible. This installation provides a reimagining of their lives, naming the unnamed and, in Himid's words, 'exposing how the moneyed classes all over Europe spent their loot, flaunted their power and wealth using African slaves . . . the installation show[s] how this was disguised and glamorised.'

Lubaina Himid has long been one of the unsung heroines of Black British art, whose work tells powerful stories about the hidden histories of people and places that impact the social, political and cultural realities confronting Black lives. She has said that her work 'is trying to fill the gaps in a history which is there in front of us but is somehow obscured or perceived as clear and completed when it is not.'[1] Her work 'challenges the order of things, [taking] back that which has been stolen to call to question those who are in power and make them answerable.' She creates paintings, drawings, prints and installations, weaving together a language that is political and uncompromising in its intention to tell uncomfortable historical truths around the social, political and economic histories of enslavement.

Born in the then British protectorate of Zanzibar to an English textile-designer mother and Zanzibarian teacher father, Himid moved to England with her mother as a baby after her father's death. She came to prominence as an artist during the 1980s, as one of the most prolific artists and organisers within the Black Arts Movement, playing an additional vital role as a curator. Himid, who has been deeply engaged with the lack of representation of Black and Asian women in the art world, championed these artists through her curation of important exhibitions such as *Five Black Women* at the Africa Centre and *Black Women Time* at the Battersea Arts Centre in 1983, and two years later the *Thin Black Line* exhibition at the Institute of Contemporary Arts.

In 2017, Himid made history by winning the Turner Prize, the first Black woman to do so, after decades of institutional dismissal and marginalisation. The *Financial Times* art critic wrote that 'the Turner jury has chosen its most worthy winner in years'.

Himid has been an inspirational role model in the Black arts community, working to make Black artists more visible. After years of not being recognised for her significant contributions, she has been awarded the CBE for her services to art and was elected Royal Academician in 2018.

Dame Kelly Holmes DBE

(b. 1970) athlete, mental health campaigner

THE EXPRESSION OF shock, incredulity and jubilation on Kelly Holmes's face as she crossed the finish line in the 800- and 1500-metre finals in the Athens Olympic Games in 2004 is caught in some of the most iconic images of that summer's Games. That smile expressed vindication of what Holmes knew about herself and her abilities as a middle-distance runner, of her resilience and dedication to her sport. It was the end of a long road of setbacks, of injury and illness and mental health challenges. The story of how she overcame adversity has become one of the most inspirational stories in sport.

Born in Kent to an English mother and Jamaican father, as a girl Holmes was a talented athlete and joined the Tonbridge Athletics Club when she was twelve, becoming the Kent and English schools 1500 metres champion when she was thirteen.

The year 1984 was pivotal for Holmes. The seeds of the dream to compete for and win Olympic gold were planted when she watched Sebastian Coe win the 1500-metre final at the Los Angeles Games. Afterwards, a talk about careers in the armed forces at her secondary school captured her interest – a section on physical training instructors (PTIs) made her realise that this was the job she wanted to do. After winning the national schools' championship a second time, she joined the Women's Royal Army Corps, missing the PTI intake, working instead as a lorry driver for Military Transport in Hampshire. A warrant officer at the Royal Army Physical Training Corps, Kriss Akabusi, who would become European and Commonwealth 400-metre hurdles champion, encouraged her to take up athletics again. Joining the Southampton Athletics Club and the Army squad in 1989, she won the 1500 metres in the Inter-Service Championship.

Watching an old rival compete in the 1992 Barcelona Games reignited her Olympic ambitions; with silver medals in 1500 metres from the European and World Championships, along with a Commonwealth gold medal under her belt, she set her sights on Atlanta 1996. She came fourth in the 800 metres, and thus began a period of setbacks that impacted on her career for the next eight years. Favourite to win gold at the 1997 World Championship, she tore an Achilles tendon and ruptured her calf in the 1500-metres heats. She injured her back in the 1999 inter-counties cross-country championships, damaging the femoral nerve in her right leg, losing sensation down that side of the body. In the Games in 2000 she tore her calf but won bronze in the 800 metres. The Epstein Barr virus ruined her 2001 season; ovarian surgery and a 2003 diagnosis of iliotibial band friction syndrome, a common runners' injury causing pain on the outside of the knee, began to take a toll on Holmes mentally. It was another torn calf before the games in Athens that caused her to begin to self-harm. It was an outlet for her misery, frustration and anger over how she believed her body was betraying her. The cycle of setback, recovery, building up of strength and confidence, only to have another setback and start all over again takes courage, fortitude and resilience.

At thirty-four, she was the oldest competitor in her event – pushing herself in the pre-Games training, she was both hopeful and pessimistic. When she raced and won in both events, the whole country was with her.

Retiring a year after her historic wins, Kelly Holmes became a dame. She has advised the government on school sports and founded the Dame Kelly Holmes Trust to support athletes who were having difficulty coping with retirement. She speaks about her mental health challenges, works with charities and makes documentaries on the subject.

Darcus Howe

(1943–2017) civil rights activist, writer, broadcaster

IN MARCH 1981, at least twenty thousand Black people marched through London, protesting against the haphazard police investigation into the deaths of thirteen Black teenagers and young men in a fire in New Cross, London, which was widely suspected to have been a racist attack, and demonstrating against national indifference to the episode. They marched for over eight hours, from Fordham Park in New Cross to Hyde Park in central London. The People's Day of Action was the largest political mobilisation of Black people ever seen in the UK, and was a powerful political statement against the marginalisation and discrimination the Black community had suffered.

One of the organisers of the march was Darcus Howe, who was determined to force the political establishment to acknowledge the deaths at New Cross and to ensure a fair inquiry would investigate the cause of the fire and that those responsible would be brought to justice. The march caught the police off-guard in terms of the sophistication of its organisation. They did not understand who they were dealing with – a passionate political activist, and an experienced organiser of campaigns and marches, who had the ability to harness the anger of the people into political action.

Howe had been one of the principal motivators behind the Black Power movement in the 1970s, and maintained, as his biographers have written, a deep belief in the potential of the Black working class as a progressive historical force, who could and should shape their own destinies. The impact of Howe's activism within the context of Black British resistance movements has only recently begun to be fully understood; Howe was a central force in the struggle for racial justice in Britain.[1]

Rhett Radford Leighton 'Darcus' Howe was born in Trinidad; his parents were a teacher and the headmaster of his primary school. Howe was also the nephew of the historian, writer and socialist C. L. R. James, author of the *Black Jacobins*, a history of the Haitian Revolution, when enslaved Africans defeated the French, English and Spanish in 1804 to create the first Black republic outside of Africa. James's work had a profound influence on Howe's political thinking and activities.

Arriving in London in 1961, Howe became a victim of and witness to the hostility of white Britons towards Caribbean immigrants, and the period of the late 1960s was important in terms of leading up to his eventual engagement with the Black Power movement. He argued that he was on a civilising mission in the form of campaigns against state racism, particularly police brutality. Between 1968 and 1972 he was a member of the British Black Panthers, which also included Linton Kwesi Johnson, Olive Morris and Altheia Jones-LeCointe, teaching young Black people about history and politics, and about how to organise and protect themselves against police violence and harassment. Furthermore, they projected 'political blackness' by establishing alliances with all nationalities of Commonwealth immigrants, creating grassroots community campaigns and initiatives against racist immigration policies, and mobilising local and national communities.

Howe also played a key role in the Mangrove Nine Trial in 1971, which was significant in the way Howe and Altheia Jones-LeCointe were able to demonstrate that there was 'evidence of racial hatred' among the police. Arrested after protesting against repeated police raids on the Mangrove restaurant in Notting Hill, the two represented themselves against the charges of incitement to riot. It lasted fifty-five days and ended in acquittal.

Howe established the Race Today Collective in 1973. The collective put out a magazine, *Race Today*, which supported and documented community campaigns across the country, including the campaign to seek justice after the New Cross Massacre. Based in Brixton, the collective was also there to cover the uprisings in 1981, which were described by Howe as 'an insurrection of the masses of the people'.[2]

In the 1980s he became a television presenter working for Channel 4, in a period when the channel was broadcasting exciting content that was aimed at Black and Asian viewers. *Bandung File* (1985–91) was a current affairs programme reporting on topics of interest to the Black and Asian communities; and *Devil's Advocate* (1992–6), which put public figures under scrutiny, brought interesting intellectual debate about race to mainstream television.

Darcus Howe helped to give a voice to a community and was dedicated in his mission to empower through political action, education and Black radical thought.

Rose Hudson-Wilkin MBE

(b. 1961) bishop

I N JUNE 2019, it was announced that Rose Hudson-Wilkin, then Chaplain to the Speaker of the House of Commons, would become the Bishop of Dover, making her the first Black woman to become a Church of England bishop. Since being among the first women to be ordained as priests, Hudson-Wilkin has been a trailblazing force within the Church: the first Black priest to serve as Chaplain to the Queen, and the first woman and Black person to be the Chaplain to the Speaker of the House of Commons.

Hudson-Wilkin's achievements are eclipsed by the fact that there remains a notable absence of Black and minority ethnic clergy in leadership roles in the Church of England, which continues to struggle with institutional racism. Professor Gus John, former lay consultant on the Committee on Minority Ethnic Anglican Concerns (CMEAC), highlighted this when he resigned from the committee. In his resignation letter, he protested against the Church's endorsement of the Chief Rabbi's message not to vote for the Labour Party due to its poor record on anti-Semitism, thereby effectively lending support towards the 'hostile environment' policy of the Conservative government. John noted that while there had been progress, 'the church's record on combating racism is no less woeful now than it was thirty years ago'.[1]

Justin Welby, the Archbishop of Canterbury, acknowledged the Church was still institutionally racist, saying that he personally was ashamed of the history and failure of the Church to be welcoming to Black Anglicans in terms of representation in leadership roles, and how they have been treated by the Church in the past.[2] Many *Windrush*-generation worshippers, who had been members of the Anglican Church in the Caribbean, expected entering the Church in Britain would be a continuation of the way they worshipped 'back home'. Instead, they were regarded as strangers and outsiders rather than fellow members. In the 1950s and 1960s, Caribbean Anglicans carried with them to Britain a letter of recommendation from their parish priests; a Church 'passport' that was widely dishonoured. Where Black people were looking for fellowship and acceptance, they received only rejection and hostility.

At the time of writing, out of 120 bishops, there are only 4 that come from a minority ethnic background; the most senior, John Sentamu, Archbishop of York, retired in 2020. Hudson-Wilkin, who has faced both sex and race discrimination, has been outspoken about the poor representation of Black and minority ethnic people in leadership positions in the Church, remarking that she 'longs for the day when we stop having firsts. When we stop having firsts, then we will know that it's normal. So, I long for that normality.'[3]

Born and brought up in Montego Bay, Jamaica, Hudson-Wilkin felt a call to the ministry aged fourteen, saying that she knew that 'God had called on her to preach His good news'.[4] Aged eighteen she joined the Church Army, an evangelistic society within the Anglican Church, and travelled to England to train as an evangelist, the only position open to her as a woman. When the Church began ordaining women as deacons, Hudson-Wilkin put herself forward to test her calling to ordained ministry, receiving a pushback from the Church, which suggested she should be taking care of her family. Eventually, in 1991, she was ordained as a deacon, and in 1994 as a priest. From 2008, she combined her parish work in Haggerston and Dalston, London, with her duties as Honorary Chaplain to the Queen and, from 2010, Chaplain to the Speaker of the House of Commons, leading the daily prayers and pastoral care of the members and staff of the Palace of Westminster. Both roles placed her within the heart of the establishment, a space with a sparse Black presence. Some critics asserted the appointment was born out of political correctness. Hudson-Wilkin countered this by pointing out the absurdity of appointing a person for a role who did not meet the essential criteria.[5]

As Bishop of Dover, Rose Hudson-Wilkin is continuing her call to service and for new challenges, stating, 'We are going to be a better church when we embrace the gifts and abilities we all bring to the church.'[6]

Eric Huntley and Jessica Huntley

(b. 1929/1927–2013) activists, publishers

I N THE POLITICAL and cultural struggles of the Black British communities against discrimination since the mid-1960s, the names Eric and Jessica Huntley feature prominently. As activists in Guyana, they were leading campaigners against the exploitation of workers, colonialism and imperialism. In Britain, they were grassroots activists, participating in and leading numerous campaigns, locally, nationally and internationally, against the commonality of oppressions that faced people of the African diaspora. The Huntleys are also known for introducing the works of Black authors to the British public via their publishing company, Bogle-L'Ouverture Publications, which was responsible for promoting and disseminating literature that presented positive representations of African people, offering alternative perspectives and analyses of the history and culture of Black people throughout the diaspora. It was one of the first Black-owned independent publishing companies in Britain.

Born in the then colony of British Guiana, Eric and Jessica's relationship was underpinned by political engagement from the start of their marriage. Both were members of the left-wing

People's Progressive Party (PPP), the first mass party in Guyana, of which Eric was a founding member. Jessica co-founded the Women's Progressive Movement, a women's group within the party, travelling the country organising meetings and campaigning on behalf of the PPP. Although the PPP won the first election based on universal suffrage in April 1953, it was suspended by the British colonial government six months later, bowing to pressure from the US government who feared the growth of socialism in the Caribbean. Guyana was placed under a state of emergency, and Eric was arrested for breaking the restriction orders and sent to prison, along with other PPP members. Unable to secure employment after his release, Eric travelled to Britain in 1957, with Jessica joining him a year later. For several years they worked to save up enough money to send for their two sons.

In London, the Huntleys continued their political activism, supporting the Communist Party and campaigning for Guyanese independence, later turning their attention to how racism and discrimination affected the lives of Caribbean immigrants. As race and immigration dominated the political agenda during the 1960s, they became more actively involved in issues that affected the Caribbean community, participating in many grassroots campaigns.

The Huntleys were committed to campaigning for Black children to receive a good education and were involved in various organisations to ensure they did not become victims of the British school system's discriminatory practices. They aimed to educate and empower the Black community in setting up means of supplementary education. They also co-founded or were involved in various organisations that created a system of defences against police harassment and the notorious 'sus' laws.

These organisations often worked in alliance with other Black grassroots groups across the country and internationally. The Huntleys' home became an important space for political meetings and discussions.

In 1968, the Huntleys became publishers when their friend, the historian Walter Rodney, was declared persona non grata and refused entry into Jamaica, where he had been teaching, due to him sharing knowledge and ideas, which Rodney called 'grounding', with the working poor and the Rastafarians. The Huntleys challenged Rodney's censure by publishing the lectures, entitled *The Groundings (With My Brothers)*, he had given to the local Kingston community. At the time, they were determined that as many people as possible read the book, despite neither having any publishing experience nor the money to cover printing costs. They named the company Bogle-L'Ouverture, after two African Caribbean freedom fighters.

Publishing for the Huntleys was a political act that could enable books of all genres to be made accessible, and could centre Black intellectual thought, poetry, children's literature and biography. Bogle-L'Ouverture was critical in providing a platform for Black writers who could not find a mainstream publisher for their work. Initially, the Huntleys sold books from their home, eventually moving to commercial premises, which became known as 'The Bookshop', and was renamed the Walter Rodney Bookshop in honour of their friend, who was assassinated in 1980.

The bookshop also served as a cultural hub for the community, where parents and teachers could seek advice on new ways to teach subjects. In her excellent biography on the Huntleys, Margaret Andrews describes how Jessica Huntley influenced teachers into making their curriculums more inclusive, exposing them to Black writers and artists.

In 1982, Bogle-L'Ouverture, New Beacon Books (founded by John La Rose) and Race Today Publications launched the International Book Fair of Radical Black and Third World Books, which was joint-directed by Jessica and John La Rose. The fair facilitated collaboration between Black-led publishers and was held annually until 1991, and then biannually until 1995. Taking place in London and cities across England, it was a truly international event for writers, publishers, booksellers, artists and filmmakers.

In 2012 Eric and Jessica Huntley donated their personal papers, covering over fifty years of campaigning for social and racial justice, and the business records of Bogle-L'Ouverture Publications to the London Metropolitan Archives, the first major deposit from the African Caribbean community to that repository.

Professor Augustine 'Gus' John

(b. 1945) academic, equality and human rights campaigner

Pᴏғᴇssᴏʀ Gᴜs Jᴏʜɴ is a key figure in the struggle for social justice and equality in education, emerging through grassroots activism to challenge and campaign against the systemic structural exclusion of Black people within British society. He was involved in the Black education movements of the 1970s and 1980s that encouraged and empowered Black British communities in inner cities to channel their anger into community cohesion, which John termed 'organisational vibrancy'. He urged people to take responsibility for their own education, seeing this as integral to the emergence of Black British identities.

He is also responsible for the establishment of the first supplementary school in the late sixties, created to tackle the underachievement of Black pupils in mainstream schools by nurturing a stronger sense of cultural identity. Throughout the 1980s, Gus John was involved in coordinating the Black Parents Movement in Manchester, founded the Education for Liberation book service and helped organise the International Book Fair of Radical Black and Third World Books in Manchester, London and Bradford.

Today, Professor John is known as a leading education consultant and academic, who continues to speak out against injustice. He is a respected public intellectual and media commentator who remains a powerful advocate for community empowerment and children's education rights.

Born in Grenada, Professor John came to Oxford from Trinidad in 1965 as a theology student and was a friar in the Dominican order. Uneasy with the Church's links with apartheid South Africa, he left the order, becoming involved in youth and education work. While working as education secretary at the Oxford Committee for Racial Integration, he saw that the difficulties that Black pupils were experiencing in school were a consequence of the prevailing belief that Black children's lack of understanding of the British system was due to a lack of intellectual ability. This experience set John on his path of political and community activism, which has been a key feature of his work ever since. He became interested in youth development and the empowerment of marginalised groups. He was then part of a group of researchers for the Campaign Against Racial Discrimination (CARD), documenting forms of discrimination experienced by Black Britons in housing, employment and education. This evidence was presented to the Harold Wilson government, which led to the enacting of the 1968 Race Relations Act.

In 1968, concerned with the level of discrimination experienced by Black students in education, he and some colleagues founded the first supplementary Saturday school in Handsworth, Birmingham.

In 1971, Gus John went to Moss Side, an area synonymous with Manchester's African Caribbean communities. The high unemployment and continuous police harassment of Black Britons, young and old, were occurrences similar to those he had witnessed in London and Handsworth. Children were being placed in educationally subnormal classes; as John had seen in Oxford, this was not because the students were deficient; rather, he said, 'the schooling system refused to believe that those children were coming with a language of their own that was not standard English.'[1] John worked alongside grassroots organisations, campaigning against racial discrimination in housing. When a regeneration scheme moved households out of Moss Side in an attempt to further marginalise Black families, Gus John applied for funding to set up a hostel for young Black people who, anxious to maintain links with friends and family in the area, were sleeping rough, leaving them in danger of becoming involved with the police.

Like Brixton, Toxteth, Handsworth, St Pauls and Chapeltown, Moss Side erupted in violence between April and August 1981 as a consequence of racism and oppressive forms of policing in Black communities. In the aftermath of the uprisings, John was a key figure in the establishment of the Moss Side Defence Committee, which offered legal support to young people who were arrested or challenged police violence, and sought to contest press coverage of the disturbances as mindless acts of violence. For John, to call the disturbances 'riots' devalued and detracted 'from the righteous political component of the whole thing'.[2] The committee was also responsible for confronting the Hytner Inquiry report, which was set up by the government to investigate the Moss Side uprisings and their causes, by writing a critique of the inquiry and how it saw the disturbances in isolation from everything that had taken place prior.

Later, in 1989, John was appointed director of education for the borough of Hackney, becoming the first Black Briton in the UK to hold such a position.

Since 1996, Gus John has worked as an education consultant in Europe, Africa and the Caribbean. He has chaired roundtable discussions with the National Union of Teachers, producing a charter on promoting the achievement of African Caribbean boys. In 1999, John declined the CBE, stating to accept would be an insult to the struggles of African people such as himself who have worked all their lives trying to humanise British society and combat racism. Similarly, in the wake of the *Windrush* Scandal in 2018, he declined to attend the government reception celebrating the seventieth anniversary, stating that Theresa May's policies had denied the *Windrush* generation its fundamental human rights, and to accept the invitation would have been a 'shameful betrayal'.[3]

Linton Kwesi Johnson

(b. 1952) poet, activist

I N THE 1970s, Linton Kwesi Johnson emerged as a poet who articulated many of the political and social concerns of the times. His early poems dealt with the experiences of being African Caribbean in Britain in the 1970s and 1980s, reflecting the pain and suffering of his generation, giving warnings in his verse that racial oppression would not be endured by Black youth; that their anger and frustration would eventually explode and they would fight back.

Johnson is one of Britain's most respected poets, and for many he is Black Britain's poet laureate. His work has gained international attention, and in 2002 he became the second living poet – and the first Black poet – to be published in the Penguin Modern Classics series. Johnson writes and performs in Jamaican patois, using different spellings to emphasise the Jamaican accent, maintaining a strong connection to his heritage and representing the Caribbean immigrant experience in Britain. Johnson is the creator of the music form dub poetry, a term he coined in 1976, performing his verse to reggae, and has produced bestselling albums.

Linton Kwesi Johnson was born in Chapelton, Jamaica, and came to England as an eleven-year-old to join his mother

Sylvena, a machinist and dressmaker, in 1963. A top pupil in Jamaica, like most Black children during that period he was placed in the bottom stream at Tulse Hill School, which he later recalled as traumatic.

As a student at Tulse Hill School, Johnson first encountered the British Black Panther Party when one of its members, Altheia Jones-LeCointe, was a guest speaker at his sixth-form debating society. He became an active member of its Youth League, and began attending meetings, sold copies of the *Black People's News* and publicly condemned state violence against Black people, including the sus laws, and daily discrimination in employment and housing. In study groups he read texts by C. L. R. James, W. E. B. Du Bois and Frantz Fanon, which broadened his political consciousness and influenced his writings. He felt compelled to write for his community and in its own idiom, using poetry as a revolutionary weapon. For Johnson, his art was 'a political act and a cultural weapon in the black liberation struggle', believing at the time that a Black poet did not have the luxury of 'art for art's sake'; it should be used to highlight particular movements and record certain events in service to the struggle.[1]

Johnson was a member of the Race Today Collective, described by Leila Hassan as the 'centre of black liberation in England' and co-founded by former Panther Darcus Howe, whose aim was to secure immigrants their full citizenship rights and help facilitate a multicultural society in Britain and end state-embedded hostility. Johnson was the arts and poetry editor of its journal *Race Today*, which served as the voice of Black British politics, featured articles on the anti-racist campaigns, and covered strikes that were being held around the country by immigrant workers against discrimination in pay and working conditions.

Johnson's first poems appeared in *Race Today*, combining his poetry with his political activity. The radical journal then published his first collection of poems, *Voices of the Living and the Dead* (1974).

Dread Beat and Blood (1975) and *Inglan is a Bitch* (1980) chronicled the harsh lives Black people were living in Britain. His poem 'Sonny's Lettah' protested against the sus laws, which were being used mercilessly against Black men by racist police, through a son's letter to his mother from Brixton Prison, while 'Forces of Victri' celebrated the Notting Hill Carnival, which the government tried to ban in the 1970s, and where people often clashed with police. 'Fite Dem Back' responded to the growth of the National Front and its attacks on Black and Asian people. Johnson's poems were testimony to the violence and bloodletting, capturing the 'dread' days in Britain in his verse.

In 1977, Johnson won a Cecil Day Lewis fellowship and was writer-in-residence for Lambeth and education officer for the Keskidee Arts Centre in Islington. Writing music reviews for Virgin Records led to his first album, *Dread Beat an' Blood* (1978), credited to Poet and the Roots (1977), with Dennis Bovell arranging his compositions. Subsequent albums *Forces of Victory* (1979) and *Bass Culture* (1980) raised his profile. He founded his own record label LKJ to produce 'thinking man's reggae', and to this day he still tours and his records still sell.

He wrote campaigning poems for Blair Peach, the teacher killed by police at an anti-racist demonstration in Southall in west London; he also wrote the song 'New Cross Massakah' for the thirteen teenagers killed in a fire in New Cross, south London, believed to have been started by racists. He was a steward at the People's Day of Action in 1981, when twenty thousand people marched in protest at the state handling of that tragedy.

As a poet, critic and performer, Linton Kwesi Johnson is literally a voice of his generation, using poetry and music to fight back.

Claudia Jones

(1915–64) radical intellectual, journalist, activist, communist, feminist

C LAUDIA JONES IS credited with being one of the most important Black radical thinkers, activists and organisers in African diasporic history.[1] Her activism has left an indelible mark on two countries. As a leading member of the Communist Party of the United States she focused on workers' rights outside of the party and women and Black people's rights within it. In Britain, she committed herself to campaigning on behalf of the Caribbean community: she used journalism as community activism by establishing the *West Indian Gazette*, Britain's first Black newspaper, giving form to the Black British community's political voice; and by founding the London Carnival, forerunner to the Notting Hill Carnival, which tackled racial hatred through cultural expression and celebration.

Jones, born Claudia Vera Cumberbatch in Port of Spain, Trinidad, joined her parents in Harlem, New York, aged nine, after they were forced to emigrate to America to look for work. Her family lived in poverty; their apartment was so damp that Claudia contracted tuberculosis and had to leave school to convalesce for a year. She could not attend her high school graduation because her family could not afford the graduation gown; her mother died when she was fourteen.

A key event that may have sparked her commitment to civil rights was the Scottsboro Nine case of 1931, one of the most notorious cases of the 1930s, in which nine African American youths were falsely accused of raping two white women and were tried without adequate counsel. False accusations and hate crimes against African Americans were common in the United States; mob lynching and destruction of Black towns by white 'vigilantes' resentful of Black progress and competition were reflective of the racism that overshadowed the era. Jones involved herself in campaigning for the Scottsboro Nine, attending rallies in Harlem and writing articles in support of them.

Jones became a member of the Communist Party of the United States of America (CPUSA), which at that time was one of the few organisations that was multiracial and committed to improving women's status. She believed that socialism held the promise of liberation not just for Black women but for the Black people as a whole and for the multiracial working class, and she joined the Young Communist League in 1936.

By 1937, aged twenty-two, Jones was on the editorial staff of the *Daily Worker* in New York, and over the next ten years her exceptional understanding and interpretation of Marxist theory, as well as her charisma, her eloquence and her talents as a writer and organiser, saw her rise quickly though the Communist Party ranks, becoming national director of the Young Communist League in 1941 and executive secretary of the Women's Commission. Her campaigning against discrimination towards Black workers and promotion of equality attracted the interest of the FBI; from 1943 onwards she was among the subversives they felt 'might be considered for custodial detention'.[2] It was during this time that the process to have her detained and deported was initiated. Jones was outspoken about anti-Semitism and the Cold War, and called for an end to the lynching and terrorism that Black people were subject to at the hands of white people in the United States. She never missed an opportunity to make an impact whenever she had a platform to advocate for the rights of the underprivileged in American society.[3] Not being a naturalised American provided the government with a way to silence her and end her activities in the States.

In 1948 she was arrested for the first time on immigration offences and charged with a deportation order back to Trinidad; the CPUSA launched a legal defence to have the order deferred. By 1955, during which time she was imprisoned on a number of occasions, she had lost the fight to remain and, since she was born under British colonial rule in Trinidad, she was deported to Britain, whose authorities felt her activities could be better monitored in London than in Trinidad.

Arriving in London in December 1955, Claudia Jones gave a succinct summary of the main reasons for her deportation:

I was deported from the USA because, as a Negro woman Communist of West Indian descent, I was a thorn in [the government's] side in my opposition to Jim Crow racist discrimination against sixteen million Negro Americans in the United States . . . for my work to redress these grievances, for unity for Negro and white workers, for women's rights and my general political activity.[4]

After Jones arrived in London, she became acutely aware of the poverty, alienation and discrimination that Caribbean immigrants were experiencing. She saw London as another site of struggle, where Black people felt powerless against the colour bar that was still being operated overtly and covertly in public spaces, employment, housing and education. People were being intimidated by Oswald Mosley's British Union of Fascists, which would place its lorry in what is today Windrush Square in Brixton, where many Caribbeans had made their home.[5] Calls for control on Black immigration in the newspapers and television were regular.

Almost immediately after her arrival, Claudia Jones began organising the London Caribbean community; one of the major tools of mobilisation was the *West Indian Gazette*, which she founded in 1957 and launched in March 1958. The newspaper became what Carole Boyce Davies, Jones's political biographer, has described as one of the defining forces of the Caribbean community in the 1950s and 1960s. It reported on the gains of various independence movements in the Caribbean, Pan-Africanist and anti-colonial struggles, and Black success in culture and sport.[6] It served as the political educator for a beleaguered, battered and uninformed community subject to racial discrimination and violence. During the racially motivated attacks in Notting Hill and Nottingham in 1958 and the racist murder of Kelso Cochrane in 1959, the *Gazette*'s office was filled with concerned people seeking advice and guidance, and was also where Jones would meet politicians from the British Caribbean, including Norman Manley (Jamaica), Cheddi Jagan (Guyana) and Eric Williams (Trinidad and Tobago).[7] The *Gazette* was also a vehicle for promoting Black artistes, including Cy Grant, Nadia Cattouse, Edric Connor and Nina Baden-Semper, and the works of writers such as George Lamming, V. S. Naipaul and Andrew Salkey.

After the violence of 1958, Jones conceived the idea of a carnival as a way to heal the community through its common African ancestry. She envisaged it as being held indoors, and in January 1959 it took place in St Pancras Town Hall, London, and was televised by the BBC. Subsequent carnivals were held in various halls until 1966, when it became an outdoor event. The carnivals had a significant impact in introducing Caribbean culture into the British experience.[8] Jones felt that Caribbean traditions had much to offer the world in terms of creating a culture of human happiness over the ignorance and pain of racism. In these early carnivals, famous Trinidadian calypsonians such as the Mighty Sparrow were brought over to perform. Jones believed that culture was an important tool in the community's development, that it would help educate the various Black British communities about each other and develop an awareness of their own cultural histories.[9]

Claudia Jones's death at the age of forty-nine ripped a hole in the fabric of Caribbean society. In the eight years she lived in England she had her finger on the pulse of British society, using her remarkable gifts to create unity and strength within the early Black British communities.

Sheku Kanneh-Mason MBE

(b. 1999) cellist

IN 2016, SHEKU Kanneh-Mason became a household name when his performance of Shostakovich's Cello Concerto No. 1 won him the BBC Young Musician of the Year competition, the first Black musician to win the award. The young cellist gained further international acclaim when he performed at the wedding of the Duke and Duchess of Sussex in May 2018, to an estimated global audience of 3 billion.

His first album, *Inspirations*, debuted at number eighteen in the mainstream charts, and to date has accumulated 60 million streams and has sold over 120,000 copies, earning him the Brit Breakthrough and Artist of the Year awards.

Kanneh-Mason's success within the classical music arena is down to his extraordinary talent and commitment to his art. Additionally, he is one of seven siblings who are all talented classical musicians. Isata, the eldest, is a successful pianist and recording artist, who was a finalist in the keyboard category of the Young Musician competition in 2014. Sheku's brother Braimah plays the violin; sisters Konya and Aminata both play the violin and piano; and Jeneba and Mariatu both play the piano and cello. All the siblings have attended the Royal Academy of Music.

Born in Nottingham to Stuart Mason, a business manager, and Dr Kadiatu Kanneh, a former lecturer, Sheku and his siblings were introduced to classical music and had their talents nurtured by their parents, who had played instruments as children. Sheku became inspired to learn the cello when he was six, after listening to a recording of Jacqueline du Pré's 1965 performance of Elgar's Cello Concerto, which Sheku has said 'directly connected with his emotions'. He won a scholarship to the junior academy of the Royal Academy of Music aged nine, after attaining the highest marks in the country for his Grade 8 cello examination.

As one of seven siblings who are classical musicians, Sheku did not consider what they did as particularly unusual. In an interview with the *Financial Times*, Sheku's mother showed how committed she and her husband were to the vision of what music could add to their children's lives. She was determined never to point out to her children the lack of Black people in classical music – a strategy that has worked out for them.

Jackie Kay CBE

(b. 1961) poet, author

JACKIE KAY IS an award-winning writer of fiction, poetry and plays, whose work explores the complex issue of identity, often drawing on her own life. Her writings underline the impossibility of separating race from one's gender, sexuality or class, and challenges simplistic definitions of race.

Born in Edinburgh to a Nigerian father and a Scottish mother, Kay was adopted as a baby by a white couple and grew up in Bishopbriggs, a suburb of Glasgow. As a gay woman of African Scottish heritage, much of her work addresses the representation of the racial and sexual 'other', which is linked to her own multiple identities. Professor Alison Lumsden has remarked that 'Kay's concern with identity is hardly surprising; as a Black woman adopted and brought up in Glasgow by white Scottish parents, she is uniquely placed to comment on the interface between personal and cultural identity.'[1]

In her work, Kay challenges and confronts those who find her blackness and Scottishness difficult to reconcile, and calls out racism and othering:

'Where do you come from?'
'I'm from Glasgow'
'Glasgow?'
'Uh-huh, Glasgow'

(from 'So You Think I'm a Mule', 1985,
The Adoption Papers, Newcastle: Bloodaxe Books, 1991)

The second voice in the poem refuses to offer any assistance to the interrogator's attempts to satisfy her need to 'other' her and to fix her identity as decidedly not Scottish. As the cultural critic Hazel Carby has noted, 'The question "where are you from?" is not to elicit information, but to confirm a hypothesis.' Kay refuses to be othered; rather, she embraces, celebrates and retains her Scottish cultural identity, demonstrating that Scottishness is not synonymous with whiteness, that her identities have become a hybrid, and that there is no one way to write about this hybridity.[2]

Kay sees poetry as a powerful means of giving voice to the voiceless. She has said it 'manages to say in words things you can't otherwise say . . . it manages to express people's love, people's grief, people's loss and intense moments of their lives and . . . expresses for us what usually cannot be articulated.'[3] The fact that Scotland had so few Black people when she was growing up spurred Kay to begin writing 'because there wasn't anybody else saying the things I wanted to say and because I felt quite isolated being in Scotland and being black . . . [it was] out of that sense of wanting to create some images for myself.'

Kay's dual heritage and her adoption inspired her first collection of poems, *The Adoption Papers* (1991), which established her fame as a poet. The poet Patience Agbabi wrote that Kay 'raised the literary bar . . . in a Britain when it was a radical act to say, "I am a Black woman", Jackie Kay answered, "Mammy why aren't you and me the same colour". She spoke not only to people like me, young Black British writers adopted or fostered in a white family, but to all writers, all people.'[4]

Written in Glaswegian dialect, *The Adoption Papers* is partly an autobiographical work. It explores Kay's own life and consists of three voices: the birth mother, the adoptive mother and the daughter, each of whom expresses their own particular fears and desires, which eventually contribute to the adult the adopted daughter will become. The collection, which also explored the impact of Thatcher's policies on those who stood outside its norms – LGBTQ people, poor people and people of colour – was a great success and won Kay the Scottish Council Book of the Year.

Kay's writings explore these recurring themes of identity, race relationships and family ties. Her first novel, *Trumpet* (1998), is an account of a Black male jazz trumpeter called Joss Moody, who after his death is discovered to have been a woman. The novel concerns itself with how the self, specifically gender, is constructed. Based on the real-life story of the jazz musician Billy Tipton who had assumed a male identity for decades, Kay suggests in this novel that gender can be invented. As in *The Adoption Papers*, there are multiple voices to tell the story.

Since 2016, Kay has been the Scots Makar (poet laureate) and was appointed a CBE in 2020 for her services to literature. Her memoir *Red Dust Road* (2010), recounting her search for her biological parents, was adapted for the stage and premiered at the Edinburgh International Festival in August 2019.

Sam King MBE

(1926–2016) RAF veteran, activist, politician

W HEN SAM KING and his fellow passengers disembarked from the SS *Empire Windrush* in June 1948, they symbolised the ushering in of a new chapter of Caribbean migration to Britain, transforming the country's social, cultural and political landscape. King was one of the key spokespersons of *Windrush* and devoted much of his time to preserving the memories of the people who arrived on that voyage, and to reminding people of the contributions of Caribbean servicemen to the war effort.

Born in Priestman's River in Portland, Jamaica, Sam King worked on his father's banana farm as a boy; he was at school when the Second World War broke out in Europe. King remembered how his teacher would keep the class informed of what was happening overseas by reading the daily reports in the newspaper. Four years into the war, aged eighteen, King answered an advert in the *Gleaner* that was calling for volunteers to join the RAF. He sought permission from his mother, who told him, 'Son, the mother country is at war, go!'

He underwent the selection process in Port Antonio and left Jamaica for Britain in October 1944, arriving in Greenock near

Glasgow in November of that year, where he was shocked by the devastation that German bombing had caused. He and the other recruits were sent on to the military camp at Filey in Yorkshire for training; King was then sent to RAF Hawkinge in Folkestone, where he served as an aircraft fitter and was sent to work at various RAF camps across the country. After the war ended, King returned to Jamaica. He wanted to remain in the RAF, but since he wasn't married to an Englishwoman and hadn't been selected to attend university, he, along with other Caribbean servicemen, had to leave.

In Jamaica, King found it difficult to settle back into civilian life, describing himself as a 'haunted and shattered man, trying to come to grips with various possibilities'.[1] Living in England had changed him, and he was anxious to seek out opportunities that lay beyond the island he grew up on. He heard a troop ship bound for England was coming to Jamaica. The SS *Empire Windrush* sailed from Jamaica on 24 May 1948, and King was one of its passengers.

King returned to a 'mother country' that had changed from a welcoming and grateful nation to one that was resentful and hostile towards the influx of Caribbean immigrants. Finding accommodation became one of the biggest challenges; to counter this, King and some friends clubbed together to purchase a house in Camberwell, south London, where new arrivals could stay until they found work and housing. After serving four more years in the RAF, King was demobbed in 1952 and found a job at the Post Office, which he held for thirty-four years, starting as a postman and eventually becoming a manager.

The discrimination experienced by Caribbeans in the 1950s and 1960s politicised King. He became acquainted with Claudia Jones, a Trinidadian activist who had been deported from the United States because of her communist links. In England, with the aim of uniting immigrants against discrimination, she launched the *West Indian Gazette* and the *Afro Asian Opinion*, and King became the circulation manager of these publications. He helped Jones to organise the first West Indian Carnival which was held in St Pancras Town Hall in London in 1959, and later became the Notting Hill Carnival.

King was elected councillor for the Bellenden Ward in Southwark in 1982. Six months later he was elected Mayor of Southwark, the first man of Caribbean heritage to hold that office. In 1996 he co-founded the Windrush Foundation with Arthur Torrington, a charity set up to preserve the memories of the men and women who came to Britain on that famous ship after the war, while also campaigning for greater recognition to be given to the men and women from the Caribbean who served in the First and Second World Wars. King was the first to have coined the term '*Windrush* Generation', decades ago.

King and Torrington brought together dozens of King's fellow *Windrush* passengers for anniversaries, including the fiftieth anniversary in 1998, of the ship's arrival. They built the platform on which all other *Windrush* organisations or projects now operate. They were first to have promoted *Empire Windrush* as the 'iconic' image of the Caribbean presence in the UK and from 1995 established what can be termed '*Windrush* good-will', which determines how other *Windrush* organisations now function. Like the Windrush Foundation, those organisations utilise the original photographs that are associated with the ship and its passengers.

In his later years King visited many schools, museums, churches and community organisations, giving talks and presentations, and was interviewed extensively about his life and experiences. Sam King was anxious to pass on to the next generation the story of *Windrush*, ensuring that the reasons why post-war Caribbean migration changed and benefitted Britain remain in the national consciousness.

Kwame Kwei-Armah OBE

(b. 1967) playwright, director, actor, broadcaster

KWAME KWEI-ARMAH HAS said that having his trilogy of plays – *Elmina's Kitchen* (2003), *Fix Up* (2005) and *Statement of Regret* (2007) – run at the National Theatre is his 'proudest achievement'.[1] Inspired and influenced by African American playwright August Wilson's ten-play cycle known as *The Pittsburgh Cycle*, the pieces examine different aspects of Black life in Britain in settings that touch upon history, memory, masculinity, aspiration, identity, belonging and racial trauma. His plays show how history and heritage affect the present, and he is not afraid to tackle difficult topics, fostering debate and portraying the different sides of these issues through human relationships.

Kwei-Armah emerged as a major British playwright when *Elmina's Kitchen* was celebrated and hailed a critical success, winning him the Evening Standard Award for Most Promising New Playwright of 2003. It was staged at the National Theatre and later the Garrick Theatre, which made it one of the very first plays by a Black British playwright to be staged in the West End.

Kwame Kwei-Armah's sense of social responsibility and the importance of education and hard work are principal themes that inform his work. In the introduction to his collected works, Kwei-Armah wrote that 'it has been ingrained in me by my brilliant mother that whatever occupation I found myself in, serving the greater community through that occupation had to be a goal, an aim. Anything else was selfishness.'[2] Growing up in Southall in west London, he was exposed to the racial tensions and violence that were a constant feature of the 1970s and 1980s, being chased by skinheads, his home being ransacked by the police. He experienced colourism (discrimination based on skin colour from people of the same ethnicity); and in time he would explore these issues in his writing. Kwei-Armah, whose birth name is Ian Roberts, changed his name after researching his ancestry and learning about his enslaved ancestors. In an interview with Bernardine Evaristo, Kwei-Armah explained that it was an act of self-determination, a gift of culture and heritage to himself and his children that celebrates his African-ness.[3]

The objective in writing the trilogy was to document the Black British experience in the first decade of the new millennium. 'Whether they were critically successful or not,' he wrote, 'would be secondary to the achievement of having something that my great-grandchildren could read and say, "That was my ancestor's view of the Britain he found at the turn of the century."'[4]

Kwei-Armah's work and that of his close contemporaries, Roy Williams and Debbie Tucker Green, rode on an upswing of mainstream visibility, their work exhilarating contributions to the canon of Black British theatre. For the past fifty years African and Caribbean communities had been demanding space for their stories and experiences on the British stage and had faced significant obstacles to gain respect and recognition for their work.

Theatre scholar Lynette Goddard attributes the mainstream recognition that Black British playwrights achieved in the first decade of the twenty-first century in part to the Arts Council's commitment to recognising the fundamental role that Black arts could play in diversifying culture through a range of initiatives.[5] The other part can be attributed to attempts to address institutional racism in British theatre. Sir William Macpherson's report for the Stephen Lawrence Inquiry concluded that the police investigation into the racist murder of the teenager was tainted by institutional racism. This led to many establishments reflecting on their policies and procedures; the report of the Eclipse Conference, held in 2001, 'discussed and devised strategies to combat racism in British theatre . . . to explore ways to develop our knowledge and understanding of African Caribbean and Asian theatre.'[6] The deadline for the report's recommendations to be implemented coincided, Goddard notes, with Kwei-Armah's breakthrough play.

Kwei-Armah, who gained national fame as the paramedic Finlay Newton in the BBC drama *Casualty* (1999–2004) began his playwriting career as writer-in-residence at Bristol Old Vic, where he wrote his first play, *Bitter Herb*, and two musicals, *Blues Brother, Soul Sister* and *Big Nose*. *Bitter Herb*'s dominant theme is how race is understood in family life. It portrays a middle-class Black family, the McKennas, whose eldest son is killed in a racist attack, and his character is tainted by rumours that he was a drug dealer. Kwei-Armah shows how a family who strived to fit in are forced to see themselves in racial terms. This is further complicated by their white adopted daughter, Jaime, being selected to be the family media representative. The play explores the awareness of wider inequalities as the family navigates the criminal justice system and the theme of belonging on the grounds of race.

In his trilogy, Kwei-Armah is fundamentally concerned with the long-term effects that enslavement, colonisation, institutionalised racism and discrimination have had on the Black British male identity, and how these effects have partially determined his circumstances. *Elmina's Kitchen*, set in a Caribbean takeaway, revolves around a father's attempts to prevent his son from being tempted into a life of crime, and is a warning of the darker side of aspiration, of criminal shortcuts to material wealth. *Fix Up*, set in a financially failing independent Black bookshop, explores how the owner can be a father to his community but not to his mixed-race daughter, who he gave up for adoption and who forces him to acknowledge the sins of his past. *Statement of Regret*, shown during the year of the bicentenary of the abolition of the British slave trade, explores race relations within a political thinktank, examining the social and historical tensions between African-born Britons and Caribbean Britons.

In his newer works, Kwei-Armah moved away from his investigation into how the past influences the present, contemplating instead the future of racial identity in Britain and the United States, where he was artistic director of Center Stage in Baltimore. His works *Let There Be Love* (2008), *Seize the Day* (2009) and *Beneatha's Place* (2013) offer an optimistic outlook of what it means to be Black in the new millennium.

In 2017, Kwei-Armah was appointed the artistic director of the Young Vic Theatre, London, becoming the first African Caribbean director to run a major British theatre.

John La Rose

*(1927–2006) poet, writer, publisher,
political and cultural activist*

JOHN LA ROSE is recognised as having been one of Britain's
leading Black British public intellectuals; Linton Kwesi
Johnson called him the 'elder statesman of Britain's Black
communities'.[1] His cultural, literary and political contributions were immense; throughout his life in Trinidad and
Britain, he either founded or was allied to numerous movements and campaigns for social and racial justice and
community empowerment. For forty years, through education, culture and politics, La Rose fought to change the
world.

La Rose was born in Arima, Trinidad, the son of a teacher
and cocoa trader. As a young man he was involved in the
burgeoning labour and cultural activism of the British
Caribbean of the 1940s as it moved from colonial rule towards
independence. Interested in Marxist and anti-colonial literature, he was an executive member of the Youth Council of
Trinidad, and helped found the Workers Freedom Movement,
editing its journal *Freedom*. He also assisted in the founding of
the West Indian Independence Party in 1956.

La Rose worked as a teacher in Trinidad and Venezuela before migrating to London in 1961. His political and anti-colonial activities in Trinidad prepared him for the political struggles he embraced in the UK, which concerned education, workers' rights, publishing, policing and immigration.[2] La Rose arrived in Britain a few years after the Notting Hill and Nottingham 'race' riots and the racist murder of Antiguan-born Kelso Cochrane, and at a time when Black communities were beginning to organise politically in defence of their interests. La Rose joined the likes of Claudia Jones and Amy Ashwood Garvey in becoming the voice of an emerging Black British political consciousness during the late 1950s and early 1960s.

In 1966 he founded New Beacon Books, the UK's first specialist Caribbean publisher, bookseller and international book service. Its creation was part of La Rose's ambition to achieve long-term change for Caribbean people in Britain, a vehicle by which to 'give an independent validation of one's own culture, history and politics; a sense of self, a break with discontinuity', by publishing affordable books for Black people in Britain and globally. New Beacon Books reprinted classic works by C. L. R. James and new works by, among others, the great Guyanese historian Ivan Van Sertima.

That same year, along with writers Edward Kamau Brathwaite and Andrew Salkey, La Rose established the Caribbean Arts Movement, a forum for artists and writers living in England. Through talks, discussions, conferences, recitals and art exhibitions, the movement provided an opportunity to explore new directions in Caribbean arts and culture, and had a major impact on Caribbean cultural identity in Britain.

La Rose was a prime mover in the Black education movement of the 1960s and 1970s, campaigning against the practice of placing disproportionate numbers of Black children in schools for the educationally subnormal (ESN), and establishing the George Padmore supplementary school, the first of its kind. He was a co-founder of the Caribbean Education and Community Workers' Association, which drew national attention to the ESN school crisis by publishing Bernard Coard's influential and ground-breaking book *How the West Indian Child Is Made Educationally Subnormal by the British School System* (1971).

In 1975, La Rose co-founded the Black Parents Movement after a Black schoolboy was assaulted by police outside his school in Haringey, with the aim of combating the brutalisation and criminalisation of young Blacks and campaigning for decent education. The Black Parents Movement's alliance with the Race Today Collective and the Black Youth Movement put La Rose at the forefront of the most powerful cultural and political movement organised by Black people in Britain, which campaigned for better state education, against police oppression and supported the Black working-class struggle.[3] This alliance organised the Black People's Day of Action in 1981, at which over twenty thousand people marched in protest against the mishandling of the police investigation into an arson attack in New Cross, south London, that left thirteen Black youngsters dead.

La Rose was chair of the George Padmore Institute, established in 1991 as an archive and library that could house materials relating to the Black community of Caribbean, African and Asian descent in Britain and Europe. Many talks and presentations were given at the institute, featuring prominent Black figures, postgraduate students and early career researchers. Often, they were presented and chaired by La Rose himself.[4]

With Bogle-L'Ouverture Publications and Race Today Publications, he organised the International Book Fair of Radical Black and Third World Books (1982–95). After the withdrawal of Bogle-L'Ouverture, La Rose was the sole director. The book fair enabled exchanges between writers and publishers, musicians, artists and activists from all over the world.

John La Rose saw culture as an essential tool to be put to use for enlightened engagement.[5] He once said, 'At the heart of my own experience is the struggle for cultural and social change in Britain, across Europe, and in the Caribbean, Africa and the Third World.'[6]

David Lammy

(b. 1972) politician

WHEN TOTTENHAM MP Bernie Grant died suddenly in 2000, David Lammy, at the age of twenty-seven, beat Grant's widow to win the vacated parliamentary seat. Grant, one of the first Black MPs to enter Parliament in 1987, was one of the most charismatic Black political leaders of modern times, and a committed social and racial justice campaigner. Grant's impact on British politics had been tremendous, and Lammy had big shoes to fill.

Two decades on, Lammy has carved out his own distinctive path as MP for Tottenham. He has emerged as an outspoken politician and prominent social and racial justice campaigner. Born in Archway and raised in Tottenham, a barrister by training and a self-described 'son of the *Windrush*', Lammy has developed a passionate and uncompromising stance against injustice, especially regarding the issues he holds closest to his heart.

Having held ministerial roles in both the Blair and Brown governments, since 2010 Lammy has found his political voice as an opposition backbencher, offering sharp criticisms on many key social issues, including knife crime, the 2011 riots, the Grenfell disaster and Brexit. Having campaigned for Britain to remain in the European Union, Lammy was a leading critic of the leave campaign's tactics, and the racism that underpinned them. His election in 2019 to represent the people of Tottenham for the seventh time (and counting) is a sign of the support and respect of his constituents.

Lammy has also established himself as a criminal justice reformer, speaking out against the inequalities inherent within the criminal justice system, particularly in relation to the experiences of Black and minority ethnic people. In 2017 he authored a report, 'The Lammy Review', on the treatment of and outcomes for Black, Asian and minority ethnic people in the criminal justice system. The report revealed what many already suspected: that there are significant problems within the criminal justice system that mean it does not operate in a fair way; and that there is a racial bias that permeates every aspect of it. Lammy's forensic investigation revealed dispropor-tionately low numbers of BAME people within the system, coupled with low representation of that group in senior staff positions. The report paints a bleak picture of deep inequal-ities, and putting in place Lammy's recommendations to dismantle them is an ongoing battle.

Lammy has been one of the Conservative government's harshest critics since it was made public that its 'hostile envir-onment' immigration policy resulted in the deportation of many now adult 'children of the *Windrush* generation'. The lack of access to healthcare, benefits and loss of employment had a destructive effect on the lives of those pinpointed by the policy, which Lammy saw as a betrayal by the government of thousands of innocent people. His powerful condemnation of the government was widely broadcast and commented upon, and his deep anger was inspired by that felt by the victims. He has consistently called the government to task on their handling of the scandal, pressuring it to do right by those caught up in it.

Similarly, Lammy felt personally connected to the 2017 tragedy of the Grenfell Tower fire, in which seventy-two people perished. His friend and mentee, Khadija Saye, a promising young artist, was one of its victims. Lammy called Grenfell 'an atrocity' that speaks to the issues around class, race and a broken social contract. He is convinced that the people who died in the tower are victims of 'corporate manslaughter' and has vowed to continue to speak up for the victims and their families, and to ensure such a tragedy is not repeated.

A former higher education minister, Lammy has been forth-right in his criticisms of Oxford and Cambridge's poor record on recruitment of Black British students. He accused the universities of being 'complacent' in their efforts to widen participation and access, continuing to draw from a 'privileged minority' from southern counties. The data, which Lammy forced Oxford University to publish via freedom of information requests, supports Lammy's assertions: more than one in four Oxford colleges failed to admit a single Black British student in the years between 2015 and 2017. Cambridge's record was not much better; between 2012 and 2016, many of their colleges had admitted no Black British students, or as few as one a year.[1] In drawing attention to the inequalities inherent in the country's leading universities, Lammy demonstrates how the homogeneity of these structures is sustained, and who benefits from it.

While David Lammy's profile may now be at its highest since he entered Parliament, it must not be forgotten that he has been consistent in his activism, including when the cameras were not on him. The recent social and political crises have permitted him to show what he has been doing quietly for many years – giving voice to the voiceless.

Marai Larasi MBE

(b. 1969) activist, campaigner against violence

THE REVELATIONS AROUND the now disgraced film producer Harvey Weinstein shone a light on the endemic sexual harassment, abuse and inequality in the film industry. In response, Hollywood celebrities founded the Time's Up movement, and at the Golden Globes awards ceremony in 2018, it chose to highlight and express support for gender and racial-justice activism, with actors attending the ceremony with campaigners as their guests for the evening. For her guest, *Harry Potter* actor Emma Watson chose renowned feminist activist Marai Larasi, in order to amplify the work she has done for decades, and continues to do, to campaign against violence towards women and girls.

Until 2019, Larasi was the executive director of Imkaan, the only UK-based women's organisation that specifically addresses issues of violence against Black and minority ethnic women and girls, dealing with domestic violence, forced marriage and 'honour-based' violence, and representing the expertise and perspectives of frontline specialist BAME organisations.[1] Her activism is rooted in Black feminist resistance and community organising, in the tradition of activists such as Claudia Jones and Olive Morris.

Larasi was born in London to Jamaican parents and spent her teenage years in Jamaica before returning to Britain. While working for women's refuge centres, she noticed that Black and minority ethnic women's needs and experiences in mainstream services were not being prioritised.[2] She understood that the journeys of BAME women were being shaped by marginalisation and exclusion in different ways to their white counterparts. Consequently, joining Imkaan allowed her to focus her work primarily on BAME women and girls, striving to ensure their experiences influenced policy to help prevent further stigmatisation and marginalisation. Imkaan positions its aid within an intersectional framework, considering how race affects survivors' experiences of violence and the support they receive.

Data currently shows that twenty-two BAME refuges across the country have had their funding cut or have been taken over by generic organisations in the last twelve years.[3] Larasi has said BAME services are essential for the ways in which they assist with language barriers and provide culturally specific support to the women they serve. At the time of writing, London boroughs with diverse populations are commissioning domestic violence refuges with no BAME-specific component.[4] The importance of specialist organisations that cater for Black and minority ethnic communities cannot, according to Larasi, be overstated.

Larasi is also concerned with media representations and reporting of domestic violence. In 2012, she gave evidence at the Leveson Inquiry into the culture, ethics and practices of the press. In an opinion piece for the *Guardian* newspaper, she wrote that if the inquiry's recommendations were to address ethics and standards effectively, then it must look at the way the media treats women. She pointed to how media reporting of violence against women tended to blame the victims, uphold myths about certain offences (for example, the rape is always violent and normally committed by a stranger) and exoticise types of violence committed against minority ethnic women. This negative or dismissive treatment, she argued, only serves to diminish these victims' experiences, discouraging more women from coming forward.[5]

Larasi acts locally but thinks globally, living in the UK but working as part of a worldwide community of BAME women and girls in her endeavour to end violence. 'If we are to end violence against women and girls, we need to create seismic shifts across our social norms,' she has written. 'This is not just about transforming belief systems and behaviours in terms of gender . . . it means addressing other norms . . . around ethnicity, class and disability, all of which contribute to holding oppressive systems in place.'[6]

Doreen Lawrence, Baroness
Lawrence of Clarendon OBE

(b. 1952) campaigner for social and racial justice and police accountability

B ARONESS LAWRENCE OF Clarendon's life as an activist and campaigner came about through the murder of her son, Stephen, in a racist attack in 1993.

Over the course of criminal and civil investigations into the murder, which initially brought no convictions, institutional racism within the Metropolitan Police – its attitude towards Stephen, his family and the Black community – was revealed to be the most significant factor in the Lawrence family's inability to secure justice. Despite many setbacks, Doreen Lawrence has been on an unrelenting quest for the truth and justice for her son, at great personal cost, so that what happened to him would never be forgotten. She has shone a light on racist practices within the police force with a view to eradicating those practices, and for families of murder victims to be treated with compassion, empathy and respect. Doreen and Neville Lawrence (Stephen's father) took on one of the country's most powerful institutions and forced it to acknowledge that its practices were dysfunctional and racist.

Doreen Lawrence (née Graham) was born in Jamaica and emigrated to Britain when she was nine years old. When she was seventeen, she met and married Neville Lawrence, a painter and decorator. They had three children: Stephen, Stuart and Georgina.

In April 1993, Stephen was fatally stabbed when he was attacked by five white men while waiting for a bus with his friend, Duwayne Brooks, in Eltham, south-east London. Although the police received anonymous tip-offs identifying the killers, the police did not arrest or question them until the Lawrences met with Nelson Mandela, who was visiting Britain at the time. Mandela drew attention to Stephen's murder and the lack of arrests, which embarrassed the police who belatedly detained the suspects, by which time much of any incriminating evidence had been destroyed. The suspects, Neil and Jamie Acourt, David Norris, Luke Knight and Gary Dobson, were charged with Stephen's murder, but the prosecution was dropped on the basis that evidence given by Brooks was not reliable.

In 1994, the Lawrences were determined to get justice for their son and launched a private murder prosecution against three of the suspects – Luke Knight, Gary Dobson and Neil Acourt. In 1996, the trial began but soon collapsed due to inadmissible evidence, and all three suspects were acquitted. The inquest into Stephen's death, which began in 1993 but had been halted several times, concluded that he was killed 'in an unprovoked racist attack by five youths'.

Mr and Mrs Lawrence, who were never satisfied with the investigation into Stephen's murder, continued to lobby for an inquiry into the police handling of it. In 1997, the then Home Secretary Jack Straw announced there would be a judicial inquiry led by Sir William Macpherson into how Stephen's murder was investigated, and what could be learned from it. The results of the inquiry vindicated what Doreen and Neville Lawrence had been claiming for years – that the police investigation was affected by 'a combination of professional incompetence, institutional racism and a failure of leadership'.

Lord Macpherson made seventy recommendations that the police should implement to improve relations with the African Caribbean community. These recommendations included establishing victims' rights, a redefinition of the term 'racist incident' and a review of the Victim Charter, especially in relationship to racist crimes. Crucially, it was recommended that there be a reconsideration of a change to the 'double jeopardy' law, enabling the appeal court to allow a new prosecution of an accused person after an acquittal where new and viable evidence is presented.

In 2011, new technology in forensic analysis of evidence meant that it became possible to charge two of the suspects of Stephen's murder. After nineteen years, in 2012, Gary Dobson and David Norris were convicted. The other three suspects remain free.

To honour Stephen's life and aspirations, Doreen Lawrence opened the Stephen Lawrence Centre and established the Stephen Lawrence Charitable Trust, a social enterprise delivering employment and enterprise programmes and support for those interested in pursuing a career in architecture, a profession that Stephen had hoped to pursue.

Doreen Lawrence was awarded the OBE for her services to community relations and became a Labour peer in 2013. She helped to establish the Stephen Lawrence Research Centre at De Montfort University in Leicester, where she serves as chancellor. It contains archives of the history of the family's campaign for justice, and focuses on research on race, the history of Caribbean communities in Britain, and the psychology of racial violence – all under-researched topics.

In 2018, twenty-five years after Stephen was killed, the government announced that a national day of commemoration would take place annually to remember Stephen and his life, and to reflect on how his death changed Britain.

Andrea Levy

(1956–2019) author

A
LL OF ANDREA Levy's books have received critical acclaim, but it was *Small Island*, her epic tale of first-generation Jamaican immigrants in post-war Britain, that established her as a gifted chronicler and observer of the experiences of Caribbean immigrants and their children, and as a talented historical novelist. The novel also launched her into the literary big league, winning the Orange Prize, the Whitbread Book of the Year and the Commonwealth Writers' Prize in 2004.

Using her own experiences of growing up in Britain and that of her family, she created interesting, relatable yet complex characters through which she explored identity, belonging, Britishness, displacement and the inheritances of enslavement.

Andrea Levy was born in London in 1956 to Jamaican parents; her father, Winston, had arrived in England on the *Windrush* in 1948; Andrea's mother, Amy, joined him six months later. Of mixed Scottish, African and Jewish heritage, they were professionals who were unable to find work in Britain that reflected their education and training. They were light-skinned Jamaicans who did not identify as Black. The entrenched social and racial hierarchies in Caribbean society had birthed colourism (discrimination based on skin colour among people of the same ethnicity), which discriminated against darker-skinned people and gave greater social and economic benefits to lighter-skinned people, who made up the middle class in Jamaica. Levy's parents discouraged her and her siblings from having friends who were not light-skinned; Andrea recalled that her mother was happy to be bringing her children up with white children.[1] Being light-skinned did not protect Levy from racism, which she described as having a 'profound effect on her', making her hate herself.

Levy would later explore the effect of colourism, and its impact on the protagonists' life chances, in her second novel, *Never Far from Nowhere* (1996).

The acceptance of her identity as a Black woman came about through a moment of personal crisis. At a racism awareness course while at her job, she was forced to confront her blackness, at a time when she was afraid to even call herself a Black person:

> We were asked to split into two groups, black and white. I walked over to the white side of the room. It was, ironically where I felt most at home – all my friends, my boyfriend, my flatmates were white. But my fellow workers had other ideas, and I found myself being beckoned over by people on the black side. With some hesitation I crossed the floor. It was a rude awakening. It sent me to bed for a week.[2]

Levy credits writing as the way she learned to explore and resolve her complicated relationship with blackness, her upbringing and her family background. Her novels address the silences over colourism, the experiences of Black British people and the shared history of enslavement.

Writing helped Levy gain a much deeper understanding of her historical roots, her heritage and herself. Her works are novels, but in another sense they are historical research projects that draw on the richness and beauty of the places and people she wrote about to find answers to understanding why, as a child, her white friends had no curiosity about the Caribbean, but only wondered why Black people were in Britain; and why it had been so difficult for her to accept her own blackness, a legacy of enslavement that had helped to maintain division and power.

Through her work she re-established the historical links between Britain and the Caribbean that had been forgotten or hidden. The journalist and writer Gary Younge wrote that she 'pushed at every level for a fuller, more rounded, more inclusive version of our national story'.[3]

Small Island and her fifth and final novel, *The Long Song* (2010), set in post-emancipation Jamaica, have both been made into well-received television adaptations, and *Small Island* has also been adapted into a successful stage play.

A year after her death, Levy's literary archive was acquired by the British Library, and it has been described by curator Zoë Wilcox as a rich and important resource that gives incredible insight into the thought processes and working practices of 'an extraordinary writer whose literary significance will be celebrated for years to come'.[4]

Sir Steven McQueen CBE

(b. 1969) artist, director, screenwriter

O F THE ADJECTIVES used to describe Steve McQueen's work, 'uncompromising' is the one encountered most often. Uncompromising in his portrayal of sexual addiction, institutional violence, war, imprisonment and even traditional school portraiture, McQueen has established a trademark in giving a visual poetry to these themes by rooting contemporary art in the cinematic. Today, he is recognised as one of the world's leading artists and filmmakers, and has gained national and international acclaim for his work, winning the Turner Prize in 1999 and the Academy Award for Best Picture for his 2013 film *12 Years a Slave*. In the 2020 New Years' Honours, it was announced that McQueen would be awarded a knighthood for his services to the film and art industries.

Born in west London, of Grenadian and Trinidadian parentage, McQueen, who studied at the Chelsea College of Art and then at Goldsmiths for a degree in fine art, explored themes of violence, homoeroticism, race, fate and survival in his early film installations.

His first film, *Bear* (1993), is a ten-minute short of an encounter between two men. One of them is McQueen; both are naked, circling each other, not speaking. Ambiguous in its nature, the viewer isn't certain what the men's intentions are: do they intend to fight or to kiss?

His film short *Deadpan* (1997) reimagines the hurricane scene in Buster Keaton's silent film *Steamboat Bill, Jr* (1928). In the original film, Keaton stands in front of a house collapsing over him as its facade is blown down by strong winds. He is left unharmed, however, as he was standing exactly under an open window. McQueen cast himself in the Keaton role, remaining in the wreckage, seemingly unfazed, with the stunt being filmed from different angles. By transforming a comedic and well-planned stunt scene into a representation of indifference at a time of near-disaster, the installation was part of his entry that helped him win the Turner Prize in 1999.

In 2006 McQueen was appointed an Official War Artist by the Imperial War Museum, commissioned to create a work to commemorate the British soldiers who died in the Iraq War. The result was *Queen and Country*, presenting the portraits of the soldiers as stamps. The critic Sarah Crompton called the installation 'an astonishingly powerful piece . . . a simple idea that symbolises the power of communication'.[1] McQueen said the work was about remembrance and acknowledgement.

Since 2008, Steve McQueen has directed four feature films that have won him international acclaim and are notable for their vision, concept and subject matter. *Hunger* (2008), his first major feature film, is a portrayal of the Irish political prisoner Bobby Sands's hunger strike, which eventually killed him. Described as an 'unforgettable portrait of battered and self-battering masculinity', the film won numerous awards including the Camera d'Or at Cannes and a BAFTA for McQueen. *Shame* (2011) is an unflinching study of sex addiction and how it imprisons and consumes those who suffer from it. *12 Years a Slave* (2013) is as challenging as his first two movies, an adaptation of Solomon Northrup's book of his experience of being kidnapped in nineteenth-century New York and sold into slavery. The film portrays uncompromisingly the realities of enslavement; its brutality, destructiveness and its impact on enslaved and enslaver. This film, which inspired debates across the United States and Britain, won the Academy Award for Best Picture, making Steve McQueen the first Black director to win the award.

Widows (2018) is a heist thriller based on the 1980s Lynda La Plante UK television series that centres on the widows of a criminal gang who are forced to stage a robbery to help clear their debts. The film, which explored themes of corruption and inequality, was a critical success.

McQueen continues to inhabit the worlds of both art and film; he does not like being labelled an artist turned filmmaker. In 2019, he unveiled his latest installation at Tate Britain, *Year 3*, which features more than seventy thousand Year 3 pupils with their teachers from state and private primaries, faith schools and pupil referral units. Clarrie Wallis, senior curator of contemporary British art at Tate, has called it one of the most ambitious portraits on citizenship ever undertaken.

Dr Harold Moody

(1882–1947) physician and activist

LIFE FOR BLACK and Asian Britons in the early twentieth century was profoundly affected by racial discrimination. The colour bar, which affected every level of British society, prevented them from seeking recourse for their grievances or living their lives unrestricted by race. They found it tough to obtain decent jobs and accommodation, and were prevented from participating in many aspects of life, from fighting for British boxing titles, to joining the armed services, to serving in positions of authority. Racist legislation was enforced, such as the Coloured Alien Seamen Order of 1925, which gave the police powers to impose restrictions on the employment of African West Indian and Asian seamen, even though, as citizens of empire, they were British. People were refused entry in restaurants, hotels and public houses; racial politics was a prominent aspect of life in Britain that was nearly impossible to overcome.

It was within this context that Harold Moody, a Jamaican-born doctor living in Camberwell, south London, founded the League of Coloured Peoples with the aim of improving conditions for Black people in Britain. Born in Kingston, Moody came to Britain in 1904 to study medicine. As a citizen of empire and brought up in the British tradition, he expected to receive a warm welcome from the mother country, which he assumed was as familiar with Jamaica as he was with England. He quickly came up against the pervasiveness of racism in London and the hostility levelled towards him because of his race. His brilliance as a student brought him no appreciation of his abilities; despite coming top of his class at medical school, he couldn't find a position at any hospital after graduating, so he eventually set up his own practice in Peckham.

In 1931, Moody felt there was a necessity for an organisation that could bring together a group of individuals who wanted to do something about the racism present in British society. A devout Christian, Moody envisaged this organisation in the charitable tradition based on Christian humanitarianism, and he created the League of Coloured Peoples. With it, he endeavoured to bring Black people together to protect the social, educational, political and economic interests of Black Britons, to improve relations between the races, to open doors that were closed to Black and Asian people, and to interest the league's membership in the welfare of coloured peoples throughout the world. A further aim was later added: to offer financial support to coloured people in difficulty.

Its membership was comprised of Africanists from the West Indies and Africa, including the Jamaican writer and poet Una Marson, the Trinidadian writer and historian C. L. R. James, the Ghanaian political activist and journalist Desmond Buckle, the Grenadian-born anti-colonialist Samson Roberts, and Jomo Kenyatta, later the first indigenous prime minister of Kenya. The diverse political stances of its membership, from communist to right wing, meant there were often strong disagreements among the executive.

The League of Coloured Peoples issued a quarterly magazine, the *Keys*, to raise funds and inform people about cases of discrimination on a range of issues. It formed an opposition to racism and the colour bar in British society, noting that 'our brothers and sisters are daily meeting with racial discrimination in their search for work' in London, Liverpool and Cardiff especially.

Among a variety of activities the league sought to advance the fortunes of Black seamen. It investigated and reported on the oppression and destitution they were experiencing after being forced to register as 'aliens'. Working with the Coloured Colonial Seamen's Union, it helped bring to light the terrible social and economic conditions of the Black community in Cardiff and other cities, noting how many of them were living below the poverty line. In London, the league supported non-white nurses in their search for employment in hospitals and helped to organise events such as Christmas parties and day trips for 'coloured children'.

Through his leadership of the league, Harold Moody became one of the most influential Black men in Britain. By 1943 the league was the most important organisation working for improved race relations in Britain, addressing racism in the armed forces and the Colonial Office. Moody had been instrumental in the setting up of two commissions: the Asquith, concerning the development of higher education in the colonies; and the Elliot, to consider the development of universities in West Africa. In all of his actions and campaigns, Moody was led by his strong belief that education was the key weapon to combat racism and the colour bar.

Olive Morris

(1952–79) anti-racist, feminist activist

OLIVE MORRIS, WHO died in 1979 aged just twenty-seven, dedicated her life to community empowerment and activism. Yet Morris's contributions are little known outside of the community in which she lived. Her activism was part of a national Black freedom movement against racism, sexism, poverty, unemployment and economic exploitation in Britain, a narrative that is largely unknown. Olive Morris should be as well known as Darcus Howe or Angela Davis, but her legacy and her life are mostly remembered by those with whom she campaigned and who knew her. This must change.

By the late 1960s, Black[1] communities in Britain were under siege, the victims of popular and institutional racism. Discrimination in housing, employment and policing was having a destructive impact on those communities. Racism was becoming more forceful and permissible; Enoch Powell's powerful 'Rivers of Blood' speech in 1968, an incendiary and provoking attack on racial integration, influenced white supremacist groups such as the National Front to incite violence against these communities with impunity. Black children were being classed as 'educationally subnormal', and unemployment was rife among African Caribbean youth. Consequently, Black organisations promoting collective action against these injustices began to emerge, advocating self-defence and self-reliance.

It was within this very fraught time of heightened racial tensions that Morris came of age politically. She was born in St Catherine, Jamaica, and came to England with her family when she was nine, settled in south London and left school without any qualifications. In 1969, while hanging out with friends at the age of seventeen outside Desmond's Hip City, one of the first Black-owned record shops in Brixton, she became caught up in an incident of police brutality.

One of the key strategies in which the police engaged to oppress Black people was applying the nineteenth-century stop and search laws, known as 'sus' laws, which permitted them to arrest anyone who they 'suspected' of committing a crime. Clement Gomwalk, a Nigerian diplomat, fell foul of the law that day. He was arrested and beaten by two policemen after they pulled him over in his Mercedes and accused him of stealing the car. Morris tried to stop the attack and was kicked and beaten to the ground. In prison, she was stripped naked, hit and threatened. A photograph taken of her after she visited the hospital showed her covered in bruises and her face swollen. She was charged with assaulting a police officer and engaging in threatening behaviour, and received a suspended sentence.

Morris began to contest injustice, throwing herself into the struggle by joining and organising support groups. Joining the British Black Panther Party Youth League, she learned to arm herself physically and intellectually against police and white violence. She was encouraged to study for her A levels and to read Black scholars such as C. L. R. James, George Padmore, Frantz Fanon and Eric Williams. She was described by fellow Black Panther Farrukh Dhondy as 'very bright, very sharp'; she and other young people were equipped with the philosophical teachings of the movement, as well as the tools of revolution.[2]

Morris realised that it became necessary to address the dual oppression of being Black and female, and co-founded the Brixton Black Women's Group and the Organisation of Women of Asian and African Descent to provide advice and guidance for women around issues that impacted on their lives, such as housing, education, employment and welfare. These organisations also brought together Black women from different backgrounds and political perspectives nationally, encouraging them to set up their own study and self-help groups, and to spearhead 'stop sus' campaigns.

Morris was central to the squatters' campaign in the 1970s, calling attention to the fact that, despite the high numbers of homeless people and those on housing waiting lists, there were hundreds of empty homes. She was so skilled in the art of squatting that she made the cover of the *Squatters' Handbook*.

She continued her activism while studying social sciences at Manchester University, getting involved in community groups in Moss Side, and was an active member of the Manchester Black Women's Co-operative. She travelled to China as part of a student delegation and was impressed with how the Chinese were building a socialist society.

Olive Morris died of cancer in July 1979, leaving behind an extraordinary legacy of community activism committed to the struggle against race, sex and class oppression. In 1986, the Brixton Black Women's Group campaigned to have 18 Brixton

Hill, a local authority office, renamed Olive Morris House in her memory. At the time of writing, that building is now set to be demolished, and there are plans to lay a stone to memorialise her and set up a scholarship in her name.

Grace Nichols and John Agard

(b. 1950/1949) poets, authors

THOSE WHO HAVE recently taken GCSE English Literature will have seen that Grace Nichols's 'Praise Song for My Mother' is one of the featured poems on the GCSE syllabus. The praise song, a widely used poetic form in Africa, lauds and celebrates the attributes of gods, warriors, animals or crops. Nichols's poem is an honouring of her mother, for the love, spirituality, guidance and protection she provided for her daughter as a child, encouraging and inspiring her to 'go to your wide futures'.

The inclusion of Nichols's poem in the GCSE syllabus speaks to how central her work is to the understanding of cultural British–Caribbean connections. The poem provides an insight into her precious memories of her mother and connects the memories of her childhood in the Caribbean to her present in England. Stuart Hall once said that the Caribbean is 'the first, the original and the purest diaspora' – Nichols's poetry is of that diaspora.[1] Influenced by Caribbean rhythms and Guyanese culture and history, women's voices are central to this eminent poet's work, which articulate their experiences in poems that explore their unsung lives with humour and wisdom.[2]

She was born in Georgetown, Guyana, and her father, who was a headteacher, encouraged her to recite poems as a child. Nichols has said that she remembers being moved by the narrative and the beauty of the words.[3]

Before coming to England Nichols worked as a teacher and a journalist, writing for the *Guyana Chronicle*, where she met her husband and fellow poet, John Agard. The worsening economic and political climate in Guyana influenced their decision to emigrate to Britain, joining Agard's father, who had emigrated in the 1960s. They arrived in 1977, at a time when racial discrimination and violence directed at Black and Asian communities were at their peak. Nichols's poems in this period are characterised by themes of alienation and displacement, of being away from one's home and culture, and show how fear of immigrants, of colour, can act as an obstacle to real multiculturalism.

Nichols's poetry also explores the trauma of Caribbean enslavement (*I is a Long-Memoried Woman*), rebels against Western images of beauty (*The Fat Black Woman's Poems*) and reflects upon the history of the Caribbean (*Startling the Flying Fish*). Her poems examine the relationship between poetry and history, migration, women's voices and the Caribbean, which is filtered through memory, time and place. Her work has won many awards, including the Commonwealth Poetry Prize.

'The first line in our history books I seem to remember,' recalls John Agard, 'was, "West Indian history begins in 1492 with the arrival of Columbus." That very Eurocentric view, [that] nothing existed until the European entered the arena.'[4] This provided the inspiration for his poem 'Checking Out Me History': the memory of how colonial education 'bandage up me eye to me own history'. The poem examines the omissions of Black historical figures from

African, Caribbean and indigenous histories, how people from former Caribbean colonies were forced to learn British history and nothing about their Caribbean heritage.

An award-winning playwright, poet and children's author, John Agard's poetry explores cultural difference, ethnicity and the fluidity of identity. His poems are conversational and humorous, offering satirical observations on the absurdities of racial stereotyping and othering, subverting accepted opinions about race and class. Like Stuart Hall, Agard views identity not as 'an already accomplished fact . . . instead, as a production which is never complete'.[5]

Born in Guyana, Agard grew up in Georgetown, where he developed a love of language through listening to the cricket commentary on the radio and began writing poetry as a teenager. Patois and Caribbean speech patterns also shape his performance style. Agard worked for the Guyana *Sunday Chronicle* as a features and sub editor before he moved to England in 1977 with his wife Grace Nichols, with whom he sometimes collaborates.

His Guyanese and British identities have allowed him to mix cultures and languages in his poetry; he invented the term 'poetsonian' to express his dedication to his Caribbean heritage. A play on 'calypsonian', Agard wanted the term to be 'a signal to people that a poet is not just a person dishing out a cerebral pain for the sake of it, but is actually delighting in language and hoping the delight will become infectious.'[6] The academic critic and poet David Dabydeen has described Agard's poetry as 'a wonderful affirmation of life, in a language that is vital and joyous'.[7]

Agard's poetry also explores the Caribbean, its culture, history and mythology, bringing Caribbean poetry into a wider consciousness in Britain and internationally. He unpicks British culture as an insider and outsider using humour, which he says is a 'powerful weapon which can awaken people's minds'.[8]

Agard has visited thousands of schools delivering workshops, performing his poems and talking about the Caribbean. In 2012, he was awarded the Queen's Gold Medal for Poetry, the second Black poet to receive the honour.

Chinyere (Chi-chi) Nwanoku OBE

(b. 1956) musician, academic

IN 2014, THE African American novelist and critic Candace Allen, who is based in London and is a great fan of classical music, lamented over how little the genre had changed in terms of diversity among the audiences and performers, and questioned what could be done to institute change. One of the explanations she put forward for the lack of representation was the removal of music from the core curriculum, correctly arguing that you cannot develop an interest in that which you have never heard. It's an argument Chi-chi Nwanoku shares with Allen; when Sheku Kanneh-Mason won the BBC Young Musician competition in 2016, she maintained that it was due in part to the commitment of his parents to ensure that classical music played an integral part of their lives; that from a very young age they had introduced music into the home and encouraged their talents, which secured them scholarships to the Royal Academy of Music, as well as being outstanding in other subjects. The Kanneh-Masons are exceptions to the rule, though; it is rare to have an entire family possess the talents they have. That said, classical music has an air of exclusivity attached to it that helps present it as a predominantly white musical genre and industry. Research by King's College London has found that the proportion of African and Caribbean members of orchestras, students and teachers at conservatoires is well below the national average at less than 2 per cent; and after their education, they continue to encounter barriers to the sector, which is seen as middle-class.[1]

Chi-chi Nwanoku is trying to redress these imbalances. An accomplished double-bass player, she has performed in leading ensembles and orchestras in the UK and Europe and is also Professor of Historical and Double Bass Studies at the Royal Academy of Music. Known for her work in championing diversity in classical music, Nwanoku, whose mother was an Irish nurse and her father a Nigerian doctor, grew up in Berkshire and was fascinated at first with the piano, which she discovered at a neighbour's home. She would come and play so often that the neighbour wheeled the piano up the road and gave it to her.[2] An injury at eighteen ended what was a promising athletics career, and she decided to concentrate on her music, taking up the double bass, which she studied at the Royal Academy of Music.

The seeds for Chineke! were sown after a conversation with the then culture minister Ed Vaizey. When he asked her why she was the only person he saw regularly on the international concert platform, she realised he was referring to the fact she was the only person of colour.

'It should not be a novelty or a surprise,' Nwanoku told the *Evening Standard*, 'to see one black face on a stage playing Beethoven to a high standard. I was shocked I hadn't thought of it before. I realised I was being prepared for this all my life.' And so Chineke! was born to celebrate diversity in classical music, with the founding of the adult and youth Chineke!

orchestras. It is, as Nwanoku said, 'a glimpse of what orchestras might look like tomorrow'.[3]

The supportive environment created by Chineke! has begun to reap rewards for the musicians involved. In 2018, four Chineke! junior musicians reached the category finals in the BBC Young Musician competition. When the orchestra debuted at the BBC Proms in 2017, 4.2 million viewers tuned in to see it. Chi-chi Nwanoku's advocacy has discovered that the level of talent among Black classical musicians not only exists but is strong. She continues to campaign for more ethnic minority players in major ensembles, calling for blind auditions, and for better representation at the top of the industry, which she says will inspire others to believe that they can get there too.

David Adetayo Olusoga OBE

(b. 1970) historian, broadcaster

O N 7 JUNE 2020, protestors in Bristol tore down the statue of Edward Colston, long celebrated as one of the city's famous sons, whose philanthropy was rewarded by numerous buildings in that city being named after him. As board member and deputy governor of the Royal African Company, Colston had overseen the transportation of an estimated 84,000 Africans to the Caribbean, 19,000 of whom drowned en route. For many years, Colston's statue had been at the centre of fierce debate as to the legitimacy of its presence in a place that has struggled to come to terms with its history as one of the leading British slave-trading cities.

While the action was condemned by some politicians and commentators as simply a criminal act, historian David Olusoga was thinking about the why: why people could not understand that the statue, in the way its presence condoned Colston's crimes, was an outrage? He was also thinking about the historical symmetry and symbolism of the event. The protestors were making history by confronting history. Many of these protestors were of African heritage, descendants of the enslaved speaking up for the silent victims. Olusoga spoke about what he personally felt about living in a city that had been unable to agree in the past about how to represent Colston and his crimes. He linked that discourse to previous efforts at campaigning for a history that brought Black Britons from the periphery of British history to inside it, putting back into focus the uncomfortable histories of slavery and imperialism.

As a popular historian, writer and broadcaster, David Olusoga has been disrupting established British historical narratives, bringing to light the 'dark shameful chunks' that have been removed from our history, and promoting the over-looked contributions of Black and Asian Britons to the national story.

Born in Nigeria to an English mother and Nigerian father, and migrating to Britain when he was a young child, Olusoga said he got into history as a way to make sense of the forces that had affected his life. Growing up on a council estate in Gateshead in the north-east of England, he experienced 'racism from my schoolteachers, from bus drivers, from the people I passed in the street'.[1] His home was attacked by the National Front so often that his family was eventually forced to relocate.

After gaining a degree in history from the University of Liverpool, Olusoga worked for the BBC as a television producer, and in 2014 began exploring the themes that have character-ised his work to date. He presented the documentary *The World's War: Forgotten Soldiers of Empire*, which explored the multiracial dimension of the First World War, which saw four million troops and ancillaries from India, Africa and the Caribbean serve on behalf of their colonial masters – an aspect of the history that was seldom discussed outside universities.

Against the backdrop of Black British-led organisations

having to crowdfund to establish a memorial in recognition of the service of African and Caribbean troops in both world wars in this country, Olusoga's programme helped reinforce the importance and value of an inclusive narrative. *Fighting for King and Empire: Britain's Caribbean Heroes* (2015) focused on the experiences of the remaining living veterans such as Sam King and Allan Wilmot (who contributed to the programme) as part of the efforts to keep the contributions of Caribbean servicemen alive in the public consciousness.

The dominant and comforting narrative of British abolitionism was also undermined by Olusoga's BAFTA-winning series *Britain's Forgotten Slave Owners* (2015), as he laid bare the depth and breadth of British slave ownership, as seen through the slave compensation records, the study of which was a major research project at University College London. By examining the experiences of the enslaved, and following the money paid to compensate the slave owners, Olusoga painted a vivid picture of the spread of slavery profits into the British economy. The programme took on further resonance as an insensitive tweet in 2018 from the UK Treasury revealed that the £20 million borrowed to compensate the slaveowners in 1833 had only finally been paid off in 2015, which meant that living Britons had paid to end slavery. That the enslaved themselves received nothing except an extra four years of apprenticeship showed, as Olusoga remarked, how poorly slavery and slave ownership are understood.[2]

Black and British: A Forgotten History (2016) was in part Olusoga's homage to the pioneering historians of the 1970s and 1980s. Peter Fryer, James Walvin and Folarin Shyllon, to name a few whose work he was building upon, had initiated what Olusoga termed as 'the wider process of historical salvage

[that] recovered lost people, reclaimed lost events . . . a wave of new research that [was] in part an attempt to compensate for the failures and myopia of so-called mainstream history'.[3] Like these historians, Olusoga demonstrated the global nature of British history, which explained its Black presence from as far back as the Roman era.

Olusoga's programme *The Unwanted: The Secret Windrush Files* (2019) was made in direct response to the 2018 *Windrush* Scandal in which thousands of Black Britons were made homeless, jobless or deported to the Caribbean as a consequence of the immigration policies of the Conservative government. In the programme, Olusoga traced seventy years of government hostility towards Caribbean migrants, showing their attempts to restrict their entry despite their right as British citizens to live here. Once again, he disrupted the romantic national myth of *Windrush* as simply the arrival of these men and women coming to Britain for a better life.

When Olusoga has been asked whether he is a historian or a Black historian, he responds that he is both; he has the archetypal British identity, whose duty is to bring up from the past the richness and full complexity of our humanity.[4]

Phyllis Opoku-Gyimah 'Lady Phyll'

(b. 1974) LGBTQI activist

PHYLLIS OPOKU-GYIMAH, KNOWN as Lady Phyll, is a leading voice in the fight for equality for the Black LGBTQI
community.[1] As co-founder and executive director of UK Black
Pride, her mission is to provide shelter against discrimination
experienced by that community and a place for that community to express confidently who they are.

The idea to create Black Pride came to Opoku-Gyimah in
2004 while running an online social group called Black Lesbians
in the UK, and she decided to organise a coach trip to Southend
to enable the group members to meet in person. Bringing along
a DJ, volleyball, badminton sets and dominoes to make the
trip more fun, the success of that outing made Lady Phyll realise that this could be the beginning of something bigger.

Opoku-Gyimah, who was born in London to Ghanaian
parents, remodelled these gatherings into Black Pride, an
organisation that celebrates LGBTQI people of African, Asian,
Caribbean, Middle Eastern and Latin American descent. Today,
it's the largest such group in Europe, staging networking and
social activities that culminate in a free annual event. Black
Pride celebrates the achievements and contributions of Black

LGBTQI people, and has also created a space for those people to talk about their intersectional difficulties. It has helped to make inroads in terms of raising visibility and eradicating all forms of bigotry.

Opoku-Gyimah, who is also the head of equality and learning for the PCS (Public and Commercial Services) Union, famously turned down the MBE in the 2016 New Year Honours, citing the continuing persecution of LGBTQI people in the Commonwealth. She was not keen to accept an award 'linked to colonialism and its toxic enduring legacy . . . where LGBTQI people are still being persecuted, tortured and even killed because of sodomy laws.'[2] Opoku-Gyimah challenges homophobia in Africa through her association with the Pan-African organisation Out and Proud Diamond Group, and the UK-based Justice for Gay Africans.[3]

UK Black Pride won the Black LGBT Community Awards in 2006 and 2007, and the *Pink Paper*'s Readers' Award and the Stonewall Community Award in 2011. In 2018, Opoku-Gyimah co-edited *Sista!*, an anthology of writings by LGBT women of African and Caribbean descent, which offers unique perspectives on their experiences, and explores how they navigate acceptance and belonging within and outside their communities. In August 2019, Lady Phyll was appointed executive director of the Kaleidoscope Trust, a charity advocating human rights for LGBTQI people globally. With Black Pride, she wants to achieve 'equal rights for all, and human rights respected. Ensuring the safety of young LGBT people and making sure we can eradicate domestic violence and other forms of violence in the LGBT BME community.'[4]

Olivette Otele

(b. 1970) academic historian

I N OCTOBER 2018, the Royal Historical Society (RHS) published a landmark report on race, equality and ethnicity in UK history academia, which outlined in stark detail the level of under-representation of African and Caribbean scholars and students within universities in Britain, and the institutional racism Black and ethnic minority historians experience in teaching and research practices. Among the report's key findings was the realisation that, of the 3115 academics currently employed in university history departments, only fifteen identify as Black African or Caribbean.[1] As academic historians in the UK remain overwhelmingly white, the notion of history as a 'white' discipline continues to prevail, presenting obstacles to diversity and inclusion. Consequently, Black students are deterred from the subject, and history remains the third least popular subject among this group.

The same month the report was published, Olivette Otele was awarded a professorship and chair in history at Bath Spa University, becoming the first Black female professor of history in the UK. Otele's appointment gave the content of the Royal Historical Society's report more urgency and offered a message to

UK institutions to do more to widen its staff, curricula and participation. At the same time, her appointment reflects the necessity of having a more representative academe and the introduction and production of more inclusive narratives of the past.

Otele, who was born in Cameroon and brought up in Paris, specialises in collective memory and geopolitics related to Britain and France's colonial pasts. She explores the links between history, memory, memorialisation and politics in relation to transatlantic enslavement. She has said the lack of equal representation in academia was one of the things that motivated her to become a historian. As a child growing up in Paris, like most children of African heritage it was drilled into her that she would always be compelled to prove her competency. 'I knew that,' she is quoted as saying, 'given the society we live in, if I worked hard as a black woman, I would only have half the reward. So, to have equal reward, I would have to work harder than my white counterparts.'

For six years Otele was associate professor of history at Université Paris XIII, and during those six years she commuted each week to Paris from her home in Newport while her partner raised their two sons. She described those years as 'exhausting and expensive' but demonstrated her strength of will – the need to succeed within her field despite the obstacles. The findings of the RHS report reflect Otele's own experiences in academia, which she describes as a place of a 'polite kind of racism and micro aggression', and in general a lack of support for Black academics.

In late 2019 it was announced that Otele would take up the post of Professor of the History of Slavery at the University of Bristol in January 2020, to lead research on the links between the city of Bristol and transatlantic enslavement.

By the early eighteenth century, Bristol was one of England's leading slaving ports, responsible for around a fifth of the voyages enslaved Africans were forced to take on British ships. In 1750 alone, Bristol ships transported 8000 of the 20,000 enslaved Africans sent that year to the British Caribbean and North America. The trade and trafficking in Africans enriched the city and its residents, and its historical connections to Africa and the West Indies are present throughout the city, in its architecture, public buildings, economic institutions, street names and memorials. As one of the leading slave-trading nations, evidence of this past is present throughout the whole of Britain; however, it remains contentious in the way it is remembered, discussed and taught. Over the past several years, reports of some of the problematic ways in which enslavement is taught in schools show that more work needs to be done in terms of providing better contextualisation, as well as a better understanding of this history and its legacies.

Professor Otele has said that she wants to produce 'a rigorous and extensive piece of research that will be relevant to the city, to the university and that will be a landmark in the way Britain examines, acknowledges and teaches the history of enslavement.' Unsurprisingly, there has been resistance to the research that Professor Otele is undertaking; the main complaint being that there is no point in rehashing the past, which casts Black people as perpetual victims. This is an argument, Otele feels, that can only come from people with privileged backgrounds. She counters it with the assertion that 'the legacy of racism feeds into eugenics, which feeds into discrimination and racism, which feeds into the fact that many people of African descent are from the working class. So, there is a clear link between past and present.'

Professor Otele aims to work with Black historians from outside of the university who have been producing their own histories with the aim of embedding them within the city's historical timeline. This may go some way to making history a more inclusive and equitable discipline, as recommended by the Royal Historical Society's 2018 report.

Horace Ové CBE

(b. 1939) film and documentary maker, photographer

A N INTERNATIONALLY RENOWNED photographer and film-maker, whose film *Pressure* (1976) was the first feature-length film by a Black director in Britain, Horace Ové has combined the genres of documentary and drama to give a voice to the Black British experience during the 1970s and 1980s, via themes of generational differences, music, culture and Black political struggle. In a career spanning over five decades, Ové has been the creative force behind a series of ground-breaking and genre-breaking films, documentaries and television dramas, which have featured the work of some of the leading Black actors and writers working in Britain. Alongside his film career, Ové is also one of the most important chroniclers of Black history through his photography, capturing the birth and development of the Notting Hill Carnival and prominent figures of the Black British community.

Born in Trinidad, Ové emigrated to Britain in 1960 to study painting and interior design but wanted to study film. To raise money for film school, he took parts as an extra in European films. Being cast as an extra in the epic film *Cleopatra* (1963), starring Elizabeth Taylor, was a turning point for Ové; after leaving Rome, he returned to London to study at the London School of Film Technique. Exposure to the filming techniques of European directors gave Ové an advantage over his peers and influenced his *vérité* style, remarking that '[European film-makers] were making films about real people and what was going on in their heads, their minds, their dreams . . . and so up until today I'm still stuck with it.'[1]

An early film that displayed the documentary style he was developing was *Baldwin's Nigger* (1969), in which Ové filmed the writer and activist James Baldwin giving a lecture to West Indian students while visiting London. Comparing the social and political struggles of Black people in the USA and the UK, Baldwin, along with the comedian and activist Dick Gregory, engages in a dialogue with West Indian students on a range of topics including race, culture and identity.

Ové's next film, *Reggae* (1971), was the first in-depth film on reggae music to be produced. It was filmed at Wembley Stadium during the 1970 Caribbean Music Festival and documented the first large reggae concert held in Britain. The film explores the history and growth of reggae as a musical phenomenon and features performances by Toots and the Maytals, Millie Small and Desmond Dekker. Poverty is a topic that influences reggae lyrics, and it is also featured in the documentary, in which scenes of extreme economic hardship in the Caribbean are juxtaposed with concert footage. In this documentary, Ové demonstrates how the music provided a social commentary on the issues that impacted on people's lives.

In *Pressure* (1976), Ové explores what it meant to be young, Black and dispossessed in 1970s Britain. Set in Ladbroke Grove in west London, where many Caribbean migrants settled during the 1950s, it focuses on Tony, a teenager who attempts to navigate his way through the hostile environment of 1970s London. His blackness and Britishness deemed incompatible and unacceptable by society, he becomes politicised as he is treated with suspicion by potential employers, the police and parents of white friends. The film lays bare the structural racism experienced by Black Britons; and the British Film Institute, nervous about the film's frank depictions of discrimination faced by Britain's Black communities, shelved it for three years. Similarly, with the BBC drama *A Hole in Babylon* (1979), a fictionalised account of the Spaghetti House Siege of 1975, Ové wanted to provide a sympathetic portrayal of the attempt by three Black men to rob an Italian restaurant in Knightsbridge to finance a Black supplementary school, which escalated into a six-day siege. Part drama and part documentary, using archival news footage, the programme sought to understand the men's motivations for the robbery, which they claimed was political. Ové's drama looked beyond the headlines, which had dubbed the men as 'black criminal gangsters', and attempted to offer a different point of view, linking their actions to the structural problems faced by second-generation Caribbean youth.

Ové also directed several episodes of *Empire Road* (1978–9), the first long-running drama that addressed Britain's multiracial society, and starred Norman Beaton (*Desmond's*), Joseph Marcell (*The Fresh Prince of Bel Air*) and Rudolph Walker (*EastEnders*). Ové made his mark on the series by filming in actual street locations. In the Channel 4 film *Playing Away* (1986), which Ové directed and Caryl Phillips scripted, this comedy drama explores the culture clash that takes place when the residents of an affluent, fictional Suffolk village invite a

West Indian cricket team to play a match to highlight the village's 'Third World Week'.

In 1986, the British Film Institute named Ové Best Director for Independent Film and Television, and he is the only non-Jamaican to have received a Doctor Bird award from the Jamaican film industry for his contribution to Caribbean filmmaking. His photography has been displayed in major exhibitions and retrospectives around the world.

David Oyelowo OBE

(b. 1976) actor, producer

As a leading actor working in film and television today, David Oyetokunbo Oyelowo is doing what he had promised himself he would do: creating the films he wants to see by changing the demographic of decision-making in film and television. Oyelowo's profile as an actor was significantly enhanced by his portrayal of Martin Luther King in *Selma* (2014), for which he received a Golden Globe Best Actor nomination. Oyelowo's portrayal of the civil rights leader was extraordinary, achieving the difficult task of humanising one of the greatest historical figures of the previous century.

Oyelowo's professional experience mirrors that of his contemporaries: Idris Elba, David Kaluuya, Chiwetel Ejiofor and David Harewood; Black British actors who left Britain for Hollywood because the lack of opportunities in British film and television were stagnating their careers. Since settling in the USA, Oyelowo has acted in films that have enabled him to demonstrate his range and take on roles that are not always specific to his ethnicity; rather, they are roles that reflect the humanity of the character.

Born in Oxford, moving to Nigeria when he was six and returning to England when he was a teenager, Oyelowo trained at LAMDA and spent three years with the Royal Shakespeare Company. Oyelowo has credited Adrian Lester's performance in the film *Primary Colours* (1998) as impactful on his understanding of the kind of career he wanted to have, one that did not restrict him as an artist to clichéd, peripheral and stereotypical roles that are often given to Black actors. Asking his agent to put him up for roles that white actors were auditioning for, Oyelowo won the lead role in an RSC production of *Henry VI* and thereby became the first Black actor to play an English king in a major Shakespeare production, for which he won critical praise and the Ian Charleson Award for best performance by an actor under thirty in a classical play.

His role as Danny Hunter in the BBC drama *Spooks* was typical of the kind of roles Oyelowo was actively seeking out – roles that were not 'race specific' and that enabled him to practise his art of evoking the lives of people. Despite outstanding performances in dramas such as the 2009 BBC adaptation of Andrea Levy's novel *Small Island*, Oyelowo moved to the United States with his family because he still wasn't being afforded the opportunity to express his full potential, not only as an actor but also as a decision maker and cultural curator. This is exemplified in an anecdote he shared with the audience at the BFI Black Star Symposium. Having written a twenty-page treatment on Bill Richmond, the eighteenth-century African British boxer, his idea for a film was rejected on the grounds that historical dramas work only when the topic is 'ripe for a revisit'. Oyelowo described the term 'revisit' as the most dangerous of words; so much of Black British history has never been visited – 'if we are only looking at things that need to be revisited,' he remarked, 'you are wiping me out of this country's history.' Those who determine what gets made are powerful, and if the decision makers are not representative, many stories will go untold.

Being in a more powerful position as an acclaimed actor and producer means that David Oyelowo has been able to have more influence in what stories are being told, becoming part of new creative partnerships with other Black filmmakers such as Lee Daniels, who directed him in *The Butler* (2013) and *The Paperboy* (2012). He credits Disney's vice president of production, Tendo Nagenda, as the primary force behind *The Queen of Katwe* (2016) getting made. The reason Nagenda championed this story of a young Ugandan girl who discovers she is a talented chess player and who is mentored by Oyelowo's character is because he had lived in Uganda and wanted to see himself reflected on film. This picture bears the hallmarks of a film being told from a Black perspective, which is rare in Hollywood.

Oyelowo has been intentional in seeking the female perspective by backing and working with female directors such as Ava DuVernay, who directed him in *Middle of Nowhere* (2012), and Amma Asante, whom he worked with on the romantic drama *A United Kingdom* (2016). The way to 'do diversity' is to have Black professionals on board and embedded in the decision-making process. This is the only way things will change.

Fundamentally, Oyelowo is keen for his children to see him at the centre of the narrative – as the protagonist – and for the future generation of Black actors not to allow themselves to be placed in a box that they did not create for themselves.

George Padmore

(1903–59) Pan-Africanist, journalist, author

G EORGE PADMORE WAS a communist and Pan-Africanist, who was one of the key figures in the anti-colonial movements in Britain in the 1930s and 1940s. During that time, there was a growing number of African and Caribbean political activists and intellectuals living in Britain who were deeply committed to critiquing and eventually breaking the power of colonial authority. Padmore was dedicated to self-government for colonial people and trade union rights, and was one of the key organisers of the Fifth Pan-African Congress held in Manchester in 1945. The years he spent as advisor to Kwame Nkrumah both before and after Ghanaian independence have memorialised him as 'one of the fathers of African emancipation'.

Padmore was born Malcolm Ivan Nurse, into a middle-class, radical-thinking family in Trinidad; his father, a schoolteacher, had joined the Pan-African Association in the early 1900s, which was founded by Henry Sylvester Williams, a Trinidadian who was training to become a barrister in London. Williams had convened the first Pan-African Conference in London in 1900 to 'secure political and civil rights for Africans and their descendants throughout the world', and to investigate the situation of Black people in the British Empire.

While studying medicine in the United States, Nurse was exposed to the racial politics and became a member of the Communist Party. Changing his name to George Padmore, in 1929 he travelled to Moscow as its rising star, an expert on race and colonialism, someone the party believed could lead the work of the Communist International (the global umbrella organisation for national communist parties) on the 'Negro Question'. He became editor of the *Negro Worker*, the Communist International trade union newspaper written for working-class Black people around the world. Based in Hamburg, Germany, Padmore was responsible for writing about the condition of Black people in Africa, the Caribbean, the USA and Europe. While there, he organised the first international conference of Black workers, which inspired his book, *The Life and Struggles of Negro Toilers*, published in 1931, discussing how millions of Black workers were being exploited throughout the USA, the Caribbean and Africa.

Within two weeks of Hitler becoming chancellor in 1933, Padmore's office in Hamburg was raided and, after three months in prison, he was deported to the UK as a British colonial citizen. It was during this period that Padmore became disenchanted with communism and more active in Pan-Africanist activism. Concerned with Italy's intention to invade Abyssinia, he joined the International African Friends of Abyssinia, which had been set up by his friend C. L. R. James, to whom he had reconnected when he returned to London. James introduced him to Amy Ashwood Garvey, co-founder of the Universal Negro Improvement Association, along with her ex-husband Marcus, the future President of

Kenya Jomo Kenyatta, the Sierra Leonean trade unionist I. T. A. Wallace-Johnson, the Guyanese-born Pan-African activist Ras Makonnen, and the President of the Colonial Seamen's Association Chris Braithwaite. Together they founded the International African Service Bureau in 1937, which broadened the scope beyond campaigning for Abyssinia's sovereignty and addressed the oppression of Black people globally. The bureau discussed the work and struggles of African people throughout the diaspora, and maintained close links with activists in the Caribbean, the USA, Latin America and Europe.

After the war, Padmore was part of the organising committee, along with Jomo Kenyatta, Peter Abrahams and Kwame Nkrumah, for the Fifth Pan-African Congress, which opened in October 1945, with over two hundred delegates representing trade unions, farmers, students, political organisations and Black organisations in Britain. The conference was significant for creating a framework for decolonisation; many of the delegates who attended the conference became leading political activists against colonial rule in their own countries. For example, Kwame Nkrumah's political education was certainly advanced by Padmore and his colleagues. The two men maintained many years of correspondence through which Padmore advised Nkrumah and visited the Gold Coast (later Ghana) as his guest, assisting him, when he became President of Ghana, to achieve his dream of a united Africa.

Padmore was, as the historian Leslie James observes, a deeply political person. He was committed to a Pan-Africanist vision that saw people throughout the African diaspora emancipate themselves from colonial and racist domination. His articles and essays were printed regularly in the United States, Britain, West Africa and the Caribbean, linking liberation struggles

ormzy performs on the Pyramid stage during day three of Glastonbury Festival at Worthy rm, Pilton, on 28 June 2019. (© *Jim Dyson/Getty Images*)

Darcus Howe *(right)* and poet Linton Kwesi Johnson *(left)* at the *Race Today* office on Railton Ro: Brixton, 1979. *(© Adrian Boot/www.urbanimages.tv)*

Gus John, 1979.
(© Brian Shuel/National Portrait Gallery, London)

Sheku Kanneh-Mason during his performan: of Elgar's *Cello Concerto in E Minor* at the B Proms at the Royal Albert Hall, London, 20 *(© Christopher Christodoulou)*

Olive Morris in about 1978 at a rally outside the Brixton Tate Library, where she and other protesters accused the Special Patrol Group, an arm of the police department intended to combat public disorder, of targeting the Black community. (© Lambeth Archives)

Grace Nichols by Maud Sulter, 2001.
(© National Portrait Gallery, London)

Horace Ové in Soho Square, London, in January 2004. (© Sal Idriss/National Portrait Gallery, London)

George Padmore, 12 November 1957.
(© Los Angeles Examiner/USC Libraries/Corbis via Getty Im

...yll Opoku-Gyimah.
(© *Rachel Adams*)

...cia Rigg talking at a rally on 25 October 2014 in Trafalgar Square, London, campaigning
...nst deaths in custody. (© *Janine Wiedel Photography/Alamy Stock Photo*)

Mary Seacole.
(© Winchester College/In aid of Mary Seacole Memorial Statue Appeal, Mary Evans)

Sharon White, 2016.
(© Simon Fredrick/National Portrait Gallery, London)

Yinka Shonibare, 20
(© Sal Idriss/National Port: Gallery, London)

Benjamin Zephaniah, 1980s.
(© Miriam Reik)

Bill Richmond by Robert Dighton, published March 1810.
(© National Portrait Gallery, London)

Drawn, Etch. & Pub. by Dighton 6, Char' Cross March. 1810.

A STRIKING VIEW of RICHMOND

taking place across the world, and having a significant effect on the development of Black political thought. As historian Bill Schwarz writes, he 'expressed the elementary truth that colonialism has neither moral nor intellectual justification'.[1]

Professor Sir Geoff Palmer OBE

(b. 1940) grain scientist, human rights and racial equality activist

PEOPLE FAMILIAR WITH the world of brewing and grain science will know the name and the accomplishments of Professor Sir Geoff Palmer, and his ground-breaking research and exceptional achievements in the brewing industry. He is credited with the discovery of the barley abrasion process – a method that demonstrated that bran, not the germ, produced the most enzymes that changed growing grain into malt, which is stimulated to speed up the malting process. This process has been adopted by the UK's biggest breweries.

In 1998 he received the American Society of Brewing Chemists Award of Distinction. This award is considered the 'Nobel Prize of brewing', and Palmer is the first European and the fourth person to receive it. Palmer was also the first African Caribbean scholar to be appointed a professor in Scotland, at Heriot-Watt University, where he was offered his own personal chair in recognition of his contributions to grain science and his reputation for attracting students and funding for research. His exploration into a species of sorghum native to Africa helped resolve a crisis in Nigeria when his findings discovered it could be substituted for barley. This encouraged Guinness and Heineken to use it in their breweries in Africa.

In addition to his scientific work, Palmer is a human rights and anti-racist activist who has written extensively on race and racism, and campaigns for better historical truth-telling regarding Scotland's role in slavery. In 2007, coinciding with the bicentenary of the abolition of the British slave trade, Palmer published *The Enlightenment Abolished: Citizens of Britishness*, in which he interweaves his personal narrative as a Jamaican British immigrant with the history of British slavery, and a focus on how the Scots who left their homeland to become slavers in Jamaica left their indelible mark. Palmer notes how the tobacco trade in Chesapeake, Virginia, was dominated by Scottish merchants, who became millionaires and invested their wealth into cities such as Glasgow, whose streets still bear their names. In the Caribbean, a third of the slave plantations were owned by Scots; British enslaved workers were clothed mainly in Scottish linen.

The former chattel enslaved eventually became British subjects, and the belief of British subjecthood became embedded into their identities. The imperial legacy that connected the Caribbean to Britain influenced the return of Caribbean British subjects to the 'mother country' to benefit from opportunities that could not be offered at home. As the Jamaican poet Louise Bennett remarks in her famous poem, which offers some stinging insights concerning the historical conditions that occasioned this migration, it was 'colonization in reverse'.

Born in St Elizabeth parish, Jamaica, Palmer's migration story exemplifies the pain of ruptured family relationships and cultural alienation. He arrived in London in 1955 to be with his mother, whom, seven years after she had left Jamaica for

London, he did not recognise. She had arrived in the first wave of migration in 1948 and had spent the interim working at menial jobs to save up the £86 fare to pay for her son to join her. Classed as 'educationally subnormal', Palmer's skill at cricket got him out of his secondary modern school and into Highbury Grammar, where he played against teams from Eton, Harrow and Winchester. Years later, Palmer would write about his concerns regarding the ignorance of Caribbean culture in British schools, explaining that the educational system was failing students. The cultural and historical biases that Palmer had himself experienced as a boy, which classed him as educationally subnormal, were racist and damaging.

As popular racism was being whipped up by right-wing politicians and the press, leading to the first immigration controls against Commonwealth citizens in 1962, Palmer found his life frightening at times. 'I didn't want to get up in the morning in the sixties,' he once said, 'because I would see a newspaper headline [saying] 500 more people arrive – and I feared that would encourage someone to try and kill me. Therefore, one of the things I had to develop was a sense of belonging, and you need that to succeed.'

Palmer credits his success with the support he was given by mentors, family (in particular his aunts and his mother) and colleagues, who he calls 'good Samaritans', throughout his life and career. Professor Garth Chapman, who gave him his first job as a junior technical assistant, encouraged him to complete his university entrance exams, after which he gained an undergraduate degree in botany at the University of Leicester, and then went to Heriot-Watt College (now University) and Edinburgh University, where he earned a PhD under the supervision of Professor Anna Macleod, an authority on brewing and distilling. He has said she looked beyond his qualifications, seeing the potential in him; since 1964, he has been at Heriot-Watt University, which he calls his 'home' and where he helped to set up the International Centre for Brewing and Distilling.

Alex Pascall OBE

(b. 1936) broadcaster, musician, cultural activist

WHEN *BLACK LONDONERS* was first broadcast on BBC Radio London on 22 November 1974, it was the first programme of its kind in Britain. It became the aired voice for the Black British community, a forerunner of Black radio. It set out to report what was happening within the community and reflect the views of Black people from all walks of life, as well as reporting on world events in the Caribbean and Africa.[1] For its first two years it was broadcast monthly; it became so popular that, by 1976, this was increased to a weekly slot. By 1978, the need for the programme was so great it ended up being broadcast daily until its cancellation in 1988.

Alex Pascall, who hosted the show during its fourteen-year run, co-produced, wrote and shaped the content of the show, which included interviews, overseas reports and special features on people and events. The show established a Black presence in British media, in a period when there was virtually nothing that provided social, political or cultural contexts to the lives of Black Britons.

Pascall, who came to Britain from Grenada in 1959, worked as a producer with the BBC's Caribbean Service. Prior to working in radio, he was a musician and singer, responsible for the creation of the Alex Pascall Singers in the 1960s, the first multicultural choir in London. Pascall is also credited with being one of the pioneers of the Notting Hill Carnival, serving as the chair of its arts committee between 1984 and 1989, and helped to establish the *Voice*, Britain's first Black newspaper, with Val McCalla.

His knowledge of Caribbean music and his experience of performance and promotion meant he was a good choice as presenter for *Black Londoners*. Prior to the show, many Black Britons did not listen to the BBC because, according to Pascall, there was nothing on it for them. *Black Londoners* – part news, part lively phone-ins, with musical interludes – quickly evolved into an international programme and was eagerly listened to by Black households. It featured interviews with guests including Muhammad Ali, Angela Davis, Alex Haley, Bob Marley and calypsonian the Mighty Sparrow. The show's influence on the Black community was significant; community leaders, local and national politicians and those seeking political office requested airtime. Pascall played music from throughout the African diaspora, and featured folklorists such as the Jamaican poet Louise Bennett, recalling that listeners went wild when she appeared on the show, as she'd never previously been on air in Britain.

Pascall used the show to protest against South African apartheid. Parallels were drawn between how Black people were being treated in South Africa and how they were being treated in Britain. *Black Londoners* played a campaigning role in its public support of the anti-apartheid movement, publicising its demonstrations and other London-based activities, urging its listeners to support them. Pascall invited on to the programme members of South African liberation movements exiled in Britain, giving them airtime to discuss their struggles. Broadcasting under restrictions by the BBC to be politically neutral, Pascall recalled that:

> You had to be careful on the radio not to voice anything controversial against the powers that be ... We allowed those who wanted to make their comments [about apartheid] to be free to comment ... for instance the Mighty Sparrow's 'Isolate South Africa', a powerful song ... Every time I played it, the South African embassy wrote to the BBC to get rid of me![2]

For Pascall, the legacy of *Black Londoners* was that it informed and educated the Black community about common African diasporic struggles.

The profound disadvantages in employment, housing and educational attainment experienced by Black Britons in the 1970s and 1980s saw them venting their anger in a series of explosive uprisings in major cities in England in 1981. *Black Londoners* was one of the few programmes that could provide context to the uprisings. With only his microphone and tape recorder, Pascall went to Brixton and was invited to speak to people involved. The marginalisation, the anti-immigration rhetoric – in 1978, Margaret Thatcher had remarked in an interview that people feared being 'swamped by people with a different culture' – the deaths of thirteen Black youngsters in a fire in New Cross, which was virtually ignored by the press and with no condolences offered, were too much to bear. 'The message they gave me to give Margaret Thatcher wasn't an easy one,' Pascall recalled.[3] In 1988, despite the show's popularity, the BBC cancelled *Black Londoners*, which led to a huge falling-out between Pascall and the corporation.

As a cultural activist, Alex Pascall's contributions are many and significant; but it is his involvement in creating a seminal radio programme for the Black community, 'something the establishment could not control', for which he will be best remembered.

David Pitt, Baron Pitt of Hampstead

(1913–94) physician, politician, civil rights campaigner

A GP AND A politician, David Pitt was one of the leading anti-racist and social campaigners during the 1950s and 1960s, who believed that it wasn't enough to believe that racial discrimination was wrong, but that it was vital that the law reflected that view. He was one of the spearheads of the campaign for the establishment of the 1965 Race Relations Act and was co-founder of the Campaign Against Racial Discrimination (CARD), which played a significant role in achieving racial equality through legislative change. Elevated to the House of Lords in 1975, Pitt became the second person of African heritage to become a peer.

Born in Grenada, Pitt had been active in Caribbean politics in the 1940s after he returned to the Caribbean upon receiving his medical degree from the University of Edinburgh in 1938. He supported the idea that the Caribbean should establish a federation that was politically autonomous from Britain, and he co-founded the West Indian National Party to achieve this aim. Unfortunately, many Caribbeans did not share his view of a united federation and, disillusioned, Pitt moved to London in 1947 with his family, establishing his own surgery in North Gower Street in 1950. As one of the few Caribbean doctors, he was in great demand among the Black community in north London, not only in matters relating to health but also to social issues, and he became a kind of informal spokesman for Black Britons. He was also an active member of the anti-apartheid movement and the Campaign for Nuclear Disarmament.

Over time, Pitt assumed a prominent role in the struggle for racial equality. After the Notting Hill riots in 1958, he established the British Caribbean Association to improve relations between the Caribbean community and Parliament, with the aim of influencing government policy.

Pitt's effectiveness as a campaigner encouraged him to attempt to enter into formal politics, and he was selected as parliamentary candidate for the Hampstead constituency in the 1959 general election. He was the first ever Black Briton to stand as a parliamentary candidate, and subsequently was the target of an aggressive racist campaign; he and his family received death threats and the building that housed his surgery was firebombed. Pitt did not win the seat, but in 1961 he was elected as a London County Council member for Stoke Newington and Hackney North. Again, he was the first Black person to serve in a local government position, which he held until 1977.

It is estimated that one million migrants from Commonwealth nations had settled in Britain by the mid-1960s. Mainly from the Caribbean, Pakistan and India, their lives were blighted by racial discrimination in the areas of housing, employment and welfare. There had been unsuccessful attempts within the different migrant communities to protest against racist policies and to lobby government, and activists turned their attention to the ways African Americans were addressing their similar experiences.

In December 1964, Martin Luther King made a short visit to London while en route to Norway to receive the Nobel Peace Prize. Marion Glean, a Caribbean-born activist, invited him to speak with other activists, whom King warned that Britain's racial problems would worsen if organised direct action wasn't taken. Pitt and the others who were present at this meeting were inspired to form the Campaign Against Racial Discrimination to speak on behalf of all 'coloured' people, bringing together groups such as the Federation of Pakistani Organisations, the Indian Workers' Association, the West Indian Students' Union and the Council of African Organisations. Pitt served as CARD's first chairman, and throughout its early period, Pitt and other committee members spent much time putting its views to the government and the public, lobbying for amendments to the Race Relations Bill, particularly in its scope and means of enforcement. Under Pitt's chairmanship, CARD persuaded the government to pass the 1965 Race Relations Act, prohibiting discrimination on the grounds of race or national origin. By 1967, however, CARD had split, unable to sustain a united front for all immigrants and subject to internal divisions. In 1970 Pitt ran again for Parliament, in Clapham South, but lost. He never stood for another parliamentary seat; however, in 1975 he was made a life peer. As a member of the House of Lords, Pitt maintained his anti-racist politics and was known for his passionate speeches against class and race discrimination, and in support of immigration. He maintained the running of his surgery, and his medical career was as distinguished as his political one, becoming president of the British Medical Association in 1985.

Mary Prince

(1788–?) anti-slavery campaigner, author

IN 1788, IN Brackish Pond, Bermuda, an enslaved woman was born who would eventually become the first Black British woman to write about her escape from that system. Mary Prince's story of her life and experiences was published in London and Edinburgh in 1831 as *A History of Mary Prince, A West Indian Slave, Related by Herself,* and was a brutal account of slavery as seen through her eyes. It was also in essence a fierce anti-slavery message which provided a stunning rebuke to the slavery apologists. Arguably, Prince's narrative advanced the cause of slavery emancipation that was passed into law throughout the British Empire in 1833; by the end of 1831, the book had gone into a third edition, demonstrating the importance and urgency of her message. She became the first Black British woman calling for total emancipation by making a public plea for it, which she did at the end of her book.

From Prince's narrative, we learn many things about how the system of enslavement operated, and about Mary Prince herself. Her story is remarkable for the fact that enslaved women had virtually no opportunity to tell or publish their experiences. Consequently, what we get from this narrative is Prince speaking to the experiences of thousands of enslaved women, of the indignities they suffered and endured, and of the violence, both physical and sexual, to which they were subjected. Additionally, we also learn about how, in the face of powerlessness, agency and defiance were important tools for survival.

Prince's narrative, which was published by the Anti-Slavery Society, follows many of the conventional slave accounts which were being published in the United States at the time and which followed a particular trajectory: details about childhood; a description of the conditions that prompted escape attempts; the final successful escape; concluding with the subject's freed status and a condemnation of the institution of slavery. Consequently, we learn that Prince's first twelve years of life were happy insofar as she was with her mother and siblings in the home of a Captain John Williams and his wife Sarah. With the benefit of hindsight, Prince was completely unaware of her status as property, or how that status determined how her life would be. The death of Sarah Williams results in the fragmentation of Prince's family, as they were all sold to different people. Mary Prince herself was sold to a Captain John Ingham. It is here that she experienced, and was witness to, extreme acts of brutality and control. It is also where she first engaged in small acts of resistance – she even escaped for short periods, and when, on one occasion, she was brought back to the Inghams by her own father, emboldened by his presence she remonstrated with them about their conduct towards her. She announced that she 'could not stand the floggings no longer; that mothers could not save [children] from cruel masters, from the whip, the rope and the cow skin'. She referred to her condition as belonging to the general plight of enslaved workers and reported that, on that day, Ingham did not beat her. On occasion, then, Prince was able to reflect her enslavers' behaviour back at them, which allowed her a little respite.

Most enslaved workers had one or two owners in their lifetime; Mary Prince had five before she freed herself. This suggests, and her narrative bears this out, that her sharp tongue and strong will meant that although she still experienced terrible violence at their hands, she had the courage to keep challenging their behaviour.

It was with her final 'owners' that Prince finally found freedom. She persuaded D_____, with whom she had spent at least fifteen years in Bermuda and at the salt ponds of the Turk and Caicos Islands, to sell her to merchant John Wood, who was moving to Antigua. That she could convince her 'owner' to sell her to the Woods indicates her understanding of the value of her labour. In Antigua, Prince demonstrated more of her agency by marrying Daniel James, a free Black carpenter, without notification or permission. Vexed by her fiery spirit, the Woods family attempted to break her through harsh and cruel punishments, including on one occasion locking her up in a cage. Prince refused to be defeated by the Woods, rebelling against them by joining the Moravian Church, again without permission.

Mary Prince travelled to England with the Woods in 1828, where she would most likely have been exposed to the debates on slave emancipation taking place in Parliament and to the agitation for it across the country. Understanding that she was free in England, Prince escaped the Woods, seeking refuge in a Moravian missionary church in Hatton Garden, London, and later with the Anti-Slavery Society, which eventually published the account of her life. Prince knew that, by leaving the Woods, she would not see her husband and family again. A truly terrible decision to have to make in any circumstances, Mary Prince chose freedom.

Mary Prince's story gives a sense of how she overcame physical and psychological trauma and hardships. She also provides an understanding of how slavery affected human beings, both enslaver and enslaved, and how the enslaved used their environment to have some control over their futures. It highlights not only the indignities and suffering of that terrible institution, but also ways in which the human spirit could triumph.

Marvin Rees

(b. 1972) politician

I N 2016, MARVIN Rees made history when he was elected
Mayor of Bristol, thus becoming the first directly elected
Black mayor in the UK and the first directly elected mixed-race
mayor in Europe. Rees's roots are in Bristol and its community;
born to a Welsh mother and a Jamaican father, he spent his
formative years in Easton and Lawrence Weston, a place he
described as the underbelly of Bristol: two of the most deprived
wards of the city, and two of the most deprived areas in Britain.

Growing up on a council estate, Rees was constantly made
aware of being different; he was the only mixed-race child in
his class, and it was 'normal' to be racially abused. As the riots
raged in the Caribbean community of St Pauls in the 1980s, he
was asked which side he would take in a war between Black and
white people. Over time, he began to reject the idea that he
should see his mixed-race identity as a problem; rather, it was
placing people in categories that was the problem; specifically,
how they reduce and restrict people.[1]

Receiving advanced degrees in political theory and global
economic development from the University of Swansea and
Eastern University in the United States, Rees won a place on the

prestigious World Fellows Program at Yale University, working for campaign and community groups, focusing on inner-city poverty. This has helped to shape his political approach: one that is based on social justice and investing in people to develop their talents. A career including broadcast journalism, community outreach and NHS development, during which he delivered a programme for race equality in mental healthcare across south-west England, indicates that empowerment of individuals and communities is a key motivator for Rees.

Marvin Rees's electoral victory in 2016 was symbolic, given Bristol's historical trajectory. The city was at one time Britain's premier slave-trading port, and the wealth created from the trade made Bristol one of the richest port cities in Britain. Evidence of its involvement in the trade and trafficking in Africans can still be recalled in its streets, public buildings, economic institutions and memorials. Bristol still struggles to face up to its terrible history: how human suffering under-pinned the city's expansion and enriched so many people. In 1963, St Pauls received national attention when the African Caribbean community staged a boycott to protest against the colour bar that had been established by the union representing the bus company, which prevented the employment of African Caribbeans at the Bristol Bus Company.

Today, the city is characterised by significant inequalities, as outlined in the report by the Runnymede Trust and the Centre on Dynamics of Ethnicity. That report painted a stark picture of a city divided, revealing that Black and ethnic minority Bristolians face the greatest disadvantages in education and employment in England and Wales.[2] Young people from BAME backgrounds are leaving school without any qualifica-tions at a much higher rate than their white counterparts.

Rees has been keen to address the social inequalities in Bristol, which he has described as 'embarrassing'. He has been working to create schemes to improve social mobility by setting up the Bristol Leadership Programme, helping twelve high-ability people from impoverished backgrounds to develop their skills and talents through an intensive course of study and mentoring. He has also called upon the major employment sectors in the city to work together to ensure poverty and inequality are removed, while pledging to build two thousand homes, protect children's centres and tackle the effects of gentrification on communities.

Bill Richmond and Thomas Molyneux

(1763–1829 / 1784–1818) bare-knuckle boxers

P RIZEFIGHTING BEGAN AS a sport in Britain in 1719, when
James Figg (1684–1734) became widely recognised as the
first English bare-knuckle boxing champion. A cruel and
unforgiving sport, a test of mental and physical endurance,
fights would not end until one of the boxers could no longer
stand or continue, and fights could last for hours. It was not
until the late eighteenth century that the first Black prizefighter
was recorded as participating in a fight. Joe Lashley, described
as an African, fought and beat Tom Treadway at Marylebone
Fields, London, on 13 June 1791.[1] According to the nineteenth-century sportswriter Pierce Egan, Lashley 'evinced great
activity, skill and games, portraying knowledge of the art superior to most amateurs. Treadway never properly recovered from
the effects of this severe contest.'[2] Up until this fight, Treadway
had not been defeated, which suggests that Lashley was a skilled
fighter; nothing more, unfortunately, is known about him or
any subsequent fights he may have had.

The lives and careers of Bill Richmond and Thomas
Molyneux are more extensively documented, giving an insight
into the world of nineteenth-century pugilism and the Black

men who succeeded in transcending the prejudices of the crowd and established successful careers. Richmond is considered the first Black fighter to have made a mark on the sport of prizefighting, and was one of the most prominent Black men in the Georgian period. His achievements were almost impeccable, having only lost two fights in his career. Many of the Black fighters who came after him, including Molyneux, benefitted from his guidance and mentorship.

Richmond's remarkable life story begins with him being born enslaved, in 1763, in Richmond Town, Staten Island, New York, in the possession of one Revd Richard Charlton. An encounter with Brigadier General Hugh Percy, a commander in the British army during the American War of Independence, changed Richmond's fate. There are two conflicting accounts of how the two met: one account says Percy was invited to dine at Revd Charlton's home and was impressed by Richmond's manners and conduct. Another account claims that Richmond beat up three soldiers who were harassing him while he was tending to their horses; it was, apparently, his fighting ability that impressed Percy. The first appears to be the more convincing account; for motives that remain unclear, Richmond was permitted by Charlton, a loyalist during the conflict, to enter into Percy's service. Richmond accompanied Percy back to England in May 1777, where he arranged for him to receive an education in Yorkshire and an apprenticeship in cabinet making. By the mid-1790s, Richmond is documented as working as a cabinet maker in London, married and with a family.

The basis for Richmond's early fights appears to have been responses to racial abuse. Luke Williams, who has written an excellent biography of Richmond, writes that his unusual position as an educated Black man in the white-dominated society of the late eighteenth century meant he was probably racially abused often, the effects of which may have drawn him towards pugilism as a profession. His first fight was with George Moore, known as 'Docky' Moore, a fearsome fighter who insulted Richmond at the York racecourse; when the fight took place is not known, possibly in the late 1780s. Williams writes that the fight lasted twenty-five minutes, during which Richmond 'punished Docky so completely that he gave in, and was taken out of the ring totally blind'. A pattern of fights followed in which Richmond, often accosted and abused, used his fists to assert himself against racial insults from his tormentors, which, like other Black people living in England in this period, he faced daily.

Prizefighting as a profession drew Richmond to London – and into an association with Thomas Pitt, Lord Camelford, a member of the Pitt political family, for whom he possibly worked as a servant or bodyguard. Lord Camelford was a huge supporter and lover of prize-fighting, and he and Richmond attended many fights. However, it wasn't until 1804 that Richmond, who was at least forty-one, fought his first prize-fight, a decision that Williams argues was because of the fortune that he could make – boxing was the biggest and most popular sport in England, and drew supporters from all social classes. Richmond was the first Black bare-knuckle boxer to achieve fame and recognition. Although he did not win the national boxing championship, he nevertheless enjoyed a remarkably successful career, winning seventeen matches and losing only two. Money earned from fights allowed him to become land-lord of the Horse and Dolphin public house in Leicester Square, London, and to hire rooms where fighters could train.

Pierce Egan has credited Richmond with being the first pugilist who fought stripped to the waist, and suggested he was responsible for placing the boxing ring on a raised platform so spectators could have a better view of fights. He was known as one of the most skilled trainers in the country and acted as trainer and mentor to Thomas Molyneux.

Molyneux's origins are ambiguous. Various accounts claim he was born enslaved, possibly in Virginia in the USA, and that he won his freedom through fighting after defeating his enslaved opponent from another plantation, thus winning his master a considerable amount of money. It is believed that Molyneux either used his winnings to travel to England, having been told about the money pugilists could earn there, or he ended up in New York, where he fought several contests before travelling to England in 1809. Again, though, it is unclear how he made his way to England; signing on with a crew ship and earning his passage is a possible explanation. It has also been suggested he was either born free or enslaved in a northern state. In any case, Molyneux may have wanted to create an air of mystery around his early life as part of his narrative and introduction into the world of English prizefighting. Whatever the truth, Molyneux and Richmond overcame the lives they were born into, ones of incredible disadvantage that were not structured to be without bondage.

How Richmond met Molyneux is not known, but he did arrange and manage his first fight, with a fighter called Jack Burrows, in July 1810, with Burrows conceding defeat after an hour of fighting. Molyneux's style was described as unconventional but effective. In December of that year, he was matched with Tom Cribb, the current English champion, and who had beaten Richmond. Molyneux fought Cribb twice and lost on both occasions; that said, Molyneux exhibited great strength and endurance in those encounters. These fights were significant in that there was a possibility that a Black man could be crowned English boxing champion in 1810, which would have undermined the intensely negative ways Africans had been represented over time. The country's honour was literally at stake. Although Molyneux did not win either of his matches with Cribb, he demonstrated he was Cribb's equal in terms of skill, strength and endurance, and in many of the rounds was superior to Cribb. Their first match lasted thirty-nine rounds, with both men sustaining terrible injuries. Cribb was knocked out in the twenty-ninth round and did not regain consciousness for thirty seconds: the fight should have ended, but it was not stopped. Years after the fight, Pierce Egan wrote that '[Molyneux's] first contest with Cribb will be long remembered by the sporting world. It will also not be forgotten, if justice holds the scales, that his colour alone prevented him from becoming hero of that fight.'[3]

Both Molyneux and Richmond became wealthy and successful boxers in Georgian England, and Richmond, who made money from and for Molyneux, was probably the first Black boxing promoter in England. Richmond helped turn Molyneux into one of the best fighters of his time, and Richmond himself was regarded as one of the leading pugilists; he was invited to serve as usher at the coronation of George IV, himself a fan of the fights.

Marcia Rigg

mental health activist

SINCE SEAN RIGG's death in police custody in 2008, his family have campaigned for the truth to be revealed into the circumstances of his death and who was accountable for it. In the process, that search has been critical in exposing the failings of the police and the body tasked with investigating it: the (then) Independent Police Complaints Commission (IPCC). The campaign also placed the efficacy of the mental health system under the spotlight, initiating major independent reviews into related agencies. The family's fight also laid bare the similar challenges and struggles faced by other families of people who have died in police custody, as well as the disproportionate dangers faced by Black men and people with mental illnesses when they encounter the police.

Handsome, intelligent and artistic, Sean (b. 1968) had also suffered from schizophrenia for half of his life. A talented rapper and musician, during breakdowns he would become paranoid and aggressive; when he was well, he wrote and performed music, and travelled. A long-term patient, his breakdowns were usually brought about by him not taking his medication, unable to handle the side effects which brought on depression and hallucinations. Rigg carried his passport with him as identification in the event he had a breakdown, so that authorities could call his older sister Marcia, who was his next of kin and part of his care team. During a mental health crisis in London, August 2008, Sean Rigg was arrested and restrained by four police officers, and held in the back of a police van. He died of cardiac arrest while in the 'care' of the police.

Sean's death changed Marcia's life, making her an activist and campaigner, critical of the mental health system that failed her brother, and of the police who criminalised him. From the beginning, the family was keen to maintain control over Sean's image and narrative, for him not to be demonised by the media. Although they were Sean's family, they found themselves shut out of the investigation, alarmed at how the police involved were treated as witnesses, not suspects, able to confer among themselves and not being questioned for seven months. With Sean's body 'belonging to the state', the family waited seven weeks before it was released for burial; information about the detail of events around his death was incomplete, and they were highly sceptical of how a physically fit young man could collapse and die. Marcia Rigg realised they would have to engage in a mass campaign to pressure the police for answers. She spoke to various media outlets, the police met MPs and community activists, and she set up the Sean Rigg Justice and Change campaign to keep his case in the public consciousness.

The Riggs's campaigning gave rise to significant public interest, informing changes in policing practice. It demonstrated that the IPCC led a flawed investigation into Sean's death. Ruling that the police involved had no case to answer, the watchdog was forced to backtrack when the inquest into Sean's death was highly critical of the 'unsuitable level of force' used on him before his death, finding that he had been restrained in the 'prone position' for eight minutes, a length of time that 'more than minimally' contributed to his death. The inquest verdict led to the establishment of an independent commission on mental health and policing, and an external review of the IPCC's investigation.

Despite these outcomes, police accountability for Sean's death has not been achieved. Although one police officer was charged with perjury and acquitted, most recently, the officers involved have been cleared of any misconduct: a major setback for the family, and a decision regarded by the family and their supporters as proof of the ability of the police to act with impunity.

323

Ignatius Sancho

(1729?–80) writer, composer, shopkeeper

IGNATIUS SANCHO WAS a member of Georgian London's literati, a cultural icon and businessman. Because of his education, social mobility and economic stability, his life was exceptional by eighteenth-century standards. He gained posthumous fame as a man of letters, particularly his correspondence with the novelist Laurence Sterne, and he is the first known Black man to have voted in Britain. His death in 1780 was announced in the *Gentleman's Magazine*; his obituary was listed among those people deemed to be 'considerable persons'. His book, which was published two years after his death, attracted over 1,200 subscribers and sold out the first edition. During his time he was thought of as the 'extraordinary Negro', and to opponents of the slave trade became a symbol of the humanity of Africans.

From the early modern period (1500 to 1800), blackness signified colonialism, the slave trade and plantation slavery. By the eighteenth century, these economic systems, along with the English manufacturing industries that had begun to operate within a profitable interlocking network, gave rise to racist ideas, transmitted largely through the written word, with their foundations in economic and political justifications. The writer Peter Fryer noted that 'racism crystallised in print in Britain in the eighteenth century as the ideology of plantocracy, the class of sugar planters and slave merchants, that dominated England's Caribbean colonies'.[1]

The growing Black British communities tended to undermine established racial tropes. There existed a variety of experiences within these communities; enslaved servants, freedmen and women, runaways, the military, musicians, labourers and sailors lived among the indigenous population. There is evidence that they supported each other, socialised together, and had, in some cases, job and social mobility. They organised politically as the slave trade came under intense public and political scrutiny, and protest took shape in autobiographies, public correspondence and literary works.[2] Britain, and London especially, was transformed by the Black presence and alarmed those who believed Black people were becoming, as the magistrate Sir John Fielding asserted, a dangerous and corrupting presence, commenting that it was the practice of Black people 'intoxicated with liberty . . . to make it their business to corrupt and dissatisfy the mind of every fresh black servant that comes to England'.[3] Slavery was under threat while Black people shared common experiences with whites in Britain, or represented themselves, as Sancho did in his life and his letters, as people with depth, intelligence and nuance.

Ignatius Sancho is said to have been born in 1729 on board a slave ship that was sailing from Guinea to the Spanish Caribbean. According to his biography written by Joseph Jekyll, his mother died while he was an infant, and his father committed suicide to escape enslavement. Aged around two, he was brought to London and was forced to work as a slave for three sisters living in Greenwich. As an adult, Sancho recalled that the sisters 'judged ignorance the best and only security for obedience and believed to enlarge the mind of their slave would go near to emancipate his person'.[4]

During this time, he met John, 2nd Duke of Montagu (1690–1749) who lived nearby in Blackheath. Montagu admired Sancho's 'native frankness of manner as yet unbroken by servitude', and gave him books and encouraged his education.[5] After the Duke's death, Sancho ran away from the house in Greenwich and persuaded the Duke's widow to employ him as a butler. He served the Duchess until her death, upon which she left him £70 and an annuity of £30. He remained in the service of the Montagu family for twenty years.

Sancho was free to indulge in his passion for reading, the theatre and music. He composed music and appeared on the stage. He befriended David Garrick, the great English actor, was taken up by London's artistic and literary circles, and was famous enough to be painted by Thomas Gainsborough, one of the century's most important artists, in 1768. He began a friendship with the novelist Laurence Sterne (author of *The Life and Opinions of Tristram Shandy, Gentleman*) in 1766, after he wrote to express his admiration for his work and asked him to write something on behalf of enslaved Africans. Sterne replied to Sancho and kept copies of the letters, which were published in 1775.

Sancho married Anne Osborne, a Caribbean woman, and had seven children with her. He left the service of the Montagus in 1773 and used the annuity left to him by the Duchess to open a grocery shop in Charles Street, Westminster. As a business owner he was eligible to vote, which he did in 1780, the year that he died.

Sancho's achievements, his published letters and musical compositions, and the friendships he cultivated which allowed him to move within fashionable Georgian society, would not have been possible had he not taken advantage of opportunities presented to him through education. His letters show he was aware that his position in society was unusual, and that it was the moral imperative of diasporic Africans such as himself to prove to whites that Africans possessed genius. Although Sancho did not write exclusively against slavery, his writings represent an early argument against it. Historian Gretchen Gerzina notes that '[as] a quite possibly middle-class, well connected and highly literate Black man in all of Britain, Sancho's very visible existence affected how thousands of people viewed Africans and slavery'.[6]

Stafford Scott

community activist, campaigner

STAFFORD SCOTT IS a veteran community campaigner, race equality consultant and co-ordinator of the Tottenham Rights group. For over thirty years, he has been challenging discriminatory laws and policies, and holding the police to account over tactics and practices that disproportionately impact on the lives and liberties of Black British people.

As a young man growing up Tottenham, north London, he and other young Black men experienced significant levels of police harassment, which politicised him and deepened his commitment to challenging racism and racist policies, and the abuses of civil and political rights.

In 1985, Broadwater Farm resident Cynthia Jarrett died of heart failure brought on by an unauthorised police raid on her home. The police had arrested her son earlier on suspicion of theft and assault (he was later acquitted of both charges). Ms Jarrett's death, the police's disregard of the family's anguish and the poor relations between the police and the Black community were the triggers that led to the Broadwater Farm estate uprising. Police officer Keith Blakelock was killed, and three men, Winston Silcott, Engin Raghip and Mark Braithwaite, were convicted of his murder two years after the uprising.[1] Believing these men to be innocent of the murder, Scott co-founded the Broadwater Farm Defence Campaign, a lobby group established to overturn their convictions. In 1991, the campaign finally succeeded and the convictions were quashed.

Since that campaign, Scott has continued to push for racial equality and community engagement. He has worked as project director for the Bernie Grant Trust and is a race advocacy officer for Tottenham Rights, part of the Monitoring Group, an anti-racist charity that promotes civil rights and has led many campaigns to support families whose loved ones have died through racist or state violence. The Monitoring Group has represented the families of Kuldip Singh Sekhon, Ricky Reel, Stephen Lawrence and Zahid Mubarek in their campaigns to get justice for their sons.

Scott has been described as the 'corner man' supporting the families in some of Britain's high-profile cases involving deaths of people after interactions with the police.[2] Since 2011 he has been supporting the family of Mark Duggan, whose death after being shot by the police sparked the 2011 uprisings in London and other cities. Scott maintains that the police response to Duggan's shooting was the reason for the escalation of the uprisings, and that there are discrepancies and unanswered questions that have rendered the investigations into Duggan's death flawed.[3] He has also spoken of behalf of the family of Rashan Charles, who died in 2017 after he was arrested and restrained by a police officer at a shop in Dalston.

Scott is a harsh critic of the police's 'Gangs Matrix' database, which he argues racially discriminates and stigmatises young Black men and targets people who are unlikely to commit offences. The database, he says, is racialised; it captures not only the names of those alleged to have been involved in serious gang violence, but also the information of their friends and associates, with little or no evidence of them having used violence or being a gang member.

In 2020, the Metropolitan Police removed nearly four hundred names from the database; however, Scott feels they haven't gone far enough, insisting that at least twice as many names should have been removed.

Scott has said he makes no apologies for challenging the officers with whom he works. Cressida Dick, Metropolitan Police Commissioner and former operational commander for Trident, told him that he was hard work, 'but do not stop doing what you do, the Met needs people like you to hold us to account!'[4]

Mary Seacole

(1805–81) nurse, war heroine

ALTHOUGH MARY SEACOLE is celebrated today as a heroine of the Crimean War and a pioneering nurse and doctress, greatly admired in her lifetime for her service, immediately after her death in 1881 her name and exploits slipped from public memory. Approaching a century and a half after her death, though, she has achieved iconic status; her experiences make her an impressive woman in any century. She was a woman of colour who often travelled without a chaperone, who self-financed her journey to the Crimea, setting up her own boarding house to treat sick and injured soldiers, and who was a skilled medical practitioner who developed treatments for yellow fever and cholera, two of the deadliest diseases of the time. In 2004, Seacole topped the poll as the Greatest Black Briton and, in 2016, a statue of her likeness was unveiled in front of St Thomas' Hospital after many years of campaigning. The first statue of a named Black woman in Britain, it is a recognition of Seacole's many contributions to medical advancement and as a nurse.

To appreciate Mary's accomplishments, they must be understood in the context of the time in which she lived. She was born Mary Grant in Kingston, Jamaica, in 1805, at the height of slavery in the British Caribbean. The trade and trafficking in Africans would not cease for another two years; and slavery itself would not be abolished until 1838. She was the child of a free Jamaican woman of mixed heritage, who ran a hotel called Blundell Hall, where British officers and their families would meet to socialise or convalesce. Mary's mother was a doctress – a healer who combined African culture with Caribbean herbal remedies to treat ailments and illnesses, and she was highly regarded for this skill among the officers and soldiers stationed in Jamaica.

Mary's father was likely a Scottish lieutenant in the British Army. Jamaican society at that time was subject to strict racial hierarchies and one's colour determined how far one rose socially. As a woman of mixed heritage, Mary was able to enjoy certain freedoms that the majority of the (Black) population could not. She was a free person in a slave society, unable to vote or hold public office; however, as a member of the free coloured classes, she enjoyed privileges, such as being able to travel to England, which Mary undertook on several occasions in the early 1820s. She learned to be a doctress by watching her mother, observing how she treated patients and copying what she did, first using her doll as her patient. When she got older, she worked with her mother at Blundell Hall; she was often in charge of nurses and sometimes on duty herself at the wards of Up Park, the military camp in Kingston. Her parents' ties with the army and doctors meant that Mary gained invaluable knowledge and experience, which she combined with her own skill as a healer.

According to Seacole's biographer Jane Robinson, she developed her entrepreneurial spirit during a trip to London. Describing it as a place for adventurers, it was the hub of imperial commerce, and she returned a second time to sell a large stock of West Indian pickles and preserves in 1823. She was eighteen and unaccompanied, which suggests she was a confident young woman with a clear vision of what she wanted from life.

In 1836, Mary Grant married Edwin Seacole, who died in 1844. In 1851 Seacole moved to Panama, where she opened a hotel with her brother Edward. Present at the time of a cholera outbreak, she gained extensive knowledge of the disease when she had to perform an autopsy on one of its victims.

When Britain, France and Turkey declared war on Russia in 1854, many of the soldiers based in Jamaica were transferred to Europe. The Allies attacked the Russian fleet and its harbour in Sevastopol to cut off Russian supplies. They did not, however, establish enough support services for the large contingents of men employed for that offensive. Soldiers lacked food, medicine, tents and medical support. This was compounded by poor hygiene, and disease became rampant. Of the 20,000 British soldiers killed in the Crimea, 2755 died in battle and 17,580 died of disease.[1]

Seacole was convinced that her knowledge of tropical diseases could be an important contribution to the war effort. She was also excited to witness the war, writing in her autobiography that 'when I was told that many of the regiments I had known so well in Jamaica had left for England for the scene of action, the desire to join them became stronger than ever'. Confident of her abilities, she presented herself at the War Office to serve as a hospital nurse, but her offer was rejected; undeterred, she approached the quartermaster-general's department and the medical department, who also rebuffed her applications. Her attempt to appeal to the Crimean Fund also failed. Facing the fact that her skin colour was the reason for her rejection, she resolved to travel to the Crimea independently.

She set up a general store and hotel business with a Mr Day, near the British camp. Mary became a 'sutler' – a person who follows the army, selling provisions to the troops. In 1855, she opened the British Hotel near Sevastopol, tending to the sick and injured, often under heavy artillery fire. The soldiers called her 'Mother Seacole'; W. H. Russell, the first war correspondent, called her 'a warm and successful physician, who doctors and cures all manner of men with extraordinary success. She is always in attendance near the battlefield to aid the wounded and has earned many a poor fellow's blessings.'

Mary Seacole's bright personality lit up the war zone and brought comfort to the men under her care. What she had aimed to do by travelling to the Crimea was to be of some use to the soldiers and to discharge her strong sense of duty. Her interest was not in advancing hygiene in war zones, but to give comfort and solace, and to use her skills to heal the sick and injured. Mary Seacole was more than a nurse; she was an adventurer. She was celebrated by *Punch* magazine as 'our own lifeline for suffering soldiers'; she was both ahead of her time and made history on her own terms, and was literally a self-made woman.

Menelik Shabazz

*(b. 1954) film and documentary
maker, producer, writer*

M ENELIK SHABAZZ IS one of the pioneers of independent
Black British cinema. With a career spanning over forty
years, Shabazz has represented the lives of Black Britons through
his documentaries and movies in a more truthful and balanced
way, empowering their voices and offering alternatives to the
distortions presented by the mainstream media. His first
feature-length film, *Burning an Illusion* (1981), was only the
second feature to be directed by a Black individual and remains
a Black British classic.

Born Thomas Braithwaite in Barbados, Shabazz came to
England in 1961 to join his family in north London. A talented
tennis player, Shabazz found himself in a white middle-class
world, which he was both a part of and that was at odds with
his interest in the burgeoning Black Power movement of the
late 1960s and early 1970s. Reading Malcolm X and African
American history books influenced Shabazz's political awakening. Braithwaite subsequently changed his name to Menelik
Shabazz, in honour of Menelik I, Emperor of Ethiopia, and
Malcolm X (El-Hajj Malik el-Shabazz).

Being introduced to the video Portapak system as a student ignited his interest in filmmaking. The freedom the equipment offered opened a new world for him. He spent six months at the London International Film School studying with people equally passionate about film. The short period he spent there taught him enough to give him the confidence to strike out on his own as a filmmaker.

In the post-*Windrush* era, films such as *Sapphire* (1959) and *A Taste of Honey* (1961) that featured Black characters usually explored the tensions between sex and race. It was not until 1976, when Horace Ové directed the first Black feature film, *Pressure*, that the exploration of what it meant to be Black and British began to be a topic explored in British films. The thirty-minute *Step Forward Youth* (1977) saw Shabazz documenting the conversations among Black youth in Brixton. He gave them the space to talk about themselves, their experiences at school, with the police and their parents. Their stories of police harassment and racism in school were in stark contrast to the optimism of their parents who settled in Britain with the intention of helping to rebuild the 'mother country'. It was one of the first times young Black people were seen on screen giving their own perspectives on the issues affecting their lives, and instantly made an impact. The success of *Step Forward Youth* allowed Shabazz to make *Breaking Point* (1978), which was commissioned by ATV. It shone a light on how the 'sus' laws were being disproportionately used to police Caribbean youth in London and other cities, which was causing a lot of anger and bitterness in Black communities. *Breaking Point* was the first documentary by a Black director to be broadcast on British television, and was notable for its commentary led by Black scholars, lawyers and activists; its success helped lead to the repeal of the notorious 'sus' laws.

The 1980s saw the emergence of the independent film workshop movement. The newly established Channel 4 was committed to showcasing the work of filmmakers who worked outside of the mainstream broadcasting and film industries. From these new initiatives emerged Black film collectives that produced some of the most politically uncompromising Black films. Ceddo Film and Video Workshop, founded by Shabazz, Imruh Bakari Caesar and Milton Bryan, made films that offered a critique of the British establishment's treatment of its Black citizens, and documentaries on African and Caribbean politics and history. These early documentaries were born out of a compulsion to act, using the tools at hand – in this case, the camera – to give voices to the unheard, the ignored and marginalised.

Ceddo's first film for Channel 4 immediately ran afoul of objections from the Independent Broadcasting Authority. *The People's Account* (1985) documented the Broadwater Farm uprising in Tottenham. Ceddo was unwilling to retract the film's description of the police as racist and of the uprising as an act of legitimate self-defence, which resulted in the film being pulled from the schedules and never broadcast.

Shabazz is best known for his full-length feature film *Burning an Illusion* (1981), which was ground-breaking in that its protagonist was a Black woman. It centres on the life of Pat (Cassie McFarlane), who dreams of meeting 'Mr Right' and settling down. Meeting Del (Victor Romero Evans) and him moving in with her seems to fulfil her romantic fantasies initially, but relationship challenges and social forces threaten to destroy Pat's dreams. What is refreshing about the film is its ordinariness – the characters were not racialised, they were depicted as people with relatable human failings and aspirations. *Burning an Illusion* won the Grand Prix at the Amiens

International Film Festival in 1982; and Cassie McFarlane won the *Evening Standard* British Film Award for Most Promising Newcomer.

Regrettably, *Burning an Illusion* did not open doors to bigger projects for Shabazz. He channelled his frustrations into a new publication, *Black Filmmakers Magazine*, in which he showcased the world of Black cinema, and passed his knowledge and experience on to the next generation. Similarly, he set up the BFM International Film Festival to give Black independent filmmakers an opportunity to showcase their work. One of the founders of Black British cinema, Menelik Shabazz is one of its most strident voices, committed to redressing the imbalance of Black representation on film and television from the 1970s up to the present.

Yinka Shonibare CBE, RA

(b. 1962) artist

I N HIS 1998 installation *Mr and Mrs Andrews Without their Heads*, Yinka Shonibare offers a satirical rendering of Thomas Gainsborough's 1750 painting *Mr and Mrs Andrews*. The latter is an iconic representation of English gentry, and one of the most recognised eighteenth-century works of art; it is a portrait of a newly married couple that features Mr Andrews standing with his gun under his arm and his dog beside him, while Mrs Andrews is seated on a bench, in a dress of blue silk.

Shonibare's version reprises this portrait with two headless mannequins, dressed in Victorian-style West African batik costumes. He uses this clothing as a comment on authenticity; ironically, West African batik fabrics are actually Indonesian fabrics produced by the Dutch for the Indonesian market, which were then introduced into the African market when they failed to sell.

The figures are headless, which adds to their lack of identity, and their skin is an orangey tone that speaks to the ambiguity of their race. Shonibare takes the aristocratic figures from Gainsborough and dresses them in working-class fabrics from

Africa to achieve a kind of parody that examines the socio-political effects of the complex interrelationship between Europe and Africa, challenging the roles of history and positions of power, past and present.[1]

This tangled relationship between Europe and Africa, and their intertwined economic and political histories as a result of colonialism, are a theme that runs throughout Shonibare's work – as are race, class and wealth.[2] He works in the media of sculpture, painting, photography, film and installation to explore his binary Nigerian and British identities, and his creations have made him one of the most distinctive artists working today.

Shonibare was born in London and moved to Lagos, Nigeria, when he was three years old. He later returned to England to attend university. Growing up in Lagos, he experienced a lot of colonial influences – he attended Catholic school where he was taught by Irish nuns; he learned British nursery rhymes and spoke English at school while speaking Yoruba at home. He learned to navigate between two cultures, conscious of the value placed on a Western education above a traditional Nigerian one, which emphasised the power disparity between Europe and Africa.[3]

Shonibare completed his first degree at Byam Shaw School of Art (now Central Saint Martins), London, after being hospitalised for a year due to transverse myelitis, a disorder caused by the inflammation of the spinal cord, which paralysed one side of his body.

His art evolved through an interrogation of authenticity when one of his teachers expected him, as an African, to produce 'authentic' African art. Shonibare began to consider what was authentic – what was African, or European? The knowledge that African batik prints were not 'authentically' African, although appropriated as a symbol of African-ness, influenced Shonibare's thinking about the greater significance of his multicultural identity, Britain's relationship to its former colonies, and how he and African people generally find their identities within this relationship.

Shonibare has said the complexity in his work 'arises from the fact that while I critique the establishment, I also want to become part of it as well'.[4] In his piece *Diary of a Victorian Dandy* (1998), Shonibare created a series of photographs depicting himself as a dandy who is an outsider trying to gain access to the establishment. While the installation engages with the construction of identity and is a nostalgic representation of British heritage, it also reflects traits of the artist's own life within the art world, that he is the outsider who wants to be on the inside.

Shonibare was nominated for the Turner Prize in 2004, and notable commissions include *Gallantry and Criminal Conversation* (2002), which first earned him international recognition. The latter is a work inspired by the 'Grand Tour', a trip taken by wealthy young English men and women of the seventeenth and eighteenth centuries to study the art, culture and history of Europe. In his work, Shonibare explores how the Grand Tour was educational in both public and private ways: he reveals that it offered a kind of sexual tourism of Europe (adultery was called 'criminal conversation' at the time). Another work, *Nelson's Ship in a Bottle*, was the 2010 Fourth Plinth Commission for Trafalgar Square, London, where it was displayed until 2012 in close proximity to Nelson's Column. The first Trafalgar Square plinth commission from a Black British artist, today it is on permanent display outside the entrance of the National Maritime Museum in Greenwich.

In 2013 Shonibare was elected as a Royal Academician, and in 2019 he was awarded the CBE.

Paul Stephenson OBE

(b. 1937) civil rights campaigner

I N 1963, PAUL Stephenson forced the Bristol Omnibus Company to abandon its racist recruitment policy designed to exclude African Caribbeans from working as bus drivers or conductors. In so doing, he helped pave the way for Britain's first race relations laws. The boycott marked the beginning of a lifetime of activism for Stephenson, who would challenge racist policies in all areas of life and dedicate his time to working to unify Black and white communities throughout the world.

In the 1940s and 1950s, a steady stream of Caribbeans arrived in Bristol; many were invited to fill the labour shortages Britain was experiencing after the war, and to work in the newly created National Health Service. As more and more Caribbeans began to settle in Britain, however, white British people started to call for controls on migration from the Commonwealth. By 1963, six thousand Caribbean people lived in Bristol, and new arrivals were subjected to racial discrimination, finding it difficult to find well-paid jobs, and were only able to find affordable homes in the heavily bombed areas of St Pauls and Easton. In this period, Bristol became a de facto segregated city, with whites closing ranks against Caribbeans.

The city's most powerful employer, the Bristol Omnibus Company, had a colour bar, preventing Caribbeans from working as drivers and conductors. This policy had been in place since 1955, when the Transport and General Workers' Union, which represented the bus company's workers, introduced a resolution to exclude Caribbeans, thus allaying white people's fears of having to compete for jobs and protecting their wages.

Three men, Roy Hackett, Owen Henry and Peter Carty, were determined to expose the company's colour bar and the union. They established the West Indian Development Council, along with Prince Brown and Audley Evans. Paul Stephenson, formerly in the RAF, had trained in youth work and, when he came to Bristol in 1962 to work as the city's first Black youth officer, joined the organisation. Born in Essex, Stephenson was of English and West African parentage, and was influenced by the civil rights movement in the United States, thinking their tactics could be effective in Britain. Stephenson recalled, 'I was committed to what [Martin] Luther King was doing, so I decided we'd do something here . . . I learned the technique of a boycott that King and Jesse Jackson were doing; it was the boycott I was going to bring to Britain.'

Stephenson established that the Bristol Omnibus Company was operating a colour bar by setting up a job interview between the bus company and a young man named Guy Bailey. Bailey was educated, employed and a part-time student whose qualifications got him an interview as a conductor, but once Stephenson let the bus company know he was West Indian, the interview was cancelled, with the general manager confirming they did not employ 'coloureds' as bus crew.

In defiance of Bristol's racial segregation, the West Indian Development Council announced that no Black people would travel on buses owned by Bristol Omnibus. The boycott was part of a larger strategy to get national attention and for the issue to be discussed in Parliament. Stephenson enlisted the support of Tony Benn, Bristol's MP, who condemned the bus company, and contacted Harold Wilson, the Labour leader, who spoke out against the colour bar at an anti-apartheid rally in London. Learie Constantine, the cricketer, lawyer and diplomat who himself had successfully sued a British hotel for its colour bar policy in 1943, also lent his support. The boycott revealed how divisive the city was on race, with feelings running high on both sides. Stephenson saw it as racial injustice and expressed it as such: 'My line was simply this: this is an employment issue, if the unions don't like it they can go to hell . . . the employer should say "we're not accepting this kind of racism" and tell the workers, if they don't like it they can lump it!"'

As the bus company and the Transport and General Workers' Union faced local and international criticism, Bristol Omnibus was forced to end its colour bar in August 1963. Within a month, the bus company hired Raghbir Singh as its first non-white conductor, employing Caribbeans days later.

The boycott heavily influenced the 1965 Race Relations Act, which was passed by the Labour government after meeting with Stephenson, Hackett and Bailey. It forbade discrimination on the grounds of colour, race or national origins, and was expanded three years later to include both housing and employment. In 1976 the Act was amended to include direct and indirect discrimination. Harold Wilson himself conceded that without Paul's efforts, it would have been difficult for the Labour government to introduce these laws.

Stephenson continued to work as an anti-racist campaigner, again receiving national attention in 1965 for refusing to leave a public house until he was served.

In 1972, he began working for the Commission for Racial Equality, ensuring that Black and minority ethnic people were being employed by the press and being fairly covered by it. While in London he met Muhammad Ali and worked with him to set up the Muhammad Ali Sports Development Association, encouraging BAME children to get involved in sports, such as tennis, with which they were not usually associated. His work with the Sports Council saw him campaign against sporting contacts with apartheid South Africa. In 1992 he set up the Bristol Black Archives Partnership to promote and protect the history of African Caribbean people in Bristol.

Paul Stephenson has received many awards for his campaigning work in Bristol, including the Freedom of the City. In 2009 he was awarded the OBE for his services to equal opportunities, and in 2017 he was the recipient of the Pride of Britain Lifetime Achievement Award.

Stormzy

(b. 1993) rapper, philanthropist, publisher, activist

'BRITAIN IS CURRENTLY teeming with fantastic MCs,' wrote the music critic Alexis Petridis, 'but Stormzy is the only one your dad knows the name of.'

Since 2017, Stormzy has achieved a level of fame and ubiquity unheard of by a grime rap artist. That year, his first album, *Gang Signs and Prayer*, went to number one, the first album of that genre to do so.

Stormzy is also the first grime artist and the first Black British solo artist to headline Glastonbury. 'With Glastonbury I wanted to achieve something iconic,' he said, 'I wanted it to be the greatest thing I'd ever done, I wanted it to be the pinnacle of my career, my defining moment.' His set that June evening in 2019 was a celebration of Black British culture, unfiltered, pure and uncensored. What was even more remarkable was that he had released only one album – it seemed that his charisma and talent had elevated Black British music into the public imagination in a profound way.

Hailing from Norbury, south London, of Ghanaian parents, Stormzy (Michael Ebenezer Kwadjo Omari Owuo), first received attention for his *Wicked Skengman* series of freestyles, beginning in 2013, which he would upload onto YouTube. Watching them now, one is struck by his confidence and self-belief, in his lyrics, style and delivery, that compelled him to pursue his music full time and abandon a job at an oil refinery in Southampton, such was his belief in his talent. His first EP, *Dreamers Disease*, won a MOBO award in 2014 for Best Grime Act. From *Wicked Skengman* in 2013, to winning a MOBO a year later, to blowing things up with his freestyle 'Shut Up' in 2015, to headlining Glastonbury four years later, speaks to an extraordinary level of dedication and commitment, as well as the ever-growing popularity of grime music and artists such as Dizzie Rascal, Skepta, Dave and more, despite attempts to curb the music and the culture via the 696 Risk Assessment Form. Introduced in 2005, this form discriminated against urban acts by shutting down gigs at short notice, preventing artists from establishing a following and making it harder for them to raise their profile. Although it was revoked in 2017, grime artists still face challenges.

It is clear that Stormzy's ambition is not only for himself; it extends to those he sees around him and to those who will come after him. He has not been afraid to be political and to take on his critics in an environment in which young Black men who speak out against injustice are vilified.

He has been highly critical of the way the government has handled the Grenfell tragedy, winning praise and condemnation in equal measure for his performance at the 2018 Brit Awards, which called attention to the lack of progress in housing the residents who lost their homes in the fire. The condemnation has come from those who think he should stick to rapping, to know his place, and be grateful for what this country has given him. Stormzy rejects this, fully aware of the impact his voice can have, and how his platform can help create opportunities for young Black people, enabling them to realise their ambitions. The impact of his support of the Labour Party in the 2019 election, encouraging people to register to vote, cannot be underestimated; artists such as Stormzy can reach and engage with young people in a way that politicians cannot.

In 2018, he set up Merky Books, an imprint of Penguin Random House, dedicated to publishing fiction, non-fiction and poetry by Black writers. He also set up the Stormzy Scholarships to support two Black students each year who win places at Cambridge University by covering their tuition fees and maintenance. These initiatives matter when you consider the reality that many Black people face when trying to advance in publishing and in education at elite institutions, where under-representation and lack of opportunities are systemic. The pioneering publisher Margaret Busby has described the battle for better representation in publishing as being no closer to being won; a *Financial Times* freedom of information request found that, between 2012 and 2016, Cambridge colleges admitted between one and zero Black students each year. Stormzy's interventions are his attempt to change the narrative.

Stormzy is more than a rapper, more than a grime artist. He is a socially conscious and socially aware young man who wants to bring everyone along, who is invested in Black excellence. 'Being so championed by my community,' he told the writer Reni Eddo-Lodge, 'I know it's my purpose to just shine a light where I can, just whatever I can, in any way, shape or form.'

Robert Wedderburn and
William Davidson

(1762–1835/1786–1820) revolutionary radicals

B LACK AND WHITE Britons alike were drawn to radical
working-class reform movements that emerged in the
late eighteenth and early nineteenth centuries. These radicals
argued that Parliament was corrupt and did not represent the
interests of the British working people. Consequently, the
attainment of political, economic and social freedoms was
dependent upon agitation, through the dissemination of
propaganda, petitioning Parliament and, if necessary, revolution. Those who followed the radical tradition and challenged
the government risked everything in the battles to win these
freedoms.

Two Black Britons played prominent roles in this movement. Robert Wedderburn and William Davidson were revolutionary socialists, followers of the radical Thomas Spence, who
was, according to Peter Fryer, 'a kind of agrarian communist'
who advocated universal suffrage and asserted that land should
be subject to communal ownership. Spenceans were prominent
in the Spa Fields Riots of 1816 and were the most serious and
determined revolutionaries in London.[1]

Wedderburn and Davidson led or were part of independent Spencean groups between 1817 and 1820.[2] As Black Britons they represented the antipathy towards imperialism within British radicalism, which was devoted to the working-class and anti-colonialist struggles, and which both challenged the ruling class. Wedderburn and Davidson's beliefs and activities cost one his life and the other his liberty. Their political ideology, which was brutally repressed and outlawed by the government, was shaped by their childhood experiences and lives as Black men living in the Caribbean and in Britain.

Robert Wedderburn was born in Kingston, Jamaica, to James Wedderburn, a doctor and slaveowner, and Rosanna, an African-born enslaved woman. Rosanna was sold while five months pregnant with Wedderburn, and she was sold again when Robert was five, on account of her 'violent and rebellious temper'. Growing up in a slave environment, Wedderburn experienced many of its destructive elements. Freed at birth, he lived between the worlds of the free and the enslaved; he witnessed the floggings of his grandmother on numerous occasions, and as a free 'mulatto', his own status was insecure – at any time it could be revoked. The loss of his mother, abandonment by his father and witnessing countless atrocities scarred Wedderburn for life. To escape the misery of the plantation, Wedderburn joined the navy when he was sixteen, serving on a privateer and a warship, arriving in London in 1778, aged seventeen.[3] Drawn to the Black community in St Giles in London, which consisted of runaway enslaved people and former sailors, he became part of that community who made a living using their wits as entertainers, beggars and petty thieves. He became aware of the divide between rich and poor, and as part of the visible group of Blacks, mulattoes and Lascars

(Indian sailors) he would have also been witness to, and victim of, disproportionate arrests, convictions and sentences of friends and associates. As historian Ron Ramdin notes, prejudice and social injustice 'sharpened his perceptions and honed his intelligence to a militant edge'.[4]

He made a meagre living as a jobbing tailor and selling pamphlets in St Martin's Lane, London; often the recession in his trade forced him back to sea, or to Edinburgh to beg for help from his father's family, without success.

One Sunday, he heard a Wesleyan preacher at Seven Dials and became interested in the ideas of unorthodox Christianity. He became a Unitarian preacher and wrote a pamphlet that rejected traditional Christian doctrine. An encounter with Thomas Spence had a profound impact on Wedderburn. Spence was a fierce opponent of slavery and saw links between that system and the system of English landed monopoly, which he believed to be the foundation of all inequality, hardship and oppression.[5] As a man born into the slave system, Wedderburn used Spence's political ideology to help articulate his own.

Wedderburn believed in the redistribution of land and property in the Caribbean and Britain. He linked the idea of revolution in the Caribbean with revolution in England, and believed that these revolutions should come about through violent means. He wrote further pamphlets denigrating Christianity and the clergy, and found ways of getting copies out to those still oppressed by slavery in Jamaica, where they whipped up fury in the colonial assembly.[6]

Wedderburn's politically extreme rhetoric and revolutionary propaganda alarmed the government, and he was placed under surveillance. Briefly locked up in Newgate jail in London, he was charged with 'blasphemous libel' and imprisoned for two years from 1831. Little is known of his contributions after he was released.

Wedderburn was a political leader whose struggles as a Black man and a member of the English working class deeply influenced his political ideology. Reform of the systems that oppressed Black and white alike could only be resolved through revolution. His commitment to the working classes and to the enslaved was uncompromising throughout his life as a radical.

William Davidson, eventually executed for his role in the Cato Street Conspiracy to assassinate the British cabinet, was born in Kingston, Jamaica, in 1781. His mother was a Black woman; his father was possibly either Alexander Davidson, a magistrate, or Duncan Davidson, a plantation owner.[7] Acknowledged and supported financially by his father, Davidson was sent to Scotland to study law, but he ran away to sea, spending the next decade on ships between the Caribbean and Britain, either willingly or pressed into service. After he was discharged, he learned the trade of cabinet making. In 1816 he became involved in radical politics and was an admirer of Thomas Paine, author of *Rights of Man*.

Davidson moved to London, where he struggled to make a living. In the weeks before his arrest he had not worked for several months, had pawned all his tools and had been picked up for begging in January 1820. He likely encountered appalling racism, which saw his life descend from tradesman to unemployed to beggar. The government response to political protest led by the people likely developed within him a disgust of the limitations of British liberty, which influenced his political activism.

Davidson was a member of the Marylebone Union Reading Society, which was formed in response to the Peterloo Massacre of 1819, in which eleven unarmed protesters against the Corn Laws had been killed.[8] The incident had radicals all over the country attending meetings to discuss political issues, practising drills and preparing themselves for armed struggle against government forces. Davidson would hold meetings of up to eighteen people in his home, and formed a shoemaker society; such societies were being formed around the country with the aim of mobilising the people to overthrow the government, and establish a provisional government that would introduce parliamentary and other reforms.[9] His activities would earn him a place on the list of thirty-three reformers compiled from reports by informants for the Home Secretary. Robert Wedderburn was also on this list.

Davidson was targeted by George Edwards, a police spy who took the cover of a radical. It has been argued that Edwards deliberately set up both Davidson and Arthur Thistlewood, one of London's influential radical leaders, by manipulating their anger over Peterloo. Drawing their attention to a false announcement planted by the government that the cabinet would be dining at the home of the Lord President of the Council, Lord Harrowby, in January 1820, Edwards suggested they assassinate the ministers as they sat down to dinner. The trap was set; Thistlewood, Davidson and others were caught at Cato Street, where they kept their weapons and ammunition. All co-conspirators were executed on 1 May 1820.

At his trial, Davidson remained defiant, and declared: 'I would willingly die as a martyr in liberty's cause for the good of my country and to be avenged on her tyrants. I joined the conspiracy for the public good. I would not have been stopped. Oh no, I would have gone through with it to the very bottom or else have perished in the attempt.'

Dame Sharon White DBE

(b. 1967) business leader, former senior civil servant

I N 2019, SHARON White, then chief executive of Ofcom, became chairman of the John Lewis Partnership, the operator of one of Britain's leading and oldest high-end department stores.

The appointment made White the first Black woman to lead one of the country's best-known department stores. When one thinks of chief executives of multibillion corporations, white, privately educated men usually come to mind. Sharon White, the daughter of Jamaican immigrants, who grew up in Leyton, east London, has been tearing down barriers since her first jobs in the civil service. Her impressive CV, which features many high-profile appointments – including chief executive of the media regulator Ofcom and Second Permanent Secretary at the Treasury, which made her one of the most powerful women at Whitehall – means that she is exceptionally qualified to be appointed as leader of one of the highest-profile jobs in retail.

Sharon White was one of the most outstanding civil servants of her generation. She had a stellar career in the civil service, working in different government departments including the

Ministry of Justice and the Department for International Development, before being put in charge of tax and public spending. Former Chancellor of the Exchequer Kenneth Clarke is a fan, describing her as 'one of the brightest people he has ever worked with'. She has spoken about how much she enjoyed public sector work, as it provided the opportunity to work on important topics that affected people's lives.

White's parents were part of the *Windrush* generation, arriving in Britain from Jamaica as teenagers. Her father worked for British Rail and her mother was a machinist, both of them leaving education at fourteen. In interviews, she has said that she senses that she has had opportunities that her parents did not have. She gained a place at Cambridge, where she read economics, and joined the civil service in 1989 as a graduate economist in what was the Department for Education and Science and also worked at the Treasury. She analysed US welfare reform at the British Embassy in Washington, undertaking a similar role as part of Prime Minister Tony Blair's policy unit at Number 10, eventually finding her way back to the Treasury. White was a talented and respected economist in a profession dominated by a white, privately educated Oxbridge 'old boys' network. It was an environment in which she not only thrived but excelled. She has attributed this to the support of Suma Chakrabarti, the Director General of Department for International Development (DFID), who she says mentored her and recognised her skills, allowing her to progress to senior roles. In turn, White has been active in coaching and mentoring women in the early stages of their careers.

It is worth noting that White worked in a sector that she says is doing well on gender disparity, but less so ethnically. In 2019, of the 445,480 civil servants working in the UK and overseas, only 3.4 per cent (11,990) were Black.[1] Only seventy were of the most senior grade, responsible for policy work or working closely with ministers. A study commissioned in 2015 by the then Cabinet Secretary Jeremy Heywood found that Black and Asian civil servants struggle within the service. Not having equal access to promotion, receiving lower marks in perform-ance reviews and being subject to open discrimination is still a way of life in some parts of Whitehall. Just as dispiriting was the news that, in 2016, none of the 339 Caribbean British applicants for the civil service fast stream managed to secure a place. The civil service is still a long way from being more repre-sentative, and with potentially most senior officials seeing things only from a white Oxbridge perspective, it means it becomes more likely that a scandal such as *Windrush* could happen again. White supports critical discussions about culture and having a more visible diversity, which means having more senior staff from working-class backgrounds.

White's feelings about the *Windrush* Scandal were of sadness, remembering how her parents, who worried that their Jamaican nationality could put them at a disadvantage and never felt totally accepted, became British citizens. The scandal proved their fears to be correct.

As chief executive of Ofcom, White prioritised inclusion, achieving fifty–fifty gender diversity at the communications regulator through the creation of new jobs and restructuring, as well as setting targets for gender, ethnicity, disability and sexual diversity. She has taken the BBC to task for their record on diver-sity, calling for more transparency, warning that mainstream channels risk losing their Black and ethnic minority audiences if they don't reflect their audiences in their workforce.

In an interview at Whitehall in 2019, White remarked that her instinct was that she might do something commercial. Her appointment to John Lewis is a victory for allowing talent and a track record to do the talking.

Henry Sylvester Williams

(1867?–1911) lawyer, activist

A T THE END of the Second World War, colonised nations in Africa and its diaspora were making louder demands for self-determination. European powers, mired in existential crises and weakened by the conflict, were assessing the effects of the catastrophic destruction of their cities and citizens. Africans, who had fought and suffered incredible losses themselves, were looking forward to a future in which they could be in control of their destiny.

As a result, the Fifth Pan-African Congress was held in Manchester in 1945, and it was one of the most significant moments of Black solidarity in the twentieth century. The congress brought together intellectuals and activists from Africa and the Caribbean to discuss strategies that would achieve African and Caribbean liberation from colonial rule. Some of the delegates, among them Ghanaian Kwame Nkrumah, would go on to lead anti-colonial struggles in their countries and see them become independent nations in the 1950s and 1960s.

The year 1945 was decisive, therefore, in determining the freedom of Africa. The path leading to that momentous congress, however, had been laid down nearly fifty years earlier.

In 1900, the Trinidadian lawyer and activist Henry Sylvester Williams organised the Pan-African Conference in London, leading the charge for Pan-African unity across regions and ethnicities and paving the way for the Pan-African Congresses. Williams was committed to working towards ending the colonial exploitation and racism that Africans were suffering. A Black transatlantic figure, active in the USA, the Caribbean, Britain and South Africa, it was Williams who coined the term 'Pan-African', planting the seeds of a philosophy that aimed politically to unite Africans around the world.

Williams was remarkable for his accomplishments at a time when, as historian Marika Sherwood has noted, race and social class were of fundamental significance and determined what one could hope to achieve from life.[1] Born possibly in 1867 in Barbados, and raised in Arouca, Trinidad, the eldest of six children, Williams studied at the teacher training institution Tranquillity, where he met Prince Kofi Intim, son of the deposed King of the Asante. Prince Kofi had, on his father's behalf, signed along with nineteen other chiefs the Treaty of Submission to the British at Cape Coast in Ghana in 1874.[2] Prince Kofi shared his experiences of imperialism-in-action with Williams, which may have had an impact on Williams's later politics. In addition, Williams grew up in a village in which the majority of the inhabitants were African-born, many with memories of their communities and lives there, who had experienced the Middle Passage as captives and had lived through slavery. Williams's environment and his later conversations with Prince Kofi perhaps enabled him to construct an overall picture of Africa, enslavement, emancipation and colonisation.

Later on in his career, Williams became the first Black man admitted to the bar in Cape Town, South Africa, and was one of the first two elected Black borough councillors in London. As a younger man, he travelled the world learning about political activism and solicited support for the African Association, which he co-founded in 1897. This organisation was formed to encourage unity among all people who claimed African heritage, and to raise awareness about how Africans suffered under colonialism. It disseminated information on issues affecting their rights and privileges as subjects of the British Empire.

The African Association organised the Pan-African Conference to bring together all concerned about the future of Black people and to express the grievances of Black British subjects of the empire. Held in Westminster Town Hall, London, in July 1900, the conference invited delegates from the British Empire, the United States, Liberia and Haiti. They discussed a range of issues, from racial discrimination to history to culture, and called for equality of opportunity and treatment. The delegates presented papers, shared experiences and put forward solutions. The scholar and activist W. E. B. Du Bois attended that conference and organised subsequent Pan-African Congresses. The composer Samuel Coleridge-Taylor and John Archer, the future mayor of Battersea (and first Black mayor in London), also attended.

Forty-five years later, the Fifth Pan-African Congress achieved what Williams had envisaged. By no small coincidence, the local Pan-African branch Williams established in Trinidad was led by James Hubert Alfonso Nurse. Unbeknownst to Williams, who died in 1911 at just forty-four years of age, Nurse would become the father of George Padmore, who was one of the organisers of the Fifth Pan-African Congress in 1945.

Allan Wilmot

(b. 1925) Second World War veteran, entertainer

Allan Wilmot is a Second World War veteran, *Windrush* pioneer and, in the 1950s, a successful singer and performer.

During the Second World War, men and women from the Caribbean volunteered to serve, believing themselves, as colonial subjects, to be 'all in it together' with the British. Thousands came to Britain to serve in the armed forces and the merchant navy, and to work in the munitions factories, and forestry workers from British Honduras (Belize) volunteered to cut timber in Scotland.

Allan Wilmot served in both the British Navy and the RAF, with the attitude that it was a difficult and necessary job that had to be done. Today, Wilmot continues to share his story of his war service and how he broke into the entertainment business in 1950s Britain. Allan Wilmot is one of the few people still living who can testify to the contributions, which were for many years forgotten or underexplored, of Caribbeans to the war effort.

Born in Kingston, Jamaica, in 1925, Wilmot grew up in a middle-class family; his mother was one of the first social workers in Jamaica and his father was an inter-island cargo-ship captain. Jamaica in the 1930s operated under strict social and racial hierarchies. Whites held the most powerful positions from government to banking, while the Black population were forced to remain in servile roles. Brown and light-skinned people were part of the middle class, and it was near impossible for a dark-skinned Jamaican to become a ship's captain; Wilmot recalled that the highest rank a Black man could achieve in the police was sergeant-major. Consequently, Wilmot's father tried to discourage his son from following in his footsteps and go through what he had to get where he was. Nevertheless, Allan aspired to be a skipper like his father.

Britain's declaration of war against Germany was welcomed by the British Caribbeans, who saw it as their duty to help the 'mother country' through this crisis. They became immediately involved in the naval campaign that became known as the Battle of the Caribbean, as German U-boats positioned themselves in the Caribbean Sea with the aim of sinking as many supply ships as they could. The Caribbean islands, of strategic importance to Britain and the United States, were in significant danger. The German submarines sank over 300 ships, with 1.5 million tons of supplies lost. It was during this extremely dangerous period that Wilmot volunteered to serve in the Royal Navy aged sixteen, straight out of college, with the objective 'if we served and survived, we'd be able to have a start in life'. He was assigned to the HMS *Hauken*, a minesweeping vessel, as one of six Jamaicans and the only Black sailor in a crew of forty-five. Working together was vital for everyone's survival – not only were they checking for mines, but they also searched for survivors of attacked ships and acted as convoy escorts for ships sailing from Kingston to the Panama Canal.

Wilmot served on the *Hauken* until late 1943 and then joined the RAF sea-air rescue team, an elite force that specialised in rescuing downed aircraft. With ambitions to become a merchant navy deck officer, Wilmot was accepted, spending the rest of the war serving in four countries as a leading aircraftman.

Unfamiliar with the realities of working-class life in England, Wilmot was shocked to see poor people and was also taken aback by their ignorance about African Caribbean people. The worst encounters with racism came from American soldiers stationed in Britain, with whom African Caribbeans engaged in bitter clashes.

After the war, Wilmot returned to a Jamaica that was ill-prepared to accommodate its returning veterans. With the war over, Britain expected Caribbean servicemen to return home; however, the need to rebuild a battle-scarred Britain attracted many ex-RAF men to return to seek work and start a new life. After finding a position as a trainee postman, Wilmot turned to showbusiness, becoming a member of the Southlanders vocal group with his brother Harry (father of Gary Wilmot), Vernon Nesbeth and Frank Mannah. They adopted an American doo-wop style. Best known for their hit single 'Alone' and the novelty song 'Mole in a Hole', they carved out a successful career performing all over Europe and sharing the stage with Britain's most popular performers of the day, including Petula Clarke, Max Bygraves and Tommy Cooper.

As an airman and sailor, Allan Wilmot helped save the lives of tens of thousands; as time passed, he and thousands of other Caribbean volunteers were forgotten. Now in his mid-nineties, Wilmot spends his time giving countless speaking engagements, relaying stories about his experiences during the war to make sure that these contributions are not forgotten.

Simon Woolley, Baron
Woolley of Woodford

(b. 1962) political and equalities campaigner

S IR SIMON WOOLLEY's interest in politics stemmed from a trip to South America, undertaken as part of his degree course. The countries he visited were undergoing profound political and economic change, and he was witnessing history in action. The people fighting for change made him realise that when he returned to England, 'I had no excuse not to change my world.'

Today, Simon Woolley is one the leading campaigners for political and social equality. As the founder of Operation Black Vote (OBV), he calls for more diversity in politics, and is credited with helping transform the racial and ethnic makeup of Parliament, local authorities, public bodies and the magistracy.

Woolley was born in Leicester and brought up on the St Matthew's council estate, and as a young boy and man witnessed and experienced discrimination and injustice.

Woolley co-founded Operation Black Vote in 1996, a time when Black communities were continuing to feel the intense pressure of discrimination in many aspects of their lives. Unemployment among African, Caribbean, Pakistani and Bangladeshi youth was

above the national average; inner-city schools were disproportionately expelling Black pupils; immigrants and asylum seekers were
being criminalised by immigration policy; and the then
Metropolitan Police Commissioner's assertion that the majority of
muggings in London were committed by Black youths further
eroded the already poor relationship between the police and the
Black community in London.

While working as a volunteer with the political reform
organisation Charter 88, Woolley realised that any change for
marginalised groups would have to be initiated and led by
those groups. With a general election to take place a year later
in 1997, Charter 88 and the 1990 Trust, the first Black national
advocacy organisation, began to explore how that event could
be used to address the concerns of the Black community. A
study of the political and demographic data in constituencies
with the smallest majorities revealed that the Black vote was
potentially extremely influential – in up to fifty seats across the
UK, the number of African, Asian and Caribbean voters was
greater than the vote margin, and in another fifty seats, Black
voters could potentially act as kingmakers in closely fought
contests.

Operation Black Vote was launched to convince the Black
community of the power it could exert at the 1997 general
election if they became more politically engaged and registered
to vote; that they could hold politicians to the promises they
make if they won their vote, which could initiate change. It
undertook a series of initiatives – nationwide meetings, ad
campaigns, distribution of voter registration forms and parliamentary support – that got Black people registered, recognising their collective political voice, and getting politicians to
take notice.

Since then, Operation Black Vote has empowered communities by instilling better political education in the school curriculum and nurturing Black and minority ethnic civic and political talent. Of the sixty-five Black and minority ethnic MPs currently in Parliament, 10 per cent of them, including Helen Grant (Conservative), Marsha de Cordova (Labour) and Tan Dhesi (Labour), were mentored directly through the OBV leadership scheme. The scheme also launched the careers of Marvin Rees, Bristol's first Black mayor, and Baroness Warsi, the first Asian cabinet minister. The organisation has the most successful BAME political mentoring scheme in Britain.

Woolley is not only committed to bringing about change in political representation; he is also willing to highlight the lack of Black and ethnic minority representation in the positions of the most powerful in Britain. In 2017, research undertaken by OBV, Green Park (a leadership recruitment and diversity consultancy) and the *Guardian* newspaper identified 1049 individuals who are considered the most powerful people in Britain – the key powerbrokers, influencers and decision makers. Of that 1049, only 36 are BAME. The research gave a damning insight into the level of disenfranchisement, and how difficult it continues to be for BAME people to break into the elite, and how white males continue to maintain control and a 'vice-like stranglehold' at top levels.

In 2017, Woolley was appointed by the then Prime Minister Theresa May as advisory chair to the Race Disparity Audit. When May was Home Secretary, Woolley had convinced her to audit the Home Office for racial disparities; the audit had a wider remit, exposing disparities that affect people from diverse ethnic and social backgrounds, bringing together the government's data, and analysing it across a range of topics to gain a fuller understanding of the inequalities people experience. It's a framework that's been applied in Bristol and Liverpool, and other cities are interested in adopting its framework.

Of his work, Woolley has remarked, 'I'm impatient for change. I still think there are persistent inequalities when it comes to race regarding employment, education and the criminal justice system.'

Gary Younge

(b. 1969) journalist, author, broadcaster, academic

G ARY YOUNGE IS an award-winning journalist, author, columnist and former editor-at-large for the *Guardian*. He is one of Britain's leading journalists who has provided brilliant reporting and commentary on a vast range of political and social issues in Britain and internationally, and has covered some of the most important stories over the last twenty years.

Younge, whose parents were from Barbados, was born in Stevenage and was raised by his mother, a former nurse, teacher and community activist. It was her sudden death at forty-four, when Younge was nineteen, that 'made me driven in a way that had precious little to do with conventional ambition . . . felt the urgency to be a protagonist, rather than a passive recipient in my own life.'[1]

Younge's determination to be the maker of his own life has resulted in a distinguished career as a journalist, broadcaster and author. He produces in-depth journalism remarkable for its incisiveness and range. He writes with passion, knowledge and integrity on topics as diverse as American and British politics, knife crime, race, gay marriage and the phenomenon

369

of the 'incel'.[2] A columnist for the *Guardian* since 1993, Younge has sought out stories off the beaten track, and imbued them with his own distinctive, journalistic style of recounting the lives of people and of ideas, combined with social and political commentary. He has reported from all over Europe, Africa, the United States and the Caribbean; when appointed the *Guardian's* US correspondent in 2003, Younge was based in New York and Chicago.

Younge has authored five books that were conceived mainly during his period as a US correspondent, exploring and commenting on race, politics and gun violence, giving a fresh perspective on these topics seen through the eyes of an outsider, a Black British journalist.

Younge's first book, *No Place like Home: A Black Briton's Journey through the American South* (2002), retraced the routes of the original Freedom Riders of the 1960s and was shortlisted for the *Guardian* First Book Prize. His fifth and most recent book, *Another Day in the Death of America* (2016), explores the unsolved shootings of ten young people killed in a single day in the USA. For this book he received the J. Anthony Lukas Prize from Columbia University School of Journalism.

Younge's 'Beyond the Blade' series in the *Guardian* looked beyond the tabloid headlines on knife crime in Britain, taking account of the human cost, not only on the victims and their families, but also the perpetrators, their families, the emergency services, charities and other organisations that have become part of this tragic narrative. He also offered a critical analysis of the factors that contribute to what he interprets as a health and social crisis. For this series he won the Broadsheet Feature Writer of the Year at the Society of Editors National Press

Awards, and Feature of the Year from the Amnesty Media Awards for an article in the same series.

In 2020, Younge left the *Guardian* to take the post of professor of sociology at the University of Manchester, and is currently a visiting professor at London South Bank University.

Benjamin Zephaniah

(b. 1958) poet, author, broadcaster, academic

BENJAMIN ZEPHANIAH'S POETRY is a living entity that reflects Britain's ethnically diverse nature. He is the people's laureate and was a pioneer of the performance poetry scene in the late 1970s and 1980s; his talent saw him shortlisted for the chair of Professor of Poetry at Oxford in 1989. Zephaniah engages with a dual vision of British society in his poetry that is staunchly Black British; it transcends racial and cultural boundaries, and is a product of the meeting of two cultures and traditions: British and Caribbean. In 2008, Zephaniah was included in *The Times*'s list of Britain's top fifty post-war poets; he has received international acclaim and has contributed to many radio programmes and documentaries about culture, literature, politics and race.

Zephaniah's success is all the more remarkable as he had great difficulty reading and writing as a boy (a consequence of undiagnosed dyslexia), and had been written off by his teachers as a failure. He learned his poetic skills on the street, in church, from sound systems and from listening to poems by the Jamaican folklorist Louise Bennett.[1]

Born in Birmingham of Jamaican–Barbadian heritage, Zephaniah's negative school experiences were exacerbated by him having to frequently move house with his mother to escape his violent father. By thirteen he was expelled from school and got involved in petty crime, which landed him in an approved school; a later incident saw him sentenced to two years' imprisonment.

The time he spent in detention made the young Zephaniah decide to do something more constructive with his life. A lover of words and performance, as a child Zephaniah had written his first poem in opposition to a teacher who told him Christopher Columbus had discovered America. He had been performing in church since he was eleven, where he was admired for his ability to rap all the books of the Bible.[2] He became a DJ on the local sound-system scene and was popular for lacing his 'toasts' with humour and sharp social commentary. Immersion in sound-system culture made Zephaniah more confident in his writing, and in 1979 he moved to London, and the following year he published his first collection of poems, *Pen Rhythm* (1980) with Page One Books, an underground publishing house that Zephaniah had founded with some of his friends in Stratford, east London.[3] He started performing at various venues and built a large following on the performance poetry circuit. In 1985 his second collection, *The Dread Affair: Collected Poems*, caused a stir as it reflected the frustrations of a generation of Black British youth and contained a number of poems attacking the British legal system. He extended the political nature of his poems internationally with *Rasta Time in Palestine* (1990), inspired by a visit to the Palestinian occupied territories.

In 2003 Zephaniah was at the centre of a controversy when he turned down the honour of an OBE offered to him by the Blair government. He explained his reasons for rejecting the honour in an article written in the *Guardian*, describing what empire conjured up for him:

> It is because of this concept of empire that my British educa-tion led me to believe that the history of black people started with slavery and that we were born slaves, and should there-fore be grateful that we were given freedom by our caring white masters. It is because of this idea of empire that black people like myself don't even know our true names or our true historical culture . . . Benjamin Zephaniah OBE – no way . . . I am profoundly anti-empire.[4]

This position was consistent with Zephaniah's long-held anti-establishment stance, showing how he viewed the poet as a public figure.

Zephaniah's poems are defined by their rhythm and their approach to language, and are filled with hope, humour and laughter. He once called himself an 'alternative broadcaster', a social commentator and observer, covering many topics poetically, from race relations to the royal family, from the environment to politics. He also uses satire to criticise and denounce the exploitation of underdeveloped countries by the 'first world', negative stereotyping and the power of the tabloid press. His 2001 collection *Too Black, Too Strong*, inspired by his tenure as poet-in-residence at Michael Mansfield QC's Tooks Chambers, is a celebration of the best of Britain as expressed through its ethnic diversity, and is also an assertion of his Black Britishness.

Benjamin Zephaniah is an important player on the British literary and cultural scene. He is a wordsmith, a griot, who uses satire, parody and political commentary to shine a light on what unites and divides Britain.

Sources and Notes

General sources and notes are listed under the name of the Great Black Briton.

Introduction

Notes: 1 A Great Briton was defined as 'anyone who was born in the British Isles, including Ireland, and who has played a significant part in the life of the British Isles'.

2 John Cooper *et al.*, *Great Britons: The Great Debate* (London: National Portrait Gallery Publications, 2002), p. 10.

3 Reporting of the number of votes for Churchill varied – the *Guardian* reported him as receiving 456,498 votes, the *Independent* 447,442.

4 Matt Wells and Jessica Hodgson, 'BBC2 to make history with viewers' top 10 great Britons,' *Guardian* (18 May 2001), https://www.theguardian.com/media/2001/may/18/broadcasting.bbc.

5 Tristan Davies, 'The Battle of the Britons', *Radio Times* (9 October 2002).

6 Cooper *et al.*, *Great Britons*, p. 10.

7 Graeme Paton, 'Conservative Party Conference: schoolchildren "ignorant of the past", says Gove', *Telegraph* (5 October 2010), https://www.telegraph.co.uk/education/educationnews/8043872/Conservative-Part-Conference-schoolchildren-ignorant-of-the-past-says-Gove.html.

8 C. Alexander, J. Chatterji and D. Weekes-Bernard, *Making British Histories: Diversity and the National Curriculum* (London: Runnymede Trust, 2012), p. 7.

9 Akala, *Natives: Race and Class in the Ruins of Empire* (London: Two Roads Books, 2018).

10 In Fryer and Ramdin's works, Black is used as a political term to include the experiences of people from Africa, the Caribbean and the Indian subcontinent.

11 Hannah Ishmael quoted in Rob Waters, 'Thinking black: Peter Fryer's Staying Power and the politics of writing Black History in the 1980s', *History Workshop Journal*, vol. 82, no. 1 (2016), p. 5.

12 'Akyaaba Addai Sebo Interview' on the origins of Black History Month, Every Generation Media (undated), https://everygeneration.co.uk/index.php/black-british-history/bhm-black-history-month/akyaaba-addai-sebo-interview.

13 See Black British History, https://blackbritishhistory.co.uk.

14 Colin Prescod, 'Why are people always banging on about racism? Reflections on Windrush: Songs in a strange land', British Library (4 October 2018), https://www.bl.uk/windrush/articles/why-are-people-always-banging-on-about-racism-reflections-on-windrush-songs-in-a-strange-land.

15 Some excellent works on this subject include Stephen Bourne, *Black Poppies: Britain's Black Community and the Great War* (Stroud: The History Press, 2014); and David Olusoga's BBC series *The World's War: Forgotten Soldiers of Empire* (2014).

16 Matthew Weaver, 'Hate crime surge linked to Brexit and 2017 terrorist attacks', *Guardian* (16 October 2018), https://www.theguardian.com/society/2018/oct/16/hate-crime-brexit-terrorist-attacks-england-wales.

17 My thoughts here have been informed by Jon Stratton's excellent article, 'The language of leaving: Brexit, the second world war and cultural trauma', *Journal of Cultural Studies* (June 2019), pp. 1–27.

18 For analyses and accounts of the '*Windrush* Scandal' see *The Unwanted: The Secret Windrush Files*, BBC Two (24 June 2019); Frances Webber, 'The Embedding of State Hostility: A background paper on the Windrush Scandal', Institute of Race Relations

Briefing Paper No. 11, http://www.irr.org.uk/publications/issues/the-embedding-of-state-hostility-a-background-paper-on-the-windrush-scandal/; Amelia Gentleman, *The Windrush Betrayal* (London: Guardian Faber Books, 2019).

Diane Abbott

Notes: 1 Tom Peck, 'Diane Abbott received almost half of all abusive tweets sent to female MPs before election', *Independent* (5 September 2017).
2 Peck, 'Diane Abbott'.
3 Damien Gayle, 'Diane Abbott: Twitter has put racists into over-drive', *Guardian* (18 December 2108), https://www.theguardian.com/politics/2018/dec/18/diane-abbott-calls-for-twitter-to-clamp-down-on-hate-speech.
4 Diane Abbott, 'Diane Abbott on feminism in the 1980s: "It was so exciting being in a hall full of black women"', *Guardian* (1 February 2018), https://www.theguardian.com/lifeandstyle/2018/feb/01/women-1980s-diane-abbott-black-women-radical-feminism.

Victor Adebowale, Baron Adebowale CBE

Andy Ricketts, 'A third of largest charities "have all white senior leadership teams and boards"', *Third Sector* (6 June 2018), https://www.thirdsector.co.uk/third-largest-charities-have-all-white-senior-leadership-teams-boards/management/article/1475578.
Winnie Agbonlahor, 'Interview: Lord Victor Adebowale', *Civil Service World* (29 September 2014), https://www.civilserviceworld.com/articles/interview/interview-lord-victor-adebowale.

Adedoyin Olayiwola Adepitan MBE

Notes: 1 'Ade Adepitan', *Dream It – Achieve It* interview series, Arco Academy (7 May 2020), https://arco.academy/ade-adepitan-interview-full/.

2 'Ade Adepitan'.
3 'Ade Adepitan'.
4 Ade Adepitan, 'Africa with Ade Adepitan' blog (24 February 2019), http://adeadepitan.com/africa-with-ade-adepitan/.

Dr Maggie Aderin-Pocock MBE

Nicola Davis, 'Maggie Aderin-Pocock: How a space obsessed schoolgirl battled the odds to become a top scientist', *Observer* (21 September 2014), https://www.theguardian.com/science/2014/sep/21/maggie-aderin-pocock-interview-bbc-nasa-space.

'Dr Maggie Aderin-Pocock, Faculty of Engineering', Imperial College website, https://www.imperial.ac.uk/mechanical-engineering/people/meet-our-alumni/dr-maggie-aderin-pocock/.

'Dr Maggie Aderin Pocock: Career Stories on Film', Vitae UK, https://www.vitae.ac.uk/researcher-careers/researcher-career-stories/list-of-vitae-career-stories-on-film/maggie-aderin-pocock.

Notes: 1 Samara Linton, 'The future of STEM is filled with women who look like me', Fawcett Society (undated), https://www.fawcettsociety.org.uk/blog/the-future-of-stem-is-filled-with-women-who-look-like-me-shakeupstem.

Professor Hakim Adi

Notes: 1 The statistics refer to those of African and Caribbean British and other Black background. The other Black professor of history is Olivette Otele, at Bristol University. Robbie Shilliam, 'Black Academia: The doors have been opened, but the architecture remains the same', in Claire Alexander and Jason Arday (eds), *Aiming Higher: Race Inequality and Diversity in the Academy* (London: Runnymede Trust, 2015), p. 32.

Sir David Adjaye OBE, RA and Elsie Owusu OBE, RIBA

Notes: 1 Richard Waite and Bruce Tether, 'Race Diversity Survey: Is Architecture in Denial?', *Architects' Journal* (10 May 2018), https://www.architectsjournal.co.uk/news/race-diversity-survey-is-architecture-in-denial/10030896.article.

2 Waite and Tether, 'Race Diversity Survey'.

3 Katie Law, 'Elsie Owusu, the architect building a more equal future', *Evening Standard* (29 August 2018), https://www.standard.co.uk/news/the1000/elsie-owusu-architect-progress-1000-a3922536.html.

4 Oliver Wainwright, 'David Adjaye: Holocaust Memorial architect who is feted around the world', *Guardian* (28 October 2017), https://www.theguardian.com/artanddesign/2017/oct/28/david-adjaye-architect-holocaust-memorial-british-ghanaian.

5 'Interview with RIBA President candidate Elsie Owusu', *Architectural Record* (3 July 2018), https://www.architecturalrecord.com/articles/13490-interview-with-riba-president-candidate-elsie-owusu.

John Akomfrah CBE

Notes: 1 Lara Choksey, 'Windrush, welfare, and caring for history', *Media Diversified* (17 April 2019), https://mediadiversified.org/2019/04/17/windrush-welfare-and-caring-for-history/.

2 John Sutherland, review of *Handsworth Songs*, *American Historical Review*, vol. 94, no. 4 (October 1989), pp. 1042–4.

Ira Aldridge

Deidre Osborne, 'Writing Black Back: An overview of Black theatre and performance in Britain', *Studies in Theatre and Performance*, vol. 26, no. 1 (2006), pp. 13–31.

Ira Aldridge, in David Dabydeen, John Gilmore, Cecily Jones (eds), *The Oxford Companion to Black British History* (Oxford: Oxford University Press, 2007), pp. 23–5.

Bernth Lindfors, 'Ira Aldridge's Africanness', *English Academy Review*, vol. 23, no. 1 (2006), pp. 102–13.

Notes: 1 'Lolita Chakrabarti on Ira Aldridge', Old Vic Theatre (undated), https://www.oldvictheatre.com/200/lolita-chakrabarti-on-ira-aldridge.

Valerie Amos, Baroness Amos CH

Sarah Brown, 'Better Angels Interview Special: Valerie Amos', *Better Angels Podcast* (undated), https://theirworld.org/better-angels/interview-special-valerie-amos.

'Interview with SOAS Director Valerie Amos', SOAS Radio (16 December 2015), https://soasradio.org/speech/episodes/interview-soas-director-valerie-amos.

Notes: 1 Simon Woolley, 'Britain's elite is white bright – but doesn't brilliance come in all colours?', *Guardian* (25 September 2017), https://www.theguardian.com/commentisfree/2017/sep/25/britain-elite-white-men-colour-of-power-national-self-interest.

2 Valerie Amos and Pratibha Parma, 'Challenging Imperial Feminism', *Feminist Review*, no. 17 (July 1984).

3 Peter Wilby, 'Valerie Amos: The coolest of cool to handle Soas's hot potato', *Guardian* (9 February 2016), https://www.theguardian.com/education/2016/feb/09/valerie-amos-soas-london-university-director.

Kehinde Andrews

'Professor Kehinde Andrews – School of Social Sciences', Birmingham City University, https://www.bcu.ac.uk/social-sciences/about-us/staff/criminology-and-sociology/kehinde-andrews.

Kehinde Andrews, 'Racism in universities is a systemic problem, not a series of incidents', *Guardian* (23 October 2019), https://www.theguardian.com/education/2019/oct/23/racism-in-universities-is-a-systemic-problem-not-a-series-of-incidents.

Kehinde Andrews, 'France is addressing black people's invisibility in art. When will the UK?', *Guardian* (28 March 2019), https://www.

theguardian.com/commentisfree/2019/mar/28/france-black-people-art-musee-d-orsay.

Patrick Grafton-Green, 'Piers Morgan in explosive row with academic who called Winston Churchill a "racist" and compared him to Hitler', *Evening Standard* (9 October 2018), https://www.standard.co.uk/news/uk/piers-morgan-in-explosive-row-with-academic-who-called-winston-churchill-a-racist-and-compared-him-a3957396.html.

Professor Dame Elizabeth Anionwu DBE

Elizabeth Anionwu, *Mixed Blessings from a Cambridge Union* (London: Elizan, 2016).

Notes: 1 Lucy Bland, 'Mixed-race babies born after the Second World War', *History Extra* (17 December 2019), https://www.historyextra.com/period/20th-century/mixed-race-babies-born-after-the-second-world-war/.

Elaine Arnold

'Dr Elaine Arnold Presents: Separation and Loss', *Changing Chapters*, accessed on YouTube, https://www.youtube.com/watch?v=BGFnUAwVfhU.

Elaine Arnold, *Working with families of African Caribbean Origin: Understanding the Issues around Immigration and Attachment* (London: Jessica Kingsley Publishers, 2011).

Amma Asante MBE

Notes: 1 Kate Kellaway, 'Amma Asante: I'm bicultural, I walk the division that Belle walked every day', *Observer* (18 May 2014), https://www.theguardian.com/film/2014/may/18/amma-asante-belle-bicultural-ghanaian-british-director-grange-hill.

2 Emma Jacobs, 'Film-maker Amma Asante on race, Brexit and meeting Prince', *Financial Times* (10 November 2016), https://www.ft.com/content/76fc6668-a6cf-11e6-8898-79a99e2a4de6.

3 Amma Asante, 'This much I know', *Guardian* (25 May 2019),
https://www.theguardian.com/lifeandstyle/2019/may/25/amma-
asante-when-my-parents-came-to-the-uk-signs-on-doors-said-no-
irish-no-black-no-dogs.

Winifred Atwell

Stephen Bourne, *Black in the British Frame: The Black Experience in
British Film and Television* (London and New York: Continuum,
2001).

Dame Jocelyn Barrow DBE

Patrick Vernon, 'Windrush Pioneer: Patrick Vernon Interviews Dame
Jocelyn Barrow OBE', *Black History 365* (7 October 2018), https://
www.blackhistorymonth.org.uk/article/section/interviews/
windrush-pioneer-patrick-vernon-interviews-dame-jocelyn-barrow
-obe/.

Kwaku, 'Dame Jocelyn Barrow: More Needs to Be Done on Her
Lifetime Work on Racial and Multi-Cultural Awareness', *Black
History 365* (17 April 2020), https://www.blackhistorymonth.org.
uk/article/section/african-history/dame-jocelyn-barrow-more-
needs-to-be-done-on-her-lifetime-work-on-racial-and-multi-
cultural-awareness/.

Notes: 1 'Dame Jocelyn Barrow obituary', *The Times* (6 May 2020),
https://www.thetimes.co.uk/article/dame-jocelyn-barrow-obituary
-zzzxcxl6j.

2 'Dame Jocelyn Barrow obituary'.

3 Ron Ramdin, *The Making of the Black Working Class in Britain*
(London: Verso, updated edition, 2017), p. 421.

4 Angela Cobbinah, 'Life is a two way street: Interview with Dame
Jocelyn Barrow', *Camden New Journal* (24 October 2019), http://
camdennewjournal.com/article/life-is-a-two-way-street.

5 'Tributes pour in for Dame Jocelyn Barrow, "a true champion of
racial equality"', *Voice* (11 April 2020), https://www.voice-online.

co.uk/news/uk-news/2020/04/11/tributes-pour-in-to-dame-joce-lyn-barrow-a-true-champion-of-racial-equality/.

Lance Sergeant Johnson Beharry VC, COG

'Johnson's Story', British Legion (undated), https://www.britishlegion.org.uk/get-involved/remembrance/tribute-ink/marking-the-memories/johnson-beharry.

William Warren, 'Absolute Legends: The man who went from a drug dealer to being awarded a Victoria Cross', Forces.net (31 October 2018), https://www.forces.net/heritage/history/absolute-legends-man-who-went-drug-dealer-being-awarded-victoria-cross.

Dame Floella Benjamin of Beckenham DBE, DL

Notes: 1 Floella Benjamin, 'Windrush Stories: Floella Benjamin on coming to England, British Library (4 October 2018), https://www.bl.uk/windrush/articles/floella-benjamin-on-coming-to-england.

2 Floella Benjamin, 'Being a *Play School* presenter was an opportunity to change the world', British Film Institute, (20 January 2017), https://www.youtube.com/watch?v=xBitqUG-TVs.

Munroe Bergdorf

Notes: 1 Daniel Welsh, 'Munroe Bergdorf holds her own against Piers Morgan on "Good Morning Britain"', *Huffington Post* (4 September 2017), https://www.huffingtonpost.co.uk/entry/good-morning-britain-munroe-bergdorf-piers-morgan_uk_59ad217ce4b0354e440b586f.

2 Reni Eddo-Lodge, 'Why I'm no longer talking to white people about race' (22 February 2014), http://renieddolodge.co.uk/2014/02/.

3 Charlie Brinkhurst-Cuff, 'L'Oréal's firing of Munroe Bergdorf shows brands want our brown skin but not our blackness', *New*

Statesman (1 September 2017), https://www.newstatesman.com/
2017/09/l-or-als-firing-munroe-bergdorf-shows-brands-want-our-
brown-skin-not-our-blackness.
4 'Transgender hate crimes recorded by police go up 81%', *BBC News*
(27 June 2019), https://www.bbc.co.uk/news/uk-48756370.

Jak Beula Dodd

'Interview with Nubian Jak', *The Ben Cooper Show*, Camden Community
Radio (date unknown), https://www.youtube.com/watch?v=CApe
FmExLYM
Notes: 1 James Twomey, 'Grade II listed building becomes the first to
house black theatre company Dark and Light and is honoured with
a blue plaque', London News Online (5 November 2019), https://
www.londonnewsonline.co.uk/grade-ii-listed-building-becomes-
the-first-to-house-black-theatre-company-dark-light-and-is-
honoured-with-blue-plaque-2/.

Karen Blackett OBE

Nicola Kemp, 'MediaCom's Karen Blackett is a new breed of leader',
Campaign (20 March 2017), https://www.campaignlive.co.uk/arti-
cle/mediacoms-karen-blackett-new-breed-leader/1427154.
Isabelle Roughol, ' "Talent comes from everywhere": Karen Blackett on
diversity and how to make it in advertising', *Isa's Notebook* (31
October 2019), https://www.linkedin.com/pulse/talent-comes-
from-everywhere-karen-blackett-diversity-roughol/.
Margareta Pagano, 'Karen Blackett: Black, working class and successful', *Independent* (10 May 2014), https://www.independent.co.uk/
news/people/profiles/karen-blackett-black-working-class-and-
successful-9348788.html.

Malorie Blackman

Lucy Coats, 'Interview with Malorie Blackman', *Publishing Talk* (21 October 2018), http://www.publishingtalk.eu/interviews/malorie-blackman/.

Decca Aitkenhead, 'The Interview: Author Malorie Blackman on why racism now is as bad as she's known it', *The Times* (28 July 2019), https://www.thetimes.co.uk/article/the-interview-author-malorie-blackman-on-why-racism-now-is-as-bad-as-shes-known-it-vp7mq2kws.

Alison Flood, 'Malorie Blackman faces racist abuse after call to diversify children's books', *Guardian* (26 August 2014), https://www.theguardian.com/books/2014/aug/26/malorie-blackman-racist-abuse-diversity-childrens-books.

Malorie Blackman, 'Racist abuse will not stop me seeking more diversity in children's literature', *Guardian* (27 August 2014), https://www.theguardian.com/commentisfree/2014/aug/27/racist-abuse-diversity-in-childrens-literature.

Notes: 1 Malorie Blackman, 'Racist abuse will not stop me seeking more diversity in children's literature', *Guardian* (27 August 2014), https://www.theguardian.com/commentisfree/2014/aug/27/racist-abuse-diversity-in-childrens-literature

John Blanke

Notes: 1 Miranda Kaufmann, 'John Blanke (fl. 1507–1512')', *Dictionary of National Biography* (1 September 2017), https://www.oxforddnb.com/view/10.1093/ref:odnb/9780198614128.001.0001/odnb-9780198614128-e-107145?rskey=YjEenO&result=2.

2 Onyeka Nubia, *Blackamoores: Africans in Tudor England, Their Presence, Status and Origins* (London: Narrative Eye, 2013), p. 13.

3 Audrey Dewjee, 'The Historian Who First Linked John Blanke to Black British History', The John Blanke Project (November 2016), https://www.johnblanke.com/audrey-dewjee.html.

4 Kaufmann, 'John Blanke'.

5 Kaufmann, 'John Blanke'.

Dennis Bovell

Dennis Bovell, Open the Gate (undated), http://openthegate.org.uk/bookings/dennis-bovell/.

Melissa Bradshaw, 'Anti-sus sound systems: An Interview with Dennis Bovell', *Quietus* (2 February 2011), https://thequietus.com/articles/05630-dennis-bovell-interview.

'Dennis Bovell on Linton Kwesi Johnson, Lovers' Rock and Song writing', Red Bull Music Academy (24 July 2017), accessed on YouTube, https://thequietus.com/articles/05630-dennis-bovell-interview.

Notes: 1 Neil Spencer, 'Reggae: the sound that revolutionised Britain', *Guardian* (30 January 2011), https://www.theguardian.com/music/2011/jan/30/reggae-revolutionary-bob-marley-britain.

Sonia Boyce OBE, RA

Notes: 1 Celeste Marie Bernier, *Stick to the Skin: African American and Black British Art, 1965–2015* (Los Angeles: University of California Press 2018), p. 151.

2 Sonia Boyce, 'Our removal of Waterhouse's naked nymphs painting was art in action', *Guardian* (6 February 2018), https://www.theguardian.com/commentisfree/2018/feb/06/takedown-waterhouse-naked-nymphs-art-action-manchester-art-gallery-sonia-boyce.

Dr Aggrey Burke

Roxy Harris and Sarah White (eds), *Building Britannia: Life Experience with Britain* (London: New Beacon Books, 2009).

'Inside Out: Improving Mental Health for BME communities in England', National Institute for Mental Health in England (2003), https://lemosandcrane.co.uk/resources/NHS%20-%20Inside%20outside.pdf.

Mental Health Foundation website

John Gulliver, 'Psychiatrist who started a quiet revolution in medicine', *Camden New Journal* (18 October 2019), http://camdennewjournal.com/article/psychiatrist-who-started-a-quiet-revolution-in-medicine.

'A blot on the profession', *British Medical Journal* (5 March 1988), https://europepmc.org/backend/ptpmcrender.fcgi?accid=PMC2545288&blobtype=pdf.

Vanley Burke

Notes: 1 Marlene Smith, in Jonathan Watkins, *At Home with Vanley Burke* (Birmingham: Ikon Gallery, 2015), p. 22.

2 Mark Sealy (ed.), *Vanley Burke: A Retrospective* (London: Lawrence and Wishart, 1993), p. 31.

3 Winford Fagan, 'Winford Fagan in Handsworth, Birmingham, 1970', *Guardian* (11 September 2015), https://www.theguardian.com/artanddesign/2015/sep/11/winford-fagan-handsworth-photograp-vanley-burke.

4 Vanley Burke, in Sealy (ed.), *Vanley Burke*, p. 33.

Margaret Busby OBE, FRSL

Notes: 1 Marika Sherwood, *Origins of Pan-Africanism: Henry Sylvester Williams, Africa and the African Diaspora* (London: Routledge, 2011), p. 336.

2 Katie Kingshill, 'Clive Allison: Publisher whose eclectic imprint was in the vanguard of independent houses', *Independent* (7 September 2011), https://www.independent.co.uk/news/obituaries/clive-allison-publisher-whose-eclectic-imprint-was-in-the-vanguard-of-independent-houses-2350183.html.

Dawn Butler

Notes: 1 Kate Proctor, 'Lib Dem staffer apologises for saying Dawn Butler lied about racism', *Guardian* (14 October 2019), https://www.theguardian.com/politics/2019/oct/14/lib-dem-apologises-dawn-butler-lied-accounts-racism-westminster.

2 Rowena Mason, 'Dawn Butler: I'm mistaken for other black female MPs at least once a week', *Guardian* (18 February 2020), https://www.theguardian.com/politics/2020/feb/18/exhausting-battle-dawn-butler-on-calling-out-racism-in-politics.

3 Aamna Mohdin and Jim Waterson, 'News outlets criticised for mislabelling photos of black MPs', *Guardian* (4 February 2020), https://www.theguardian.com/media/2020/feb/04/news-outlets-in-racism-row-over-mislabelling-photos-of-black-mps.

4 Yas Necati, ' "Without your rights I can't have my rights": Dawn Butler on the importance of intersectionality at the UK's first transgender conference', *Independent* (12 September 2018), https://www.independent.co.uk/news/uk/home-news/dawn-butler-transgender-uk-labour-intersectionality-rights-a8534761.html.

Earl Cameron CBE

David M. Anderson, 'Mau Mau at the movies: contemporary representations of an anti-colonial war', *South African Historical Journal*, vol. 48, no. 1 (2003), pp. 71–89.

BFI Screenonline.

Notes: 1 Stacee Smith, 'Staying Power: Interview with Earl Cameron', *Black History 365* (11 August 2019), https://www.blackhistory-month.org.uk/article/section/interviews/staying-power-interview-with-earl-cameron/.

2 Stephen Bourne, *Black in the British Frame: The Black Experience in Film and Television* (London and New York: Continuum, 2001), pp. 105–6.

3 Bourne, *Black in the British Frame*, p. 109.

4 Smith, 'Staying Power'.

Betty Campbell MBE

Notes: 1 Ceri Lewis, '#towerlives: Betty Campbell's fight for childhood dream', *BBC News* (15 April 2016), https://www.bbc.co.uk/news/uk-wales-36044620.
2 Harriet Marsden, 'Betty Campbell: Wales' first Black headteacher took civil rights history into the classroom', *Independent* (25 October 2017), https://www.independent.co.uk/news/obituaries/betty-rachel-elizabeth-campbell-wales-black-head-teacher-headmistress-mount-stuart-civil-rights-race-a8008541.html.

Naomi Campbell

Liam Freeman, 'Naomi Campbell on the power of African talent to sweep racism off the runway', *Vogue* (UK) (12 April 2019), https://www.vogue.co.uk/article/naomi-campbell-on-diversity-in-fashion.
Scarlett Newman, 'Black Models Matter: Challenging the Racism of Aesthetics and the Façade of Inclusion in the Fashion Industry', MA thesis (New York: City University of New York, 2017).
'Naomi Campbell on Nick Knight', *Subjective* (ShowSTUDIO, 2015), https://showstudio.com/projects/subjective/naomi_campbell_by_nick_knight?autoplay=1.

Queen Charlotte

Notes: 1 Thabiti Asulkile, 'J. A. Rogers: The Scholarship of an Organic Intellectual', *Black Scholar*, vol. 36, no. 2–3 (2006), pp. 35–50.
2 J. A. Rogers, *Nature Knows No Color-Line: Research into the Negro Ancestry of the White Race* (New York: Helga M. Rogers, 1952), p. 93.
3 Stuart Jeffries, 'Was this Britain's first Black Queen?' *Guardian* (12 March 2009), https://www.theguardian.com/world/2009/mar/12/race-monarchy.
4 Mario de Valdes y Cocom, 'The Blurred Racial Lines of Leading Families: Queen Charlotte', PBS Frontline (undated), https://www.pbs.org/wgbh/pages/frontline/shows/secret/famous/royalfamily.html.

5 Valdes y Cocom, 'The Blurred Racial Lines'.

6 'Revealed: The Queen's Black ancestors', *Sunday Times* (6 June 1999).

7 Karen Grigsby Bates, 'Code Switch: The meaning of Meghan: "Black" and "Royal" no longer an oxymoron in Britain', NPR (29 November 2017), https://www.npr.org/sections/codeswitch/2017/11/29/567012180/the-meaning-of-meghan-black-and-royal-no-longer-an-oxymoron?t=1592050381521.

Edric Connor

Darrell Newton, *Paving the Empire Road: BBC Television and Black Britons* (Manchester: Manchester University Press, 2011).

John Cowley, 'London is the Place: Caribbean Music in the Context of Empire', in Paul Oliver (ed.), *Black Music in Britain: Essays on the Afro Asian Contribution to Popular Music* (Milton Keynes: Open University Press, 1990).

Edric Connor, *Horizons: The Life and Times of Edric Connor, with a foreword by George Lamming* (Kingston: Ian Randle, 2007).

Notes: 1 Connor, *Horizons*.

2 Stephen Bourne, *Black in the British Frame: The Black Experience in British Film and Television* (London and New York: Continuum Books, 2001), p. 82.

3 Bourne, *Black in the British Frame*.

4 Bourne, *Black in the British Frame*, p. 87.

5 Bourne, *Black in the British Frame*, p. 88.

Lloyd Coxsone

Steve Barrow and Peter Dalton, *The Rough Guide to Reggae* (London: Rough Guides, 1997).

Simon Jones and Paul Pinnock, *Scientists of Sound: Portraits of a Reggae Sound System* (independently published, 2017).

Michael De Koningh and Marc Griffiths, *Tighten Up! The History of Reggae in the UK* (London: Sanctuary, 2004).

David Katz, 'The return of Sir Coxsone Outernational, the UK's most influential sound system', *Fact Mag* (2 September 2015), https://www.factmag.com/2015/09/02/sir-coxsone-outernational-interview/.

Lloyd Coxsone – His Story (Angry People Smiling, 2018), accessed from YouTube, https://www.youtube.com/watch?v=JvqQn-osIpU.

William Cuffay

Notes: 1 Ron Ramdin, *The Making of the Black Working Class in Britain* (London: Verso, updated edition, 2017), p. 19. Other leaders of African heritage included Robert Wedderburn (1762–1835), Matthew Bogle, Benjamin Profitt and David Duffey

2 Stephen Roberts (ed.), *The People's Charter: Democratic Agitation in Early Victorian Britain* (London: The Merlin Press, 2003), p. 1.

3 Roberts (ed.), *The People's Charter*, p. 2.

4 T. M. Wheeler, 'Mr William Cuffay', *Reynold's Political Instructor* (13 April 1850), p. 177.

5 Norbert J. Gossman, 'William Cuffay: London's Black Chartist', *Phylon*, vol. 44, no. 1 (1983), p. 58.

6 Ramdin, *The Making of the Black Working Class*, p. 25.

7 Gossman, 'William Cuffay', p. 58.

8 Ramdin, *The Making of the Black Working Class*, p. 25.

9 Ramdin, *The Making of the Black Working Class*, p. 26.

10 Gossman, 'William Cuffay', p. 63.

Quobna Ottobah Cugoano

Notes: 1 Quobna Ottobah Cugoano, *Thoughts and Sentiments on the Evil and Wicked Traffic of the Slavery and Commerce of the Human Species*, ed. Vincent Caretta (Harmondsworth: Penguin, 1999), p. 7.

2 Cugoano, *Thoughts and Sentiments*, p. xi.

3 Cugoano, *Thoughts and Sentiments*, p. xiii. Lord Mansfield's great niece Dido Elizabeth Belle was of mixed parentage. The scholar

Gretchen Gerzina considers the extent to which Mansfield reconciled his affection for her and the suffering of the men and women who looked like her who came before him in court. Gretchen Gerzina, *Black England: Life Before Emancipation* (London: Allison and Busby, 1999), p. 92.

4 Hakim Adi and Marika Sherwood, *Pan-African History: Political figures from African and the Diaspora since 1787* (London: Routledge, 2003), p. 26.

5 Granville Sharp was known for his role in the Somerset case; he convinced Mansfield to issue the writ of habeas corpus, ordering Somerset be brought before the court.

6 Charles T. Davis and Henry Louis Gates, *The Slave's Narrative* (Oxford: Oxford University Press 1985), pp.183–6.

Dame Linda Dobbs DBE

Notes: 1 'Judges and non-legal members of the judiciary, by ethnicity', GOV.UK (13 January 2020), https://www.ethnicity-facts-figures. service.gov.uk/workforce-and-business/workforce-diversity/judges-and-non-legal-members-of-courts-and-tribunals-in-the-workforce/latest.

2 Paul Knepper, 'Black Firsts in British Law', LERN Grant Report, University of Sheffield Law School (2015), https://ials.sas.ac.uk/sites/default/files/files/About%20us/Leadership%20%26%20Collaboration/LERN/LERN_grant_REPORT_PK.pdf.

3 Desiree Artesi, 'Potential Difference: Dame Linda Dobbs interview', *Counsel Magazine* (June 2019), https://www.counselmagazine.co.uk/articles/potential-difference-dame-linda-dobbs.

4 Artesi, 'Potential Difference'.

5 Leah Henderson, 'The Big Interview: Dame Linda Dobbs', *Chambers Student UK* (May 2019), https://www.chambersstudent. co.uk/where-to-start/newsletter/the-big-interview-dame-linda-dobbs.

John Edmonstone

R. B. Freeman, 'Darwin's Negro Bird Stuffer', *Notes and Records of the Royal Society of London*, vol. 33, no. 1 (1978), pp. 83–6.

Francis Darwin, *The Life and Letters of Charles Darwin, Volume 1* (London: D. Appleton and Company, 1896).

Julia Blackburn, *Charles Waterton 1782–1865: Traveller and Conservationist* (London: The Bodley Head, 1991).

Notes: 1 Charles Waterton, *Wanderings in South America, the north-west of the United States, and the Antilles in the years 1812, 1816, 1820 and 1824* (London, 1825), p. 154.

2 Darwin, *The Life and Letters of Charles Darwin*, pp. 35–6.

Idris Elba OBE

Notes: 1 Maane Khatchatourian and James Bailey, 'Idris Elba "too street" to play Bond, 007 author says', *Variety* (1 September 2015), https://variety.com/2015/film/news/idris-elba-james-bond-too-street-author-anthony-horowitz-1201582692/.

2 Nolan Feeney, 'Idris Elba says there is more diversity in US TV and film than UK', *Time* (19 January 2016), https://time.com/4184830/idris-elba-diversity-tv-film-oscars/.

Edward Enninful OBE

Notes: 1 Afua Hirsch, 'Glossies so white: the data that reveals the problem with British magazine covers', *Guardian* (10 April 2018), https://www.theguardian.com/media/2018/apr/10/glossy-magazine-covers-too-white-models-black-ethnic-minority.

2 Afua Hirsch, '*Vogue*'s Edward Enninful: "Was the criticism of Meghan Markle racist? Some of it, yes"', *Guardian* (21 September 2019), https://www.theguardian.com/fashion/2019/sep/21/edward-enninful-vogue-meghan-markle-criticism-racist.

3 Dodai Stewart, 'The All Black Issue of Italian Vogue: Both a Success and a Failure', *Jezebel* (31 July 2008), https://jezebel.com/the-all-black-issue-of-italian-vogue-both-a-success-5031485.

4 Lauren Indvik, 'Edward Enninful on *Vogue*, Gen Z and what makes a great editor', *Vogue Business* (5 August 2019), https://www.vogue-business.com/companies/edward-enninful-interview-editor-in-chief-british-vogue.

Olaudah Equiano

Notes: 1 Vincent Carretta, *Equiano the African: Biography of a Self-Made Man* (Athens, GA: University of Georgia Press, 2005), p. 115.

2 Paul Edwards and David Dabydeen (eds), *Black Writers in Britain, 1760–1890: An Anthology* (Edinburgh: Edinburgh University Press, 1995), p. 54.

3 Olaudah Equiano, *The Interesting Narrative and Other Writings* (Harmondsworth: Penguin, 2003), p. 93.

4 Folarin Shyllon, *Black People in Britain, 1555–1833* (London: Oxford University Press, Institute of Race Relations, 1977), p. 226.

5 I don't mean to suggest there was a causal link between the two events, although it is possible.

6 James Walvin, *An African's Life: The Life and Times of Olaudah Equiano, 1745–1797* (London: Cassell, 1998), p. 130.

7 Walvin, *An African's Life* , p. 131.

8 Shyllon, *Black People in Britain*, p. 233.

9 Walvin, *An African's Life*, p. 160.

Bernardine Evaristo MBE, FRSL

Hannah Chukwu, 'Older Black women, who writes about that?', *Five Dials* (undated), https://fivedials.com/interviews/older-black-women-who-writes-about-that-bernardine-evaristo/.

Free Verse: Publishing opportunities for Black and Asian poets (Arts Council), https://www.spreadtheword.org.uk/wp-content/uploads/2016/11/Free-Verse-Report.pdf.

Alison Donnell, 'Writing of and for our time: Bernadine Evaristo talks to Alison Donnell', *Wasafiri*, vol. 34. no. 4 (October 2019), pp. 99–104.

'Great Writers Inspire at Home: Bernardine Evaristo on writing Britain's Black Histories' (undated), https://writersmakeworlds.com/video-bernardine-evaristo-writing-britains-black-histories/.

Notes: 1 Anita Sethi, 'Bernardine Evaristo: I want to put presence into absence', *Guardian* (27 April 2019), https://www.theguardian.com/books/2019/apr/27/bernardine-evaristo-girl-woman-other-interview.

2 Donnell, 'Writing for and of our time', p. 99.

Lenford Kwesi Garrison

Nigel Carter, 'Lenford Kwesi Garrison', New Ruskin Archives (2014), http://newruskinarchives.org.uk/wp/?page_id=757.

Notes: 1 David Olusoga, *Black and British: A Forgotten History* (London: Macmillan, 2016), p. 493.

2 Len Garrison, *Black Youth, Rastafarianism, and the Identity Crisis in Britain* (London: ACER, 1979), p. 39; Raimund Schaffner, 'Assimilation, separatism and multiculturalism in Mustapha Matura's *Welcome Home Jacko* and Caryl Phillips's *Strange Fruit*', *Wasafiri*, vol. 14, no. 29, p. 66.

3 Google Arts and Culture, 'The development of the Black Cultural Archives', online exhibition, *Google Arts and Culture* (undated), https://artsandculture.google.com/exhibit/the-development-of-black-cultural-archives-black-cultural-archives/NgJC8B5HTgpBLg?hl=en.

4 'Black Cultural Archives welcomes MPs recognition', *Brixton Blog* (25 June 2018), https://brixtonblog.com/2018/06/black-cultural-archives-welcomes-mps-recognition/?cn-reloaded=1.

5 Lauri Johnson, 'Culturally Responsive Leadership for Community Empowerment', *Multicultural Education Review*, vol. 6, no. 2 (2014)

6 Johnson, 'Culturally Responsive Leadership', p. 158.

George the Poet

Griselda Murray Brown and Lilah Raptopoulos, 'From Rap to Representation with George the Poet', *FT Culture Call Podcast*, *Financial Times* (27 October 2019), https://www.ft.com/content/5a8e2aa2-1eaf-4f4d-b12e-f536d17075ea.

Notes: 1 George the Poet, 'Concurrent Affairs', *Have You Heard George's Podcast?*, chapter 2, episode 18 (2019).

2 Tara Joshi, 'George the Poet is pushing podcasting's limits', *New York Times* (18 September 2019), https://www.nytimes.com/2019/09/18/arts/music/george-the-poet-podcast.html.

Paul Gilroy

The 2019 Holberg Conversation with Paul Gilroy (2019), https://www.youtube.com/watch?v=PBntPdPcQes.

Notes: 1 Paul Gilroy, Tony Sandset, Sindre Bangstad and Gard Ringen Høibjerg, 'A diagnosis of contemporary forms of racism, race and nationalism: a conversation with Professor Paul Gilroy', *Cultural Studies*, vol. 33, no. 2 (2019), pp. 173–97.

2 Les Back, 'Viewpoint: There Ain't No Black in the Union Jack @ Thirty', *Discover Society* (2 January 2019), https://discoversociety.org/2019/01/02/viewpoint-there-aint-no-black-in-the-union-jack-thirty/.

3 Jennifer Schuessler, 'Paul Gilroy, scholar of the Black Atlantic, wins Holberg Prize', *New York Times* (14 March 2019), https://www.nytimes.com/2019/03/14/arts/paul-gilroy-holberg-prize.html.

Bernie Grant

Notes: 1 Bernie Grant's maiden speech in the House of Commons (6 July 1987), https://kmflett.wordpress.com/2020/04/08/bernie-grants-maiden-house-of-commons-speech-6th-july-1987-berniegrant20/.

2 Thomas L. Blair, 'Bernie Grant's Black agenda forged in Thatcher's years, still relevant today', *Chronicleworld* (16 April 2013), https://

chronicleworld.co.uk/2013/04/16/bernie-grants-black-agenda-forged-in-thatchers-years-still-relevant-today/.

Stuart Hall

Notes: 1 Sam Harman, 'Stuart Hall: Re-reading Cultural Identity, Diaspora and Film', *Howard Journal of Communications*, vol. 27, no. 2 (2016), p. 114.

2 Stuart Hall, 'Critical Dialogues in Cultural Studies: The formation of a diasporic intellectual', in Onyekachi Wambu (ed.), *Empire Windrush: Fifty Years of Writing about Black Britain* (London: Victor Gollancz 1998), p. 35.

3 Hua Hsu, 'Stuart Hall and the rise of Cultural Studies', *New Yorker* (17 July 2017), https://www.newyorker.com/books/page-turner/stuart-hall-and-the-rise-of-cultural-studies.

4 Wambu, *Empire Windrush*, p. 37.

5 Stuart Hall with Bill Schwarz, *Familiar Stranger: A Life Between Two Islands* (London: Penguin, 2018), p. 173.

6 Sam Harman, 'Stuart Hall', p. 115.

7 Stuart Hall and Sut Jhally, 'The Last Interview: Stuart Hall on the politics of Cultural Studies' (transcript, undated,), p. 4, https://www.mediaed.org/transcripts/The-Last-Interview-Transcript.pdf.

8 David Morley and Bill Schwarz, 'Stuart Hall obituary', *Guardian* (10 February 2014), https://www.theguardian.com/politics/2014/feb/10/stuart-hall.

Lewis Hamilton MBE

Notes: 1 Oliver Brown, 'Lewis Hamilton carries the scars of racist abuse, says Mercedes chief Toto Wolff', *Telegraph* (25 October 2019), https://www.telegraph.co.uk/formula-1/2019/10/25/lewis-hamilton-carries-scars-racist-abuse-says-mercedes-chieftoto/.

Sir Lenny Henry CBE

'Lenny Henry on seeing comedy as a career', Chortle UK (2019), accessed from YouTube, https://www.youtube.com/watch?v= 2MQrd4hchfk.

Lanre Bakare, 'Lenny Henry: "I wish someone had taught me how to defend myself"', *Guardian* (21 October 2019), https://www. theguardian.com/culture/2019/oct/21/lenny-henry-wish-some-body-taught-me-to-defend-myself.

Lubaina Himid CBE, RA

Notes: 1 Lubaina Himid, quoted in Celeste-Marie Bernier, *Stick to the Skin: African American and Black British Art, 1965–2015* (Los Angeles: University of California Press, 2018), p. 48.

Dame Kelly Holmes DBE

Sandra Laville, 'Kelly Holmes reveals she self-harmed at the height of athletics career', *Guardian* (24 September 2017), https://www. theguardian.com/sport/2017/sep/24/kelly-holmes-tells-how-she-self-harmed-at-height-of-athletics-career.

Rob Bagchi, '50 Stunning Olympic Moments no. 34: Kelly Holmes doubles up in Athens', *Guardian* (29 May 2012), https://www. theguardian.com/sport/blog/2012/may/29/50-stunning-olympic-moments-kelly-holmes.

Darcus Howe

Notes: 1 Robin Bunce and Paul Field, *Darcus Howe: A Political Biography* (London: Bloomsbury Academic, 2013).

   2 Robin Bunce and Paul Field, 'Darcus Howe obituary', *Guardian* (3 April 2017), https://www.theguardian.com/world/2017/apr/03/ darcus-howe-obituary.

Rose Hudson-Wilkin MBE

Notes: 1 Resignation letter from Professor Gus John to CMEAC (29 November 2019), https://www.ihrc.org.uk/wp-content/uploads/2019/12/TakingAStand-ProfGusJohn.pdf.

2 Harriet Sherwood, 'Justin Welby says he's "sorry and ashamed" over church's racism', *Guardian* (11 February 2020), https://www.theguardian.com/world/2020/feb/11/justin-welby-tells-synod-he-is-sorry-and-ashamed-over-churchs-racism.

3 Harriet Sherwood, 'I'm Britain's first Black woman bishop and I long for the day when that's not unusual', *Observer* (23 November 2019), https://www.theguardian.com/world/2019/nov/23/first-black-woman-bishop-church-england-rose-hudson-wilkin-dover-racism-inequality.

4 Cole Moreton, 'Rose Hudson-Wilkin: could she be the Right Rev?', *Daily Telegraph* (5 February 2012), https://www.telegraph.co.uk/news/religion/9061674/Rose-Hudson-Wilkin-could-she-be-the-Right-Rev.html; Katie Stock, 'Rose Hudson Wilkin: My battle against racism and sexism', *Premier Christianity* (August 2017), https://www.premierchristianity.com/Past-Issues/2017/August-2017/Rose-Hudson-Wilkin-My-battle-against-racism-and-sexism.

5 Ibid

6 Sherwood, 'Justin Welby says he's "sorry and ashamed" '.

Eric Huntley and Jessica Huntley

Margaret Andrews, *Doing Nothing is Not An Option: The Radical Lives of Eric & Jessica Huntley* (London: Krik Krak, 2014).

Margaret Busby, 'Jessica Huntley obituary', *Guardian* (27 October 2013), https://www.theguardian.com/books/2013/oct/27/jessica-huntley.

Professor Augustine 'Gus' John

Notes: 1 Andy Bowman, 'A violent eruption of protest: reflections on the 1981 Moss Side "Riots", part one', *Mule* (15 August 2011),

http://manchestermule.com/article/%E2%80%98a-violent-erup-
tion-of-protest%E2%80%99-reflections-on-the-1981-moss-side-
%E2%80%98riots%E2%80%99-part-one.
2 Bowman, 'A violent eruption of protest'.
3 Gus John, 'Why I'm turning down Teresa May's invitation to celebrate Windrush', *Guardian* (21 June 2018), https://www.theguard-
ian.com/commentisfree/2018/jun/21/turning-down-theresa-may-
windrush-reception-caribbean-hostile-environment.

Linton Kwesi Johnson

Notes: 1 Dorian Lynskey, *33 Revolutions per Minute: A History of Protest
Songs* (London: Faber and Faber, 2012).

Claudia Jones

Notes: 1 Carole Boyce Davies, *Left of Karl Marx; The Political Biography
of Black Communist Claudia Jones* (Durham, NC: Duke University
Press, 2008), p. xiii.
2 Fongot Kini-Yen Kinni, *Pan-Africanism: Political Philosophy and
Socio-Economic Anthropology for African Liberation and Governance:
Caribbean and African American Contributions* (Cameroon: Langaa
RPCIG, 2015), p. 589.
3 Kinni, *Pan-Africanism*, p. 590.
4 Boyce Davies, *Left of Karl Marx*, pp. 143–4.
5 Donald Hinds, 'The *West Indian Gazette*: Claudia Jones and the
Black Press in Britain', *Race and Class*, vol. 50, no. 1, p. 91.
6 Boyce Davies, *Left of Karl Marx*, p. 172.
7 Donald Hinds, 'The *West Indian Gazette*', p. 92.
8 Boyce Davies, *Left of Karl Marx*, p. 174.
9 Boyce Davies, *Left of Karl Marx*, p. 175.

Jackie Kay CBE

Notes: 1 Alison Lumsden, 'Jackie Kay's 'Poetry and Prose: Constructing Identity', in Aileen Christianson and Alison Lumsden (eds), *Contemporary Scottish Women Writers* (Edinburgh: Edinburgh University Press, 2000), p. 79.

2 Peter Clandfield, 'What's in My Blood: Contemporary Black Scottishness and the Work of Jackie Kay', in Teresa Hubel and Neil Brook (eds), *Literature of Racial Ambiguity* (Rodopi Perspectives on Modern Literature) (Amsterdam: Editions Rodopi, 2002), p. 2.

3 Jackie Kay, in Ozlem Aydin, *Speaking from the Margins: The Voice of the Other in the Poetry of Carol Ann Duffy and Jackie Kay* (Washington, DC: Academica Press, 2010), p. 77.

4 Patience Agbabi, 'Book of a Lifetime: The Adoption Papers, Jackie Kay', *Independent* (25 April 2008), https://www.independent.co.uk /arts-entertainment/books/features/book-of-a-lifetime-the-adop-tion-papers-jackie-kay-814970.html.

Sam King MBE

Notes: 1 Sam King, *Climbing Up the Rough Side of the Mountain* (Peterborough: Upfront, 2004).

Kwame Kwei-Armah OBE

Notes: 1 Bernardine Evaristo, 'Statements of Intent: An interview with Kwame Kwei-Armah', *Wasafiri*, vol. 25, no. 4 (2010), p. 57.

2 Kwame Kwei-Armah, *Plays:1* (London: Methuen, 2009), introduction.

3 Evaristo, 'Statements of Intent', p. 54.

4 Kwei-Armah, *Plays: 1*, introduction.

5 Lynette Goddard, 'Cultural Diversity and Black British Playwrighting on the Mainstream, 2000–2012', National Theatre Black Plays Archive (undated), http://www.blackplaysarchive.org. uk/sites/default/files/bpa_essay-series-lynette_goddard.pdf, p. 2.

6 Goddard, 'Cultural Diversity', p. 3.

John La Rose

Notes: 1 Linton Kwesi Johnson, 'John La Rose', *Guardian* (4 March 2006), https://www.theguardian.com/news/2006/mar/04/guardianobituaries.socialexclusion.

2 Gus John, 'John La Rose', *Independent* (22 April 2006), https://www.independent.co.uk/news/obituaries/john-la-rose-8704221.html.

3 Johnson, 'John La Rose'.

4 Margaret Busby, 'John La Rose', *Wasafiri*, vol. 21, no. 3 (2006), p. 65.

5 Busby, 'John La Rose', p. 66.

6 Busby, 'John La Rose', p. 67.

David Lammy

Notes: 1 Richard Adams and Caelainn Barr, 'Oxford faces anger over failure to improve diversity among students', *Guardian* (23 May 2018), https://www.theguardian.com/education/2018/may/23/oxford-faces-anger-over-failure-to-improve-diversity-among-students; Rianna Croxford, 'Dearth of black students admitted to Cambridge revealed by FOI request', *Financial Times* (3 June 2018), https://www.ft.com/content/9dcd7d0a-65b3-11e8-a39d-4df188287fff.

Marai Larasi MBE

Notes: 1 Imkaan.org.uk.

2 David Batty, 'Marai Larasi: I'm hurt that this country neglects BME women', *Guardian* (12 February 2019), https://www.theguardian.com/society/2019/feb/12/marai-larasi-bme-women-services-domestic-violence.

3 Maya Oppenheim, 'Women's lives "at risk" as refuges for black and minority ethnic domestic-violence survivors face closure', *Independent* (6 July 2019), https://www.independent.co.uk/news/

uk/home-news/women-refuge-domestic-violence-refuge-bame-london-black-women-s-project-newham-cuts-a8990391.html.

4 'State of the Sector: Contextualising the current experiences of BME ending violence against women and girls organisations', Imkaan (November 2015), p. 13, https://www.dropbox.com/s/c3n2gjs4g2g37s2/IMKAAN%20-%20STATE%20OF%20THE%20SECTOR%20%5BFINAL%5D.pdf?dl=0.

5 Marai Larasi, 'The Leveson inquiry must address media treatment of women', *Guardian* (24 January 2012), https://www.theguardian.com/commentisfree/2012/jan/24/leveson-inquiry-media-treatment-women.

6 Marai Larasi, 'In the words of Marai Larasi', UN Women, Europe and Central Asia (15 December 2017), https://eca.unwomen.org/en/news/stories/2017/12/in-the-words-of-marai-larasi-the-executive-director-of-imkaan.

Doreen Lawrence, Baroness Lawrence of Clarendon OBE

'The Stephen Lawrence Inquiry' (Macpherson Report, February 1999). https://assets.publishing.service.gov.uk/government/uploads/system/uploads/attachment_data/file/277111/4262.pdf.

'Doreen Lawrence: the mother who changed the justice system', *Justice Gap* (29 March 2019), https://www.thejusticegap.com/doreen-lawrence-the-mother-who-changed-the-justice-system/.

The Stephen Lawrence Research Centre, De Montfort University, https://www.dmu.ac.uk/research/centres-institutes/stephen-lawrence-research-centre/index.aspx.

Andrea Levy

Notes: 1 Andrea Levy, 'How I learned to stop hating my heritage', *Guardian* (3 November 2014), https://www.theguardian.com/commentisfree/2014/nov/03/how-i-learned-stop-hating-heritage.

2 Levy, 'How I learned to stop hating my heritage'.

3 Gary Younge, 'After a life of striving, Andrea Levy got the acclaim she deserved', *Guardian* (15 February 2019), https://www.

theguardian.com/books/2019/feb/15/andrea-levy-fight-recogni-
tion-truly-deserved-politics.

4 Mark Brown, 'Andrea Levy's literary archive acquired by the British
Library', *Guardian* (6 February 2020), https://www.theguardian.
com/books/2020/feb/06/andrea-levy-literary-archive-acquired-by-
british-library.

Sir Steven McQueen CBE

Notes: 1 Sarah Crompton, 'Steve McQueen's Queen and Country: The
new face of remembrance', *Telegraph* (10 November 2008), https://
www.telegraph.co.uk/culture/art/3563050/Steve-McQueens-
Queen-and-Country-The-new-face-of-remembrance.html.

Dr Harold Moody

Ron Ramdin, *The Making of the Black Working Class in Britain* (London:
Verso, updated edition, 2017).

David Dabydeen, John Gilmore and Cecily Jones (eds), *The Oxford Companion
to Black British History* (Oxford: Oxford University Press, 2007).

Daniel Whittall, 'Creating Black Places in Imperial London: The League
of Coloured Peoples and Aggrey House, 1931–1943', *London
Journal*, vol. 36, no. 3, pp. 225–46.

Olive Morris

Angelina Osborne, 'The power of Olive Morris' (2 October 2018),
https://www.fawcettsociety.org.uk/blog/black-history-month-
power-olive-morris.

Tanisha C. Ford, *Liberated Threads: Black Women, Style and the Global Politics
of Soul* (Chapel Hill, NC: University of North Carolina Press, 2015).

Notes: 1 Here, 'Black' is used here in the political sense to include
African, Caribbean and South Asian communities.

2 Ford, *Liberated Threads*, p. 140.

Grace Nichols and John Agard

Notes: 1 F. S. J, Ledgister, 'Arrival Poems', *Caribbean Review of Books* (21 May 2010), http://caribbeanreviewofbooks.com/crb-archive/21-may-2010/arrival-poems/.

2 Hannah Lowe, 'Inside the Frame: Women Writers and the Windrush Legacy, Interviews with Grace Nichols, Karen McCarthy Woolf and Jay Bernard', *Wasafiri*, vol. 33, no. 2 (2018), pp. 3–9.

3 'Poems by Grace Nichols: typescript drafts including "Granny Granny Please Comb My Hair", "Break Dance" and "Cosmic Disco"', British Library (undated), https://www.bl.uk/collection-items/poems-by-grace-nichols-typescript-drafts.

4 '"Checking Out Me History" by John Agard analysis', BBC Class Clips, English Literature KS3/GCSE, https://www.bbc.co.uk/teach/class-lips-video/john-agard-checking-out-me-history-analysis/zdbkqp3.

5 Stuart Hall, 'Cultural Identity and Diaspora', in Jonathan Rutherford (ed.), *Identity: Community, Culture, Difference* (London: Lawrence and Wishart, 2003), p. 222.

6 John Agard, 'In Praise of Poetry', quoted in Leanna M. Hall, 'Caribbean Hybridity: Language and Identity in John Agard's Poetry' (undated BA thesis), p. 1.

7 'John Agard', Poetry Archive (undated), https://poetryarchive.org/poet/john-agard/

8 'John Agard'.

Chinyere (Chi-chi) Nwanoku OBE

Notes: 1 'Equality and Diversity in the Classical Music Profession: A report by Dr Christina Scharff' (London: King's College London, 2015), https://www.impulse-music.co.uk/wp-content/uploads/2017/05/Equality-and-Diversity-in-Classical-Music-Report.pdf.

2 'Meet Chi-chi Nwanoku', https://www.chi-chinwanoku.com/meet-chi-chi/.

3 Katie Strick, 'Chineke! Founder Chi Chi Nwanoku: We're what orchestras tomorrow will look like', *Evening Standard* (17 July 2018), https://www.standard.co.uk/go/london/arts/chineke-founder-chichi-nwanoku-were-what-orchestras-tomorrow-will-look-like-a3888956.html.

David Adetayo Olusoga OBE

Notes: 1 Tom Ough, 'David Olusoga: As a child I never presumed the racism I experienced would ever stop', *Daily Telegraph* (11 June 2020), https://www.telegraph.co.uk/family/life/david-olusoga-child-experienced-racism-teachers-strangers-never/.

2 David Olusoga, 'The Treasury's tweet shows that slavery is still misunderstood', The *Guardian* (12 February 2018), https://www.theguardian.com/commentisfree/2018/feb/12/treasury-tweet-slavery-compensate-slave-owners.

3 David Olusoga, *Black and British: A Forgotten History* (London: Macmillan, 2016).

4 Professor David Olusoga, 'Unlocking the links to our past and identities', *Lockdown Lectures*, University of Manchester (10 June 2020), https://www.youtube.com/watch?v=YK8GWpKCG8Q.

Phyllis Opoku-Gyimah (Lady Phyll)

Notes: 1 Here 'Black' is used in its political term to mean the African and Asian diaspora.

2 Ella Braidwood, 'Meet the UK Black Pride co-founder who turned down an MBE', *Vice Magazine* (20 February 2016), https://www.vice.com/en_uk/article/qbx94d/lgbt-history-month-phyll-opoku-gyimah-interview.

3 Kirsty Osei-Bempong, 'gal-dem in conversation with Lady Phyll, director of Black Pride UK', *gal-dem magazine* (26 June 2016), http://gal-dem.com/lady-phyll-director-black-pride-uk/.

4 Braidwood, 'Meet the UK Black Pride co-founder'.

Olivette Otele

Aamna Mohdin, 'UK's first Black female history professor to research Bristol's slavery links', *Guardian* (30 October 2019), https://www. theguardian.com/education/2019/oct/30/olivette-otele-uk-first-black-female-history-professor-to-research-bristol-slavery-links.

'University of Bristol appoints new black history professor to explore its relationship with the slave trade', University of Bristol press release (30 October 2019), http://www.bristol.ac.uk/news/2019/october/professor-of-the-history-of-slavery-.html.

Julia Llewellyn Smith, 'The privileged don't get to tell us when slavery stops hurting', *The Times* (3 November 2019), https://www. thetimes.co.uk/article/olivette-otele-the-privileged-dont-get-to-tell -us-when-slavery-stops-hurting-xlx9tsxcq.

Nadine White, 'Meet Olivette Otele, Britain's first ever Black female history professor', *Huffington Post* (8 December 2018), https:// www.huffingtonpost.co.uk/entry/britains-first-black-history-professor-on-career-motherhood-and-racism-in-academia_uk_ 5be3f540e4b0769d24c95370.

Notes: 1 'Race, Ethnicity and Equality in UK History: A Report and Resource for Change' (London: Royal Historical Society, October 2018), p. 22.

Horace Ové CBE

Paul Ward, 'Ové, Horace (1939–)', BFI Screenonline (undated), http:/ /www.screenonline.org.uk/people/id/507421/.

Sally Shaw, 'Screening Black Political Struggle on 1970s British Television: the case of Play for Today, A Hole in Babylon', *Historical Journal of Film Radio and Television*, vol. 35, no. 3 (2015), pp. 489–502.

Annabelle Alcazar, 'Horace Ové, Cultural Icon', *Caribbean Quarterly*, vol. 61, nos 2–3 (2015), pp. 143–6.

Notes: 1 Josanne Leonard, 'Interview with Horace Ove' (22 March 2009), http://josanneleonard.blogspot.com/2009/03/interview-with-horace-ove-film-maker.html.

David Oyelowo

Horatia Harrod, 'David Oyelowo: I had to quit Britain in order to succeed', *Telegraph* (15 October 2016), https://www.telegraph.co.uk/films/2016/10/15/david-oyelowo-interview-i-had-to-quit-britain-in-order-to-succee/.

David Oyelowo's speech on diversity, BFI Black Star Symposium (20 October 2016), accessed on YouTube, https://www.youtube.com/watch?v=FhFaAXfR2NU.

George Padmore

Leslie James, *George Padmore and Decolonization from Below: Pan-Africanism, the Cold War and the End of Empire* (London: Palgrave Macmillan, 2015).

Bill Schwartz (ed.), *West Indian Intellectuals in Britain* (Manchester: University of Manchester Press, 2003).

Notes: 1 Bill Schwarz, 'George Padmore', in Bill Schwarz (ed.), *West Indian Intellectuals in Britain* (Manchester: Studies in Imperialism, University of Manchester Press, 2003), p. 149.

Geoff Palmer

Geoff Palmer, *The Enlightenment Abolished: Citizens of Britishness* (Penicuik: Henry Publishing, 2007).

Stephen Mullen, *It Wisnae Us: The Truth about Glasgow and Slavery* (Edinburgh: The Royal Incorporation of Architects in Scotland, 2009).

Alex Pascall OBE

Notes: 1 Lionel Morrison, *A Century of Black Journalism in Britain: A Kaleidoscopic View of Race in the Media* (London: Truebay 2007), p. 45.

2 Elizabeth Williams, 'Anti-Apartheid: The Black British Response', *South African Historical Journal*, vol. 64, no. 3 (2012), p. 697.

3 Angela Cobbinah, 'Black Londoners: Ex-presenter Alex Pascall looks back' (28 October 2016), https://angelacobbinah.wordpress.com/2016/10/28/black-londoners-ex-presenter-alex-pascall-looks-back/.

David Pitt, Baron Pitt of Hampstead

Jeanette Arnold OBE, 'Echoes of our past: A series of reflections on prominent black people' (2014), https://jennettearnold.com/wp-content/uploads/2014/09/Echoes-A5-red.pdf.

David Dabydeen, John Gilmore and Cecily Jones (eds), *The Oxford Companion to Black British History* (Oxford: Oxford University Press, 2007).

Mary Prince

Mary Prince, *A History of Mary Prince, A West Indian Slave, Related by Herself* (London: Westley and Davis, 1831).

Marvin Rees

Notes: 1 John Harris, 'Bristol Mayor Marvin Rees: "My dad arrived to signs saying, No Irish, No Blacks, No Dogs"', *Guardian* (23 May 2016), https://www.theguardian.com/cities/2016/may/23/bristol-mayor-marvin-rees-racism-inequality.

2 Farah Elahi, Nissa Finney and Kitty Lymperopoulou, *Bristol: a city divided? Ethnic Minority disadvantage in Education and Employment* (Manchester: Centre on Dynamics of Ethnicity/Runnymede Trust, 2017), pp. 1–4.

Bill Richmond and Thomas Molyneux

Kevin R. Smith, *Black Genesis: The History of the Black Prize-fighter, 1760–1870* (Bloomington, IN: iUniverse, 2003).

Luke G. Williams, *Richmond Unchained: The Biography of the World's First Black Sporting Superstar* (Stroud: Amberley, 2015).

Pierce Egan, *Boxiana, or Sketches of Modern Pugilism*, vols 1 and 3 (London: Virtue, 1830).

Notes: 1 Joe Lashley entry in David Dabydeen, John Gilmore, Cecily Jones (eds), *The Oxford Companion to Black British History* (Oxford: Oxford University Press, 2007).

2 Egan, *Boxiana*, vol. 1, p. 477.

3 Egan, *Boxiana*, vol. 3, p. 493.

Marcia Rigg

Nina Lakhani, 'The story behind Sean Rigg's death in custody', *Independent* (2 August 2012), https://www.independent.co.uk/news/uk/crime/the-story-behind-sean-riggs-death-in-custody-7999485.html.

Sean Rigg Justice and Change Campaign, https://www.seanriggjustice-andchange.com.

Oona Ryder and Sam Swann, 'Marcia Rigg interview: Deaths in State Custody: Justice for Sean Rigg', Novara Media podcast (17 October 2018), https://novaramedia.com/2018/10/17/deaths-in-state-custody-1-justice-for-sean-rigg/.

Ignatius Sancho

Notes: 1 Peter Fryer, *Staying Power: The History of Black People in Britain* (London: Pluto Press, 1984), p. 134.

2 Fryer, *Staying Power*, p. 67.

3 Fryer, *Staying Power*, p. 71.

4 Ignatius Sancho, *Letters of the Late Ignatius Sancho, An African, in Two Volumes* (London, 1782), Letter 35, July 1766.

5 Fryer, *Staying Power*, p. 93.

6 Gretchen Gerzina, 'Ignatius Sancho: A Renaissance Black Man in Eighteenth-Century England', *Journal of Blacks in Higher Education*, vol. 21 (1998), pp. 106–7.

Stafford Scott

Stafford Scott, 'The way out of the Gangs Matrix crisis', *Amnesty Magazine*, no. 197 (21 October 2019), https://www.amnesty.org.uk/way-out-gangs-matrix-crisis.

Campaign Opposing Police Surveillance, http://campaignopposingpolicesurveillance.com/tag/stafford-scott/.

Notes: 1 Katy Stoddard, 'From the Archive blog: Anger smoulders in Tottenham: The Broadwater Farm riots of 1985', *Guardian* (8 August 2011), https://www.theguardian.com/theguardian/from-the-archive-blog/2011/aug/08/anger-tottenham-broadwater-riots-1985.

2 Steven Hopkins, 'Veteran British racism campaigner has message to Black Lives Matter ahead of London riots anniversary' *Huffington Post* (30 July 2016), https://www.huffingtonpost.co.uk/entry/london-riots-anniversary-nothing-has-changed-since-mark-duggan-shooting-claims-race-advocate-still-fighting-for-justice_uk_578f5a54e4b011978b131e84.

3 Stafford Scott, 'The investigation into Mark Duggan's death is tainted. I want no part of it', *Guardian* (20 November 2011), https://www.theguardian.com/commentisfree/2011/nov/20/investigation-mark-duggan-tainted.

4 Scott, 'The investigation into Mark Duggan's death is tainted'.

Mary Seacole

Jane Robinson, *Mary Seacole: The Charismatic Black Nurse who became a Heroine of the Crimea* (London: Robinson, 2005).

Ron Ramdin, *Mary Seacole (Life and Times)* (London: Haus, 2005).

Notes: 1 Gaston Bodart and Vernon Lyman Kellogg, *Losses of Life in Modern Wars: Austro-Hungary, France, and Military Selection and Race Deterioration* (Oxford: Clarendon Press, 1916).

Yinka Shonibare CBE RA

Notes: 1 Yema Thomas, 'Race, Class and Wealth: Thomas Gainsborough's *Mr and Mrs Andrews* (1750) and Yinka Shonibare's *Mr and Mrs Andrews Without their Heads* (1998)', Georgia State University paper (2016).

2 Yinka Shonibare profile, Royal Academy of Arts website (undated), https://www.royalacademy.org.uk/art-artists/name/yinka-shonibare-ra

3 Andrew M. Goldstein, 'Yinka Shonibare on art, Africa, and why he's so fond of the Queen', Artspace.com (20 December 2014), https://www.artspace.com/magazine/interviews_features/meet_the _artist/yinka-shonibare-interview-52566.

4 Goldstein, 'Yinka Shonibare on art'.

Paul Stephenson

Madge Dresser, *Black and White on the Buses: The 1963 Colour Bar Dispute in Bristol* (Bristol: Bristol Broadsides Co-op Ltd, 1986).

Culture Clash on the Frontline: The Story of Jamaicans in Bristol, dir. Borja Cantera (Undo Productions, 2010), accessed on YouTube, https://www.youtube.com/watch?v=HrVNhRVWHrM.

Stormzy

Reni Eddo-Lodge, ' "It's my purpose to shine a light where I can": How Stormzy is championing Black British culture', *Time* (10 October 2019), https://time.com/collection-post/5692968/ stormzy-next-generation-leaders/.

Francesca Gillett, 'Form 696 scrapped by Metropolitan Police: "racist" paperwork accused of unfairly targeting grime acts is axed', *Evening Standard* (10 November 2017), https://www.standard.co.uk/news/ london/met-police-scrap-live-music-form-696-after-it-was-criti-cised-for-being-racist-and-targeting-grime-a3688166.html.

Rianna Croxford, 'Dearth of Black students admitted to Cambridge revealed after FOI request', *Financial Times* (6 June 2018), https:// www.ft.com/content/9dcd7d0a-65b3-11e8-a39d-4df188287fff.

Robert Wedderburn and William Davidson

Notes: 1 Peter Fryer, *Staying Power: The History of Black People in Britain* (London: Pluto, 1984), p. 214.

2 Ron Ramdin, *The Making of the Black Working Class in Britain* (London: Verso, 2017), p. 20.

3 Ian McCalman, 'Antislavery and ultra-radicalism in early 19th century England: The case of Robert Wedderburn', *Slavery and Abolition*, vol. 7, no. 2 (1986), p. 100.

4 Ramdin, *The Making of the Black Working Class*, p. 21.

5 McCalman, 'Antislavery', p. 107.

6 Fryer, *Staying Power*, p. 225.

7 Ryan Hanley, 'Cato Street, and the Caribbean', in Jason McElligott and Martin Conroy (eds), *The Cato Street Conspiracy: Plotting, Counterintelligence and the Revolutionary Tradition in Britain and Ireland* (Manchester: University of Manchester Press, 2019), p. 84.

8 The Corn Laws prohibited the import of cheap wheat, keeping its price artificially high.

9 Marika Sherwood, 'William Davidson', *Dictionary of National Biography* (2004), https://doi.org/10.1093/ref:odnb/57029.

Dame Sharon White DBE

'Civil Service Ethnic Diversity Programme presents Richard Heaton (permanent secretary, Ministry of Justice) in conversation with Sharon White', Civil Service (2019), accessed via YouTube, https://www.youtube.com/watch?v=vn4uNP98mQg.

John Plunkett, 'Sharon White: from Leyton schoolgirl to Ofcom leader', *Guardian* (16 December 2014), https://www.theguardian.com/media/2014/dec/16/sharon-white-12-things-ofcom-media-regulator.

Notes: 1 'Civil Service workforce: main facts and figures', Gov.uk (26 November 2019), https://www.ethnicity-facts-figures.service.gov.uk/workforce-and-business/workforce-diversity/civil-service-workforce/latest.

Henry Sylvester Williams

Marika Sherwood, *Origins of Pan-Africanism: Henry Sylvester Williams, Africa and the African Diaspora* (New York, London: Routledge: 2011).
Notes: 1 Sherwood, *Origins of Pan-Africanism*, introduction.
  2 Sherwood, *Origins of Pan-Africanism*.

Allan Wilmot

Allan Wilmot, *Now You Know: The Memoirs of Allan Charles Wilmot* (London: Liberation, 2015).
Mark Johnson, *Caribbean Volunteers at War: The Forgotten Story of the RAF's 'Tuskegee Airmen'* (Barnsley: Pen and Sword, 2014).

Simon Woolley, Baron Woolley of Woodford

Operation Black Vote, www.obv.org.uk.
Asha Patel, '"I had no excuse not to change my world": Operation Black Vote campaigner explains how growing up in St Matthews shaped his views', *Leicester Mercury* (5 January 2020), https://www.leicestermercury.co.uk/news/leicester-news/i-no-excuse-not-change-3609879.
Leah Sinclair, 'Sir Simon Woolley: "My honour is for all of us"', *Voice* (15 June 2019), https://archive.voice-online.co.uk/article/sir-simon-woolley-my-honour-all-us.

Gary Younge

Notes: 1 Gary Younge, 'Lessons I learned about life from my mother's early death', *Guardian* (31 December 2015), https://www.theguardian.com/commentisfree/2015/dec/31/lessons-learned-about-life-mothers-early-death.
  2 'Incel' means 'involuntary celibate', usually men who blame their inability to attract a female partner on the woman rather than themselves; a phenomenon based on sexism and entitlement.

Benjamin Zephaniah

Notes: 1 Eric Doumerc, 'Benjamin Zephaniah, the Black British griot,' in Kadijah Sesay (ed.), *Write Black, Write British: from postcolonial to Black British Literature* (Hertford: Hansib, 2005), p. 193.

2 Asher Hoyles and Martin Hoyles, 'Black Performance Poetry', *English in Education*, vol. 37, no. 1 (2003), p. 31.

3 Doumerc, 'Benjamin Zephaniah', p. 194.

4 Benjamin Zephaniah, 'Me, I thought, OBE, me? Up yours, I thought', *Guardian* (27 November 2003), https://www.theguardian.com/books/2003/nov/27/poetry.monarchy.

Other 100 Great Black Britons nominations made by the public between June and December 2019

Akua Agyemfra – publisher, activist

Travis Alabanza – performance artist, theatre maker, poet, writer

Dina Asher-Smith – athlete

Rikki Beadle-Blair – actor, screenwriter, playwright, singer, choreographer, dancer, songwriter

Norman Beaton – actor

Linda Bellos OBE – politician, activist, businessperson

Nadine Benjamin – opera singer

Rob Berkeley MBE – writer, activist

Peter Scott Blackman OBE – health worker, activist, artist

Jay Blades – television presenter, furniture restorer

Barbara Blake Hannah – newsreader

Frank Bowling – artist

John Boyega – actor

Valerie Brandes – publisher

Edson Burton – writer, historian

Tafia Byfield – activist, community worker
Barbara Campbell – journalist, publisher
Hilary Carty – arts and culture director
Candice Carty-Williams – author
Sophie Chandauka – lawyer, entrepreneur, businessperson
Cavita Chapman – health worker
Linford Christie OBE – athlete
Sharon D. Clarke MBE – actor, singer
Michaela Coel – actor, screenwriter, director, producer, singer,
    songwriter, poet, playwright
Yvonne Coghill CBE, OBE – health worker, nurse
Craig David – singer, songwriter
Catherine Despard – prison reformer
Drillminister – musician
Lance Dunkley – activist
Jacqui Dyer MBE – health and social worker
Reni Eddo-Lodge – journalist, author
Cynthia Erivo – actor
Dawn Estefan – psychotherapist
Melanie Eusebe – entrepreneur, author
Clenton Farquharson MBE – community and health worker
Justin Fashanu – footballer
Mark Felix – strongman competitor
Júlio Ferreira – artist
Yvonne Field – social-justice activist
Cherry Fletcher – community worker
Peter 'Flip' Fraser – television producer, editor
Saundra Glenn – activist
Derek Griffiths – actor, television presenter
Martin Griffiths – surgeon
Donna Guthrie –activist

Zenebu Hailu – refugee, activist
Trevor Hall – civil servant
Darren Harriott – comedian
'Daddy' Ernie Harriott – DJ
Jerome Harvey-Agyei – charity worker
Maxie Hayles – author, activist
Aaron Haynes – activist
Dawn Hill CBE – activist
Layla-Roxanne Hill – writer, curator, artist
Afua Hirsch – journalist, author, broadcaster
Zita Holbourne – campaigner, activist
Leyla Hussein – psychotherapist, social activist
Ruth Ibegbuna – community and youth worker
Ajamu Ikwe-Tyehimba – artist, curator, archivist, activist
Anne-Marie Imafidon MBE – speaker, computing and mathematics child prodigy
Paul Ince – footballer
Chinyere Inyama – solicitor, coroner
Eric Irons OBE – magistrate, campaigner
Wendy Irwin – health worker
Uzo Iwobi OBE – barrister, community worker
Eddie Martin – veteran, author
Wilston Samuel Jackson – train driver
Bishop Desmond Jaddoo – activist, faith leader
Dorah Jones – campaigner
Anthony Joshua – boxer
Varaidzo Kativhu – activist
Arinzé Kene – actor, playwright
Soweto Kinch – jazz saxophonist
Agnes Koko – lawyer
Dorothy Koomson – author

Joy Bhila Kwaramba – activist, speaker, writer
Irma La Rose – activist
Labake – filmmaker
Angie Le Mar – comedian, actor, writer, presenter
Denise Lewis OBE – athlete
Miranda Lowe – curator and museum scientist
Una Marson – activist, author, poet, playwright
S.I. Martin – historian, author
Nichole McIntosh – nurse, activist
Augustus Merriman-Labor – writer, barrister
KaHun Montu Tar – pastor
Sharon Morgan – community worker
Lord Bill Morris – trade unionist
Mia Morris OBE – activist
Namron OBE – dancer
Trevor Nelson – broadcaster, DJ
Courttia Newland – author
Evelyn Ngugi – vlogger, content creator
Selma Nicholls – talent agency founder
Cécile Nobrega – educator, poet, playwright, classical
  composer
Elena Noel – campaigner
Sheila Nortley – film producer
Tony O'Connor – headteacher
Habeeb Ogunfemi – politician
John Oke – campaigner, social housing creator
Lola Olufemi – writer, activist
Femi Oluwole – activist
David Orobosa Omoregie (Dave) – rapper, songwriter
Leanne Pero – community worker, dance entrepreneur
Caryl Phillips – author, academic, playwright

Ronke Phillips – presenter
Eartha Pond – footballer
Heather Rabbatts – solicitor, businesswoman
Cyrille Regis – footballer
Claudine and Patrick Reid MBE – community workers and
    founders
Dean Ricketts – campaigner
Kano Robinson – rapper, actor
Marva Rollins OBE – education consultant
Hughie Rose – community worker
Catherine Ross – museum founder
Kenrick Sandy MBE – choreographer
George Saunders – tailor
Roni Savage – engineer, entrepreneur
Amani Simpson – activist
Skepta – rapper
Theo Sowa OBE – community and charity worker
Alistair Soyode – media entrepreneur
Alicia Spencer – health worker
Enrico Stennett – activist
Raheem Sterling – footballer
Wilf Sullivan – campaigner
Jasper Thompson – charity founder
Marc Thompson – activist
Rose Thompson – health worker, activist
Shirley Thompson OBE – composer, academic
Annalisa Toccara – content creator, activist, speaker
Natasha Trotman – artist, designer
Walter Tull – footballer, veteran
Patrick Vernon OBE – activist, health and community worker
Kit de Waal – author

Jackie Walker – activist, writer
Robin Walker – historian, author
Ewart James Walters – actor
Tony Warner – historian, author
Paulette Watson – engineer
Gloria Wildman – activist
Tony Williams – DJ
Paulette Wilson – campaigner
Wretch 32 – rapper, singer, songwriter
Ian Wright – footballer, presenter
Rachel Yankey OBE – footballer
Keisha York – health worker
Lola Young, Baroness Young of Hornsey – academic, author,
    campaigner, actor, university chancellor

100 Great Black Britons 2003 list

Diane Abbott – politician
Ira Aldridge – 19th-century Shakespearian actor
Dounne Alexander – entrepreneur
Valerie Amos – politician, Leader of the House of Lords
Viv Anderson – footballer
John Archer – politician, political activist, first known Black
   mayor
Jennette Arnold – politician
Jazzie B – DJ and music producer
Francis Barber – manservant and heir of Samuel Johnson
John Barnes – footballer
Dame Jocelyn Barrow – activist, educator, BBC governor
Dame Shirley Bassey – singer
Brendan Batson – footballer
Floella Benjamin – broadcaster, actor, author
Nigel Benn/Chris Eubank – boxers
Patrick Berry – media director
Ozwald Boateng – designer
Paul Boateng – politician
Nana Bonsu – community activist

Yvonne Brewster – theatre company founder
Frank Bruno – boxer
Queen Charlotte – wife and consort of George III
David Chase – RAF officer
Linford Christie – athlete
Samuel Coleridge-Taylor – composer
Lord Learie Constantine – cricketer, politician
John Conteh – boxer
William Cuffay – Chartist leader
Ottobah Cugoano – abolitionist, author
Craig David – singer/songwriter
Des'ree – singer/songwriter
Desmond Douglas – table tennis player
Ms Dynamite – rapper, singer, songwriter
John Edmonstone – taxidermist
Olaudah Equiano – abolitionist and author
Mike Fuller – police constable
Gabrielle – singer/songwriter
Bernie Grant – politician, activist
Jeremy Guscott – rugby player
Stuart Hall – cultural theorist, writer
Al Hamilton – sports campaigner
Ellery Hanley – rugby manager
Lenny Henry – comedian, actor
Peter Herbert – chair, Society of Black Lawyers
Rosalind Howells, Baroness Howells of St Davids – life peer,
    community activist
Paul Ince – footballer, England captain
Colin Jackson – athlete
Lee Jasper – activist, government advisor
Linton Kwesi Johnson – poet, activist

Claudia Jones – activist, editor

Janet Kay and Carroll Thompson – recording artists

Kanya King – music entrepreneur

Oona King – politician

Beverley Knight – singer/songwriter

Cleo Laine – jazz vocalist

David Lammy – politician

Stephen Lawrence – victim of racist murder

Angie Le Mar – comedian, actor

Denise Lewis – athlete

Lennox Lewis – boxer

George of Lydda – Patron Saint of England

Phil Lynott – singer/songwriter, guitarist

Oliver Lyseight – faith leader

Val McCalla – publisher

Sir Trevor McDonald – journalist, newsreader

Paul McGrath – footballer, Ireland captain

Harold Moody – campaigner, physician

Bill Morris – trade union leader

Carmen Munroe – television and stage actor

Martin Offiah – rugby player

Chris Ofili – artist

Ben Okri – poet, author

Bruce Oldfield – fashion designer

Herman Ouseley, Baron Ouseley – parliamentarian

Mica Paris – singer/songwriter

Trevor Phillips – writer, broadcaster, politician

Courtney Pine – jazz musician

Lord David Pitt – politician, GP, activist

Sade – singer/songwriter

Ignatius Sancho – diarist, composer, businessman

Tessa Sanderson – athlete

Patricia Scotland, Baroness Scotland – political, barrister

Mary Seacole – nurse

Seal – singer/songwriter

Septimius Severus – Roman emperor

Zadie Smith – author

Julius Soubise – gentleman, swordsman

Moira Stewart – newsreader

John Taylor, Baron Taylor of Warwick – politician

Daley Thompson – athlete

Walter Tull – footballer, Army officer

Randolph Turpin – boxer

Rudolph Walker – actor

Andrew Watson – footballer

Robert Wedderburn – radical leader, anti-slavery advocate

Arthur Wharton – footballer

Willard White – opera singer

Henry Sylvester Williams – lawyer, campaigner, writer

Wilfred Wood, Bishop of the Church of England – faith
    leader

Ian Wright – footballer, broadcaster

Benjamin Zephaniah – poet, writer, lyricist

Acknowledgements

From Angelina Osborne:

Writing this book is one of the hardest things I've done. Doing it in the midst of the coronavirus pandemic made it even more challenging, as I juggled writing and researching with home-schooling my son and teaching. I am therefore grateful for the support, guidance and encouragement of my editors, Rebecca Sheppard and Duncan Proudfoot. I am grateful to Patrick Vernon, who approached me in spring of 2019, asking me if I wanted to go on this journey once more, this time producing a book documenting the achievements of Black Britons. I am also grateful for his support and encouragement, and the great discussions we had about history, who gets to write it, dissemin-ate it, and interpret it.

I am grateful to all the historians, both academic and community (especially the community), and the activists – educational, cultural, social and political – who dedicated their lives and careers to researching and documenting Black British people from the Roman period to present, and from which so much of this work is drawn.

I am also blessed to be part of a terrific Black sisterhood who do the crucial work of nourishing my soul and uplifting my spirit. Thank you: June, Umi, Natalie, Rose, Amber, Astrid, Tinu, Lorna, Marie and Lanora.

Thanks also to my good friends Cha Ashworth, Jennifer Parr and Helen Corner, with whom I discussed the book ad infinitum, and with whom I wined, dined and sat in parks (socially distancing all the while) and who celebrated each milestone with me. Thanks, ladies.

Most of all I'm grateful to my family. A lot of the time, I wrote this with my late brother, Owen, in my mind, who so would have bigged me up for doing this had he been here today. Thank you for always having my back.

From Patrick Vernon:

There are so many people to thank who have been involved in the making of *100 Great Black Britons*, from its beginnings as a website to a campaign and now to a publication.

I want to acknowledge my co-author and friend Dr Angelina Osborne, who has done the vast majority of the research and writing while I have been busy as an activist and campaigner.

I want to also thank the original team back in 2003 who developed the *100 Great Black Britons* and *Every Generation* websites: Pamela Adjei, Denise Lyttle, Samantha Watson, Jacqui Walker, Tendayi Kerr and my sister Julie Vernon as the Company Secretary. Also, thanks to Angie Brooks for developing the 2003 school competition.

I want to thank Jak Beula Dodd for his support in the early days of the project, Stephen Bourne, Mia Morris and members of the BASA network. Also, thank you to Lee Jasper and Rosemary Emodi, who supported the launch of 100 Great Black Britons at the GLA in 2003.

I want to thank Melvin Bell, Andy Yeoman and the team from Focus Games for developing the latest *100 Great Black Britons* website and for their ongoing support for my work on Black history.

Also, thanks to Ceri Hands and Catherine Ritman-Smith from Somerset House and Liz Smith from the National Portrait Gallery. For the 2020 school competition, I would like to thank Karen Chouhan from NEU, Martin Spafford, Emma Winch, Francesca Wickens and Helen Sanson.

I want to thank the shortlisting panel for their advice and recommendations, which helped Angie and me to finalise the list of 100 Great Black Britons: Sharmaine Lovegrove, Nadine White, Yvonne Davis, Kenneth Olumuyiwa Tharp, Dawn Hill, Dwain Neil, Arike Oki, Dr Wanda Wyporska, Joyce Fraser and Michelle Moore. I would like to thank the staff at Black Cultural Archives for supporting the hosting of the shortlisting meeting, and I would also like to thank Dr Pen Mendonca, Sharron Wallace, Sadiki Harris, Ahmed Alaska and Shashi Loannides.

Thank you to my family, especially my parents, Norris and Avis, for being inspirational role models, and my sisters, Janet, Julie, Carol, Dawn, Hyacinth and Monica, plus my niece and nephew, Sharifa and Tendayi, and all my extended family in Jamaica and the USA. In addition, thank you to Patrice and Josephine Lawrence for their support over the years. I would also like to acknowledge my school friends who I grew up with in Wolverhampton.

Finally, I want to thank Duncan Proudfoot and Rebecca

Sheppard from Robinson for having the vision and commitment to the development of this publication, and for having confidence in both Angelina and me in our approach and perspective on this book.

Index

433

Patrick Vernon OBE is a Clore and Winston Churchill Fellow, a fellow at the Imperial War Museum and a fellow of the Royal Historical Society. Patrick was awarded an OBE in 2012 for his work in tackling health inequalities for ethnic minority communities in Britain. In 2018 Patrick received an honorary PhD from Wolverhampton University for his work on migration and cultural history. Since 2010 he has been leading the campaign for national Windrush Day and in 2018 kick-started the campaign for an amnesty for the Windrush Generation as part of the Windrush Scandal. In 2020, Patrick was selected by *British Vogue* as one of Britain's top twenty campaigners and was included in the 2020 Power List of 100 Influential Black People in Britain.

Dr Angelina Osborne is an independent researcher and heritage consultant. She received her PhD in History from the Wilberforce Institute for the Study of Slavery and Emancipation, University of Hull in 2014. She has worked on a range of projects related to the public history of slavery, memory and citizenship, and the African and Caribbean presence in Britain, and has worked on these topics with museums, libraries and archives, NGOs, community organisations, and presented programmes on slavery and the Black presence in Britain on radio and television.

Praise for *100 Great Black Britons*

'An empowering read . . . it is refreshing to see somebody celebrate the role that black Britons have played in this island's long and complicated history'

David Lammy, author of *Tribes*, in
'The best books of 2020', *Guardian*

'Timely and so important . . . recognition is long overdue . . . I would encourage everyone to buy it!'

n Butler MP

70004521194 2

Praise for the 100 Great Black Britons campaign

'I am delighted to see the relaunch of 100 Great Black Britons. For too long the contribution of Britons of African and Caribbean heritage have been underestimated, undervalued and overlooked'

Sadiq Khan, Mayor of London

'100 Great Black Britons celebrates what we have always known about Britain's history: it is irrefutably rooted in Black and global history'

Kevin Courtney, General Secretary,
National Education Union

'The story of people of African and of Caribbean descent in the UK is part of the fabric of British history. We built Britain together'

Arike Oke, Managing Director of Black Cultural Archives

'There is no more important time than now to shine a light on the huge contributions made by black Britons'

Trevor Sterling, Chair, Mary Seacole Trust

'100 Great Black Britons is needed now more than ever. Celebrating Black Britons is important not just for all our children and teachers, but for society as a whole'

Dr Wanda Wyporska, Executive Director of
The Equality Trust

'100 Great Black Britons is a vital initiative to contribute to a more representative and relevant curriculum and ensure that the impact of these inspiring individuals is fully recognised'

Liz Smith, Director of Participation and
Learning, National Portrait Gallery

100 GREAT

PATRICK VERNON & ANGELINA OSBORNE

BLACK BRITONS

FOREWORD BY DAVID OLUSOGA

ROBINSON

ROBINSON

First published in Great Britain in 2020 by Robinson
This paperback edition published in 2021 by Robinson

Copyright © Patrick Vernon and Angelina Osborne, 2020

1 3 5 7 9 8 6 4 2

A CIP catalogue record for this book is available from the British Library

ISBN: 978-1-47214-704-2

Typeset in Adobe Garamond Pro by Hewer Text UK Ltd, Edinburgh
Printed and bound in Great Britain by Clays Ltd, Elcograf S.p.A.

Papers used by Robinson are from well-managed forests and other responsible sources

Robinson
An imprint of
Little, Brown Book Group
Carmelite House
50 Victoria Embankment
London EC4Y 0DZ

An Hachette UK Company
www.hachette.co.uk

www.littlebrown.co.uk